THE ETHICAL
IN THE JEWISH
AND AMERICAN
HERITAGE

**Volume IV in the Moreshet Series, Studies in
Jewish History, Literature and Thought**

THE ETHICAL IN THE JEWISH AND AMERICAN HERITAGE

by Simon Greenberg

THE JEWISH THEOLOGICAL SEMINARY OF AMERICA
NEW YORK 1977

Library of Congress Cataloging in Publication Data

Greenberg, Simon, 1901-
   The ethical in the Jewish and American heritage.

   (Moreshet series; v. 4)
   Bibliography: p.
   Includes indexes.
   1. Ethics, Jewish. 2. Law and ethics. 3. Law—United
States—History and criticism. 4. Jewish law—Philoso-
phy. I. Title. II. Series: Moreshet (New York); v. 4.
BJ1280.G73   296.3'85   77-8481
ISBN 0-87334-002-7

DISTRIBUTED BY KTAV PUBLISHING HOUSE, INC.
NEW YORK, NEW YORK 10013

MANUFACTURED IN THE UNITED STATES OF AMERICA

Dedicated to our Parents

חיים דוד בן שמשון ז״ל	משה בן בנימין ז״ל
Hyman Davis	Morris Greenberg
שרה רבקה בת נחמיה ז״ל	בתיה בת צבי הירש ז״ל
Sarah Davis	Bessie Greenberg

In grateful and loving memory.

CONTENTS

FOREWORD

THE HISTORY OF JEWISH THOUGHT is in large measure the history
of Jewish interpretation of Scripture. From Philo and the Rabbis
of the Talmud to Rosenzweig and Heschel, the aim and technique
of *midrash* have been very much the same: the application of the
text and spirit of Scripture to the major ethical and spiritual problems confronting the Jewish community in any particular period
and context. Inevitably the *midrash* of every age has in large measure been the fruit of Jewish confrontation with alien systems or
patterns of thought and behavior. Put differently, the great Jewish
teachers of every generation have sought to formulate and articulate
an authentic Jewish response to the pattern of culture and *Weltan-
schauung* confronting them.

These responses have often been outright rejections of the
dominant cultural pattern or of one or more fundamental strands
within it. When, however, it was possible in the view of interpreters
of Judaism to bridge the ostensible gulf between their own tradition
and the dominant culture, the midrashic process often consisted
largely of a re-reading and reinterpretation of Scripture, on occasion
of rabbinic tradition as well, so that the classical principles of
Judaism were brought into harmony with those of the surrounding
milieu. But whatever the response, whether of repudiation or of
harmonization, the drive underlying the endless process of herme-
neutics was that of confrontation and response. The ethical and
spiritual constructs of the world at large could not be ignored, at
least not by those Jewish spokesmen who sought to live up to the
full measure of their responsibility as rabbis and teachers.

The need to respond to non-Jewish value systems was a consequence of being a minority that was simultaneously fired by the

conviction that the Jewish way of life must persist. It was not merely that the Jews knew that they had been enjoined to live as "a people apart" from the nations of the world (Num. 23: 9). They also knew that as heirs to the Torah and its covenant, they were bearers of a unique mission and message to the world at large. What the nature of this message-mission was, it was the duty of the Jewish teacher and thinker to reassert in contemporary idiom and concepts. However, only that restatement or reinterpretation of Jewish principle could hope to gain recognition as valid which responded to the contemporary situation with specific texts of Scripture or with fundamental principles of rabbinic tradition. It is for that reason that so much of classical Jewish philosophy is taken up with exegesis.

If this has been the case through all of Jewish history, such a reaffirmation of fundamental Jewish principles, particularly in the area of ethics and interpersonal relationships, is all the more urgent in the open society of the modern free world. In the present context, not only are many of the factors that formerly insulated the Jews from the rest of the world—and that thus contributed to ensuring the continuity of the Jewish people and of the principles of their tradition—lacking, but large numbers of Jews have consciously and outspokenly identified with at least some of the fundamental values of the society in which they live. If Judaism is to continue to speak to them as well as through them, the basic affirmations of the Jewish tradition will have to be examined anew alongside the fundamental assumptions of the wider society.

From this perspective, Professor Greenberg's present work is of particular significance, for it traces with great erudition and insight the foundations of man's ethical imperatives and the forces they have exerted in American and Jewish legal development. The volume invites the American Jew to consider the two traditions he bears and how they have interacted. The dissimilarities between the American and Jewish traditions are all too obvious. The former is above all a secular tradition, which from its inception eliminated the church from its halls of government, while the latter bases its laws and institutions on the Torah, which in turn claims divine revelation as the source of its legitimacy. The free, secular American society was an unlikely atmosphere for Judaism to flourish in. And yet Judaism has enjoyed a renascence in the United States theologically as well as communally and institutionally. In some ways the American atmosphere has proven itself to be surprisingly congenial to Jewish spiritual resurgence. Perhaps it is because of the elements shared by the two traditions. For all their dissimilarities, they have much in common: they have each been consumed by a vision of what is required of man, and neither has yet presumed to declare that its vision has been adequately served. It was and is the confluence of the American and the Jewish missions of ordering society so as to conform to ethical imperatives that assured the Jewish people of a productive place in the American tradition. It is because this work calls for a renewal of the faithfulness to those missions, so vital to the continued flourishing of the American and Jewish civilizations, that its publication is so welcome as America embarks on its third century.

Dr. Greenberg has undertaken the challenge facing the true spokesman of Jewish values in contemporary America by articulating clearly and forthrightly the common and the distinctive in classical Judaism and American democracy.

This indeed has, *mutatis mutandis,* always been the function of the Jewish philosopher-exegete and of the Jewish homiletician. Since that is the function of the Jewish teacher, it is evident that the task should be high on the priorities of the academic agenda of the Seminary that trains the transmitters and interpreters of the Jewish tradition. Indeed, it is out of the sense of mandate to articulate the affinities and differences between classical Judaism and the American democratic ethos that Professor Greenberg's work has been written and that the Seminary proudly presents it in its *Moreshet* series. The title of the series is particularly appropriate for this volume, for Dr. Greenberg confronts two discrete legacies that destiny has placed side by side and does not flinch from stating where, in his view, they coincide, where they conflict irresolvably, and where they can meet.

Dr. Greenberg's conscious concern with this task spans his service as rabbi, teacher and scholar during more than half a century. His views on the subject treated in the present volume were summed up in an earlier work in these words:

> When I say that American democracy is rooted in Judaism, I do not think primarily of the historic role played by the Bible in early American life, important as that role undoubtedly was. Nor do I mean that Americanism and Judaism are or should be identical. I mean that the political order established by the Declaration of Independence and the Constitution of the United States and the laws enacted in compliance with their spirit and letter are as full an implementation of the laws of justice and the principles of righteousness enunciated in the Torah, as has yet been achieved by any human society. But Judaism demands more of its followers than justice and righteousness. It requires them also to live lives of mercy, of love and holiness. It asks them to be ever conscious that they are always in the presence of God.

The present work provides a commentary in depth on that statement by its exploration of the relationship between law and ethics in Judaism and in America.

Had Dr. Greenberg's essays been but disquisitions on moral philosophy, they would have merited our study and our gratitude. They are that, to be sure, but they are far more than that. Fundamentally, Dr. Greenberg's essays are serious extensions of the process of *midrash* to an examination of the two traditions to which he is dedicated. He thus walks and speaks in the long and rich tradition of Jewish thought as well as in the younger but rich tradition of American thought. As exegete, Dr. Greenberg has made Scripture and rabbinic tradition speak to us afresh in moral categories that are specific and relevant to our contemporary lives. Underlying this work is the unspoken but clearly perceived conviction that Judaism must always recapture its moral message if it is to retain its hold and impact on modern man.

GERSON D. COHEN
Chancellor, The Jewish Theological
Seminary of America

INTRODUCTION

THIS IS THE SECOND volume of preliminary studies motivated by the desire to formulate a philosophy for the American Jew who wants the fact that he is both an American and a Jew to serve as a constructive and wholesome factor in integrating his total personality. The first volume, *Foundations of a Faith,* was published in 1967. It is frequently referred to in the notes to this volume. Hence its ready availability, though not indispensable to an understanding of this volume, would prove very helpful. The third and final volume should hopefully appear within the reasonably near future.

While the circumstances within which the Jewish and the American traditions came into being, and have thus far run their course, are about as dissimilar as they can be, and while they differ in many essentials, there are some striking affinities between them, some of which are discussed in the last chapter of this volume. Here I shall but briefly note that both traditions cherish the memory of a moment in time when, well-nigh simultaneously, ethical principles, and codes of law which presumably embodied them, were formally adopted. The gap between the ethical principles and the law in time became ever more visible. The history of the spiritual development of each tradition is, then, largely the history of the successes and the failures of the efforts made within each tradition to eliminate that gap. These efforts entailed controversies on the highest intellectual and spiritual levels as well as on the level of passion and vested interest. Since both traditions are rooted in written texts, these controversies involved the problem of how the literal meaning or the reasonable implications of a text may be established. Moreover, while the American tradition does not include a law which is presumed to have been divinely revealed, it does maintain that the Creator endowed his creatures with certain unalienable rights. The relationship between ethics and metaphysics is, therefore, a basic concern of both traditions.

The final, definitive word on the theme of this volume can never be spoken. All one can hope for is to make a modest contribution to the understanding of the relationship of ethics to metaphysics and of the place that the tension between ethics and law has held in the development of both these traditions, so that he may be of some help to individuals who are heirs to and who love both of them, and who seek to integrate them more meaningfully into their own lives.

Chapters one and three which first appeared in *Conservative Judaism* have been significantly revised for inclusion in this volume. I want to thank the editors of *Conservative Judaism* for permission to reprint them. Chapter two was first written for the yet unpublished volume three. Chapter four was delivered at the Seminary as the 1975 Sol Feinstone Lecture. I am deeply grateful to Dr. Gerson D. Cohen, Chancellor of the Jewish Theological Seminary, for having read the manuscript and for recommending it to be published as one in the *Moreshet Series*. I want also to thank Mrs. Dora Levine and Mrs. Elsie Knopf, who patiently typed and retyped portions of the manuscript in New York City, and Mrs. Cilla Meroz, who did the same in Jerusalem, and Mrs. Harriet Catlin for her helpful suggestions and for the care with which she saw the volume through the press.

Above all, I am grateful to the Almighty for enabling me to formulate, with what I hope is some degree of clarity, some of the intuitively conceived and rationally comprehended principles by which I have attempted to guide my life.

SIMON GREENBERG

The Jewish Theological Seminary of America
Iyyar 5734—May 1974.

1.

ETHICS, RELIGION, AND JUDAISM

The Scope of This Inquiry

IN MYTHOLOGICAL THOUGHT, SCIENCE, ethics, and religion are inextricably intertwined. The Greek philosophers started the process of differentiation. It is now generally accepted that the realm of science consists, or should consist, only of phenomena that are accessible to the senses.[1] However, concepts and hypotheses whose substantive content is not observable have proved indispensable to scientific inquiry in its effort to comprehend the "material, natural relationships between physically or objectively observable phenomena."[2] The realm of religion also includes objectively observable phenomena. However, the concepts of religion, whose substantive content is not "physically or objectively observable," are concerned primarily with man's effort to comprehend his relationship to himself, his fellow man, and the universe. The controversies between science and religion are usually due to the tendency of religionists

1

to apply religious concepts to explain relationships between objectively observable phenomena, and the inclination of scientists to apply scientific concepts to the comprehension of man's relationships to himself, his fellow man, and the universe.[3] Over the years the frequently acrimonious controversies between "science" and "religion" have had the beneficial result of sharpening rather than blurring the differentiation between them, thus assigning, as it were, to each its own significant realm of primary concern.

Ethics as a distinct discipline has followed a different course. Its practitioners could never quite agree whether it has its own clearly defined realm, or whether it properly belongs to the realm of science, religion, or the social sciences.[4] Sidgwick opens his "general account of the subject" with a typical English understatement to the effect that "there is some difficulty in defining the subject of Ethics in a manner which can fairly claim general acceptance." He points out that "ethics originally meant what relates to character as distinct from intellect," and that the "primary subject of ethical investigation is all that is included under the notion of what is ultimately good or desirable for man; all that is reasonably chosen or sought by him, not as a means to some ulterior end, but for itself."[5] Another conception of ethics views it as being "concerned primarily with the general rules of Duty or Right Action—sometimes called the Moral Code—viewed as absolutely binding on every man, and properly to be obeyed by him without regard to his personal interests: the relation of duty to the agent's private happiness being regarded as a matter of secondary concern from an ethical point of view."[6] The difficulties that Sidgwick had in 1886 in defining the subject matter of ethics have since then not been significantly resolved. "There is a tendency today, more popular than strictly philosophic, to identify as 'ethics' any personally chosen value system and code of behavior."[7] All agree, however, that the central concern of ethics is human behavior.

Every human act of which the agent is, or becomes, aware, is at the time of its performance, or preceding or following it, actually or potentially associated with a threefold awareness.

1. An awareness of an intention which the act is expected to implement.
2. An awareness of a rationale for the proposed act. That is, an awareness of how the act is expected to result in consequences that will conform to the intention.
3. An awareness of a rationale for the intention.[8]

This inquiry will be devoted exclusively to the rationale for the intention. We shall not take sides in the "great controversy as to whether Reason can ever furnish a motive for action" or whether "the recognition by Reason that a certain proposed course of action is right or wrong by itself stirs a desire for doing or avoiding it."[9] Our inquiry derives from the undeniable fact of universal human experience that the human intellect is not satisfied with knowing only the intent that motivates an act. It requires that the intent be rationalized in a manner acceptable to the agent's faculty of reason. When one becomes conscious of an intention, he must, whether he wants to or not, simultaneously or eventually have a rationalization for it which will be sufficiently satisfactory to him so that he does not feel that in acting upon the intention he will be acting or had acted irrationally.[10] Many a rationalization may in fact be naught but a delusion, a self-deception. But the very fact that human beings find some kind of satisfaction in such delusions reflects the profundity of the need.

Note that we shall be interested in the rationale for the intention and not for the act per se. The act requires its own particular rationale whereby it is reasonably associated with the intention. An agent must have a reason for choosing one of a number of alternative acts which may be available to him in order to implement his intention. An agent's wisdom and skill are judged by the extent to which the consequences of his acts conform to his intentions. His ethical sensitivity is also unquestionably reflected in his choice of means. But that problem will be of only tangential interest to us. We shall concentrate our attention upon the *intention and its rationale*.

This inquiry will therefore center around seven concepts: (1) ethical intention, (2) unethical intention, (3) moral intention, (4) subsidiary intention, (5) welfare, (6) secular rationale, (7) religious rationale. The concepts as used here are defined as follows:

1. *Ethical intention.* An intention is ethical when it intends by means of an act to advance the welfare of the object, without anticipated injury, or even with anticipated benefit, to the agent. A merchant's intention to give what would be generally recognized as true value to his customer is therefore no less ethical because the merchant intends thereby to advance not only his customer's welfare but also his own.[11]

2. *Unethical intention.* An intention is unethical when it intends to impair the welfare of the agent or an object.

3. *Moral intention.* An intention is moral when it intends to impair, or seriously risks impairing, the welfare of the agent in order to benefit an object.[12] Such intentions have been designated variously as "sentiments of beneficence," "altruism," "ultra obligations," and the like. We shall categorize them as moral intentions, even though this may at first give rise to some confusion since *moral* and *ethical* have long generally been used as absolute synonyms.[13] We choose to do so primarily because it is linguistically much more manageable than the other terms. The distinction between the moral and the ethical we consider to be of primary importance for this inquiry.[14]

4. *Subsidiary intention.* A subsidiary intention is one which subserves another intention. Thus the surgeon's intention to remove a limb, when associated with the intention thereby to save the object's life, is a subsidiary intention. Subsidiary intentions will in this essay be viewed as ethical or unethical in their own right, and not merely in their relation to the intention which they are supposed to subserve. Hence, subsidiary intentions may in themselves be unethical even though they are intended to subserve ethical intentions, or ethical even though they are intended to subserve unethical intentions.[15]

5. *Welfare.* The term *welfare* will designate those experiences which in the opinion of the agent are desirable, and which he would choose for himself whether the object does or does not agree that they are desirable. Thus the Inquisitor presumably believed he was advancing the welfare of the heretic whom he gave over to the arm

of the state to be burned, for he believed that he was thus saving his soul. The primary intention of the Inquisitor to save the heretic's soul does not transform his subsidiary intention of having him burned at the stake into an ethical intention, for surely the Inquisitor did not believe that the act of burning the heretic in itself represented an advancement of his welfare. That was to be advanced only by what followed the burning, and that was not within the power of the Inquisitor to bestow or withhold. Under these circumstances, even the primary intention of the Inquisitor may be considered as ethical only if the Inquisitor believed that he was treating the heretic as he himself would want to be treated if he were the heretic.

The case of a judge sentencing a criminal is analogous but not identical, for the judge presumably does not have the welfare of the criminal in mind when he sentences him, but rather that of society. The primary intention of the judge to advance the good of society by punishing the criminal can be designated as ethical only if the judge believes that he would want to be treated similarly if he were the criminal.

This definition of welfare contains a substantial subjective element. It accords with what seems to me to be the reasonable import of the injunction to "love thy neighbor as thyself" (Lev. 19:18). The criticism usually leveled at this biblical commandment is twofold.

(a) If to love one's neighbor as oneself means that one is to feel toward his neighbor what a normal human being feels toward himself and to do for him all that he does for himself, then this injunction requires more than can reasonably be expected from any human being in terms of both emotion and action. One cannot be commanded to love, since love is not an emotion which one can summon at will. Moreover one cannot, under normal circumstances, love his neighbor with a love equal to that which he has for himself. But even if we eliminate the emotional implications of the commandment and limit it merely to its implications in terms of action, we still cannot reasonably be expected to do for others all that we do or should normally do for ourselves. The objection to this literal interpretation of the biblical injunction seems to me to be valid.

(b) The second objection to this injunction is that it makes the tastes and ideals of the agent the standard for right or wrong attitudes toward the object. The overt manifestations of the agent's love for himself, assuming that he loves himself, may not be of the kind in which his neighbor delights. The agent may love himself in a manner in which the neighbor does not want to be loved. That, too, appears to me to be a valid criticism. Hence in his criticism of this biblical injunction, Kant concludes: "I cannot do good to any one according to my concept of happiness (except to children and insane) but only according to that of the one I intend to benefit."[16] What Kant, at this point, seems to be asking us to do is to substitute the "neighbor's" subjective opinion of what is good for him for our subjective opinion of what is good for him. However, if I am convinced that what my neighbor wants me to do for him will injure rather than benefit him—and he need not be a child or insane for me to feel that way—and I still do it, I cannot be said to be acting out of an ethical intention. In the final analysis, if my intention is to be ethical I must believe that if I were in the other man's place, I would want my fellow man to do for me what I now intend to do for him. Hence, the only reasonable interpretation of this biblical injunction seems to be that an agent is not asked to do for his neighbor everything that he (the agent) does for himself, but only those things which he (the agent) would reasonably want and expect his neighbor to do for him, if he were in his neighbor's place. This standard for behavior obviously involves a measure of subjectivity. We believe that such subjectivity is absolutely unavoidable in all human relations. Hence, the only one, in the final analysis, who can categorize the character of an intention with any degree of certainty, is the one who harbors it.

It is the function of human reason to reduce to the minimum the measure of subjectivity inherent in our actions toward our fellow men. But thus far all attempts to eliminate it completely have, I believe, failed.[17] This failure, however, has not eliminated the irrepressible need that every thoughtful person feels to rationalize, in as cogent a manner as he can, this very element of subjectivity insofar as he is aware of it.

The fact that the agent claims that his intention was ethical, and that his claim may be accepted by others, does not *ipso facto* remove blame and consequent responsibility from him for whatever untoward consequences were occasioned by the act which implemented the intention. Legal systems generally agree with the rabbinic maxim that *adam muad l'olam*,[18] a human being is always responsible for the consequences of his acts regardless of the nature of the intention that motivated them. Nevertheless, the nature of the intention that is believed to have motivated the act is usually taken into consideration by those meting out punishments or rewards. Unethical intentions that do not issue in acts, or issue in acts which cause no injuries to others, are usually not severely or at all punishable in civilized societies. When acts do produce injuries, the intention which motivated them may, but does not necessarily, affect the nature of the punishment.

6. *Secular.* The term *secular* will be used to categorize two main types of non-religious rationalizations of the ethical.

(a) Those whose components consist exclusively of phenomena that are readily or conceivably accessible to the senses.

(b) Those whose components are assumed to be necessitated by the very nature of human reason as an autonomous and fully adequate instrument for discovering the axioms—the *grund gesetze,* or self-evident principles—of ethics, on the basis of which one can then with certainty logically deduce whether an act or an intention is or is not ethical. Spinoza and Kant constructed their majestic systems of ethics upon this premise. Spinoza asserted that "the human mind possesses an adequate knowledge of the eternal and infinite essence of God."[19] It is therefore capable, by its own resources, of determining the ethical. Hence he used Euclid as his model for constructing his ethics. Just as geometry was a product wholly of human reason, and its certainty and truth were universally recognized at the time to be self-evident and beyond doubt, so his ethics were to be totally the product of human reason and their validity as certain as that of geometry.

Underlying Kant's ethical system are two basic propositions:

(a) Human reason is absolutely autonomous. It is in no way dependent upon sources outside or beyond itself for "instruction," "inspiration," or "guidance."[20]

(b) He (Kant) had discovered the fundamental rational principle from which all ethics could be deduced. Human reason is thus the legislator of the ethical and the moral.[21]

7. *Religious.* The term *religious* will be used to categorize rationalizations which include components that are not now and can never conceivably be accessible to the senses. The human mind has created concepts to refer to these sensibly inaccessible components, such as God, soul, future life. Insofar as the existence of this sensibly inaccessible component of the rationalization is conceived to be independent of man, as well as beyond the power of the human mind fully to comprehend, human reason cannot conceive of itself as being self-sufficient for the rationalization of the ethical.

From the above definitions it follows that the adjectives *ethical, unethical,* and *moral* may be appropriately used only when applied to intentions. They are misused or carelessly used when applied to the act itself or to the agent or to the rationale of the intention.

An act per se is neither ethical nor unethical. It is merely an event analogous to any natural event, such as rainfall or earthquake. Just as we do not rationally attribute ethical qualities to natural events on the basis of their consequences, so also should human acts not be ethically endowed because of their consequences. Acts of God or nature or man most often simultaneously affect more than one object, and what may constitute a favorable consequence for one may be an unfavorable consequence for another. The "angel of the Lord" who destroyed Sennacherib's army saved Jerusalem (2 Kings 19:35). An act which appeared altogether "ethical" in the eyes of King Hezekiah was certainly not so in the eyes of Sennacherib. What God intended when He "delegated His angel" to destroy the army of Sennacherib, only He could know with certainty.

Acts have both immediate and delayed consequences. The two are often contradictory, and only distantly related to the intention which motivated the act. Even the immediate consequences of an act invariably involve factors that are but tangentially related to the intent or the act itself. The selling of Joseph to the Midianites was only remotely related to his becoming viceroy of Egypt, and the Russian pogroms of the 1880s and at the beginning of the twentieth century, which were the immediate causes for the mass migration of Russian Jews to the United States, were certainly not the most important factors contributing to the present generally happy conditions of the Jews in the United States. In neither case would we say that the delayed consequences transformed the original intentions of Joseph's brothers, or of those who organized the Russian pogroms, into ethical intentions.

Intentions are not unethical because of their immediate undesirable consequences. A fireman's intention to save a child by throwing it out of a burning building is certainly ethical even though he may cause its death. The rationale for his decision to save the child by throwing it out cannot be designated as ethical or unethical, but only as the exercise of good or poor judgment.[22]

We conclude, therefore, that only the intention which motivates an act may properly be categorized as ethical, unethical, or moral.[23] And only the rationalization of the intention may properly be categorized as religious or secular.

SECTION II

The Secular Rationalization of the Ethical Preliminary Remarks

We have designated as ethical an intention to benefit an object without anticipated injury to the agent or with anticipated benefit also to the agent. Any intention, therefore, to give to the object what the group considers to be his due is ethical. It is so considered by common opinion. Society usually designates those who harbor and implement such intentions not merely as law-abiding but also as "ethical" individuals.

The adjective *ethical* is universally considered to be a commendatory appellation. The fact that we commend such intentions, and those who entertain and implement them, is *prima facie* evidence that they are not "natural" in the sense that experiencing hunger pangs is natural. We do not associate commendatory appellations with hunger, or with those who experience it. Only in the sense that it is natural for a human being to walk or talk is it natural for him to entertain ethical intentions and to strive to implement them. At any particular moment he can choose not to walk or talk. Thus, while it may be natural for a human being to harbor an ethical intention,[24] it is equally natural for him not to harbor or try to implement it. Because an individual actually has, or is somehow deluded into believing that he has, the power to choose what intentions he shall or shall not entertain and implement, we feel moved to commend him when he harbors and implements ethical intentions.[25]

We commend him because every ethical intention requires a measure of exertion either to act in accordance with it or to resist a temptation to utilize an opportunity to benefit oneself at the expense of another human being. One is tempted to keep an object which he finds even though its owner is known to him, or to take advantage of a customer's ignorance of the true value of what he wishes to buy. The Rabbis designate the resistance to such a temptation as a *mizvah,* an ethically or religiously motivated act.[26] It too requires an exertion of the will. It is this characteristic of the ethical which is reflected in the admonition of Rabbi Judah the Prince (second century C.E.) that one should "reckon the loss incurred by the fulfillment of a *mizvah* against the reward secured by its observance." He then goes on to say that one should "reckon the gain resulting from the performance of an *averah*—a transgression—against the loss incurred thereby."[27] Note that Rabbi Judah's statement indicates that the first thing one becomes aware of when faced with the opportunity to perform a *mizvah* is that it will involve the agent in a "loss." He must, therefore, by an act of will overcome his natural resistance to incurring that loss. The first thing he becomes aware of when confronted with the temptation to commit a transgression is the immediate gain he would derive therefrom. It requires an act of will to resist the temptation to acquire that gain. In both instances, therefore, we commend those who harbor and implement ethical intentions even though it may be "natural" for human beings to do so.

Because ethical intentions invariably involve either some actual loss or the passing up of an opportunity for possible gain, there are present in every society those who at one time or another violate the laws and and mores in which that society has concretized its ethical intentions. Every society has therefore found it necessary not only to formulate laws and codes of behavior, but also to establish some agency to enforce them by punishing transgressors and praising conformers. A police force alone, however, cannot assure the observance of a society's laws. Unless the laws and mores of a society are buttressed by a rationale which is acceptable to the overwhelming majority of that society, no police can long effectively enforce them. What, then, are the secular rationalizations which have been suggested for ethical intentions and their implementation?

While the formulations of secular rationalizations display a wide range of philosophical sophistication, only a few concepts are involved. The concept which is basic, and which in one form or another is the very core of all rationalizations of human action, whether secular or religious, is, and of necessity must be, that of self-interest. Hence the difference between one system of ethics and another is ultimately rooted in the concept of the self projected by each system. One's conception of what one's interests are depends upon how he conceives his "self." As Bertrand Russell somewhere remarks, selfishness per se is neither good nor bad. It depends upon the kind of self one is selfish about.[28]

The Secular View of the Self

Now the consistently logical secularist must conceive of the self in terms that are completely accessible to the senses. The self thus conceived is that tangible phenomenon of flesh and blood which thinks and feels for a definite period of time and then irretrievably ceases in any sense whatsoever to be. It disintegrates into the half-dozen or more substances which chemists have identified as constituting the human body.[29] The basic concepts which should determine the interest of such a self, to the extent that it is governed by its faculty of reason, are self-preservation and physical pleasure and pain. To such a self it should be, and is, self-evident that it should harbor and implement only those intentions which will hopefully produce for it the maximum of pleasure and the minimum of pain. "According to egoistic hedonism the rational agent regards quantity of consequent pleasure and pain to himself as alone of importance in choosing between alternatives of action, and seeks always the greatest attainable surplus of pleasure over pain."[30]

Hence the following syllogism may be said to constitute the core of the secular rationalization of the ethical.

Major premise: Everyone rightly acts in accordance with what he believes will best advance his physical well-being.

Minor premise: Harboring and implementing ethical intentions best advances one's physical well-being.

Conclusion: Therefore everyone should strive to harbor and implement ethical intentions.

The task of the philosophers of this school of thought is therefore to prove the correctness of the Minor premise, which is often referred to as the principle of "enlightened self-interest."[31]

It is not at all difficult to prove that "by and large" this principle is valid. The welfare of every individual requires that he live in a viable, stable society. That is possible only if the overwhelming majority of the members of the society almost always entertain and implement the ethical intentions approved and nurtured by the society. But the fact that something is true "by and large" does not constitute a logically cogent argument that it will be true in any given situation. By and large, most air flights end safely, but the flight-insurance companies nevertheless do a flourishing business, and rightly so. Had the experience of mankind demonstrated beyond reasonable doubt that those who entertain and implement ethical intentions thereby always advance their personal welfare, while those who harbor and implement unethical intentions always suffer, there would be no problem for the moral philosopher to ponder. When the prophet and the psalmist raise the question of the prosperity of the wicked, they do not refer to those who were delinquent in their ritual practices. They refer to those who acted unethically toward their fellow man.

> Righteous art Thou, O Lord, when I plead with Thee: yet let me talk with Thee of Thy judgments: Wherefore doth the way of the wicked prosper? Wherefore are all they happy that deal very treacherously? (Jer. 12:1).

> But as for me, my feet were almost gone; my steps had well nigh slipped. For I was envious . . . when I saw the prosperity of the wicked (Ps. 73:3).

All of the arguments leveled against faith in a just and merciful God because of the fact that many individuals who believe in Him, and who meticulously observe what they believe to be His ethical and ritual injunctions, suffer, while disbelievers who violate both His ethical and ritual laws prosper, can be used with equal cogency against the secular position, which rationalizes the ethical life on the basis of enlightened self-interest. There are too many individual instances which contradict the Minor premise.

Nor is this due to the fact that men seldom act in accordance with the dictates of reason, as Spinoza would have us believe.[32] On the contrary, reason in the service of self-interest secularly conceived, often presents a most convincing rationale for the unethical and counsels men to take "reasonable" risks. One who hesitates to take a reasonable risk in behalf of what he considers his self-interest is not acting out of wisdom but out of cowardice. Why should one not take advantage of his fellow man's ignorance or weakness when the chances of being punished by society are slight in comparison to the gain resulting from the unethically motivated act? The Kantian categorical imperative—to universalize the maxim of one's act and see what would happen if all men acted on the basis of this universalization—is so completely irrelevant to the practical daily affairs of men as to be meaningless. To counsel an individual not to take advantage of his fellow man on the basis of the far-fetched argument that if he were always to do so and everyone else would likewise always act thus, society could not exist and he would himself ultimately suffer, is to ask him to build his life on two absolutely unrealistic suppositions.[33] In the first place, enlightened self-interest would never counsel an individual always to be untrustworthy. One who is "enlightened" will choose what appears to be the appropriate occasion for his deception. Moreover, one has to have great faith indeed in the significance of his act if he is to believe that his or anyone else's occasional deviation from the "path of virtue" will bring down the whole social fabric in his own lifetime.

It has thus far never happened, and probably never will, that everyone deviated from the society's norms at the same time. Moreover, human experience has established, beyond reasonable doubt, that the stability of a social structure does not require that all its members conform to all its mores all the time. It is enough if most of the members conform to most of its mores, most of the time. That leaves ample room for most of the members to vary from one or more of its mores from time to time. Indeed, it is this very flexibility or plasticity of the social structure that makes possible simultaneously change and continuity. Hence, whatever significant relationship there exists between enlightened self-interest and the ethical intentions entertained by members of a group larger than a family is established largely by fear of the law-enforcement agencies of the society. When that fear is eliminated, enlightened self-interest has in fact proved to be "a broken reed of a staff" (2 Kings 18:21) as a support for morals and ethics.[34]

But even assuming that the individual's unethical behavior may lead to the collapse of the social fabric of which he is a part, why should that concern him? If it be argued that he may shorten his

own life in the process, then we have no less an authority than
Aristotle to the effect that the "good man . . . would prefer a short
period of intense pleasure for a long run of mild enjoyment, a twelve-
month of noble life to many years of humdrum existence."[35] And
in the matter of enjoying "intense pleasure" the wicked man acts
very much like the good man, preferring a short period of intense
pleasure to a long life of mild enjoyment. To be sure, Aristotle has
his own definition for the "good man" and the "noble life" and for
"intense pleasure." But every man certainly has the right to decide
what he considers "intense pleasure." Within the limits of the
secular he has as much right as anyone else to decide what he wants
most out of his existence upon this earth.

To the argument that by his action he may grievously impair
the welfare of future generations, which include his own descendants,
there is the well-known response attributed to Louis XV of France
when his ministers warned him that his policies would lead to the
ruin of France: *"Après mois le déluge."* Why should one determine
his action by what might or might not happen to others after he
is dead?

To counter this obvious weakness in the secularly oriented rationale of "enlightened self-interest," secularists have recourse to
formulas and dicta which in fact take them beyond the realm of
the secular. They ground their ethics in such propositions as every
rational being insofar as he is rational should intend by his act (a)
to achieve the greatest possible happiness for the greatest possible
number, or (b) to implement the concept of justice, or (c) to
achieve the good. These and similar dicta are appealed to by religionists as well as by secularists to rationalize the unethical as well as
the ethical. We shall discuss them later in section IV.

SECTION III

*The Secular Rationalization
of the Moral*

The difficulties faced by the secularist in rationalizing the ethical are compounded when he attempts to rationalize the moral; that is, an agent's intention to advance an object's welfare while being fully aware of the serious impairment that will inevitably or most likely result therefrom to himself.

André Malraux in his *Anti-Memoirs* remarks: "If it is true that for a religious spirit the [Nazi concentration] camps, like the torture of an innocent child by a brute, pose the supreme riddle, it is also true that for an agnostic spirit the same riddle springs up with the first act of compassion, heroism, or love."[36] We shall return later in this inquiry to Malraux's generalization regarding the "supreme riddle" for the "religious spirit." For the present, we are concerned only with the "agnostic spirit."

Acts of compassion, heroism, or love are acts motivated by an intention to benefit the object even while injuring the subject. To the agnostic spirit, such morally motivated acts are a supreme riddle because agnosticism offers no cogent rationale for such acts. The agnostic, like the scientist or the secular existentialist,[37] has recourse only to sensibly accessible data. On the basis of the evidence thus available, he must conclude that "there is no ultimate meaning to existence,"[38] that is to say, existence, in its most tangible physical sense, is its own ultimate meaning. Hence, any act which in any way impairs or limits one's physical existence must rationally be considered as an evil to be avoided. How then can one possibly rationalize the moral intention and its consequent act of compassion, heroism, or love?

From the fact that agnostics have no way of cogently rationalizing the moral, it does not follow that self-acknowledged agnostics do not perform acts of heroism and love. For some agnostics these acts do not constitute a riddle. If they have no acceptable rationalization for them, they do have what appears to be an adequate explanation. Human acts reflecting the moral intent are equated by them with the well-established phenomena of animals sacrificing themselves for the protection of their offspring or of their group.[39] The performance of such acts by human beings is thus explained as part of our biological heritage, like sex or fear. "To be rooted in a biological mechanism serving a biological need seems to many to be all the justification human behavior can ultimately ask."[40] These acts, therefore, require no further rationalization.

However, except for the most doctrinaire agnostics, one cannot remain impervious to the fact that no human act, and certainly not an act of love and heroism, ever remains on the purely animal, instinctive level. It is either preceded by a conscious awareness of the contemplated act and its possible consequences for the agent or is followed by an awareness and an evaluation of those consequences. The supreme riddle for the agnostic is not to explain a biologically rooted act, but to rationalize a consciously avowed moral intent which either preceded the act or which was associated with the act after it had been performed so that the agent would, if necessary, be ready to repeat it.

There are those, therefore, who declare the consciously avowed moral intent to be in essence either non-existent or irrational self-delusion. "Since reason demands nothing which is opposed to nature, it demands, therefore, that every person should love himself, should seek his own profit—what is truly profitable to him, should desire everything that really leads man to greater perfection, and absolutely that everyone should endeavor, as far as in him lies, to preserve his own being."[41] "The endeavor after self-preservation is the essence itself of a thing . . . and is the primary and only foundation of virtue."[42]

Agnostics may in theory accept the conclusion that acts of love and heroism which involve a degree of self-sacrifice are expressions of either instinctive animal behavior, or of "womanish pity,"[43] or of the suicidal drive within us.[44] This conclusion is, however, emotionally abhorrent to most agnostics. "Sacrifice," Malraux somewhere remarks, "is never contemptible." No matter what we may think of a self-sacrificing act of compassion, heroism, and love on the rational level, we cannot, on the emotional level, resist the apparently ingrained reaction of admiration, and even of awe, in its presence, even if the act is performed by one whom we otherwise hold in utter contempt, such as a Nazi. The agnostic is thus torn between the emotional reaction of awe and the rational reaction of disparagement. And just as the religious believer in a just and loving God seeks ways to bridge the gap between God's justice and love and the presence of evil in the world, the agnostic tries to find a rationally acceptable role for moral intentions and acts in a world whose ultimate arbiters he believes to be meaningless blind force and matter.

Hence, having decided that "there is no ultimate meaning to existence," agnostics "call upon men to create with lucidity their own private meanings and purposes in the knowledge that no power in the cosmos will deliberately sustain or validate them."[45] But within such an intellectual framework, the rationally least defensible "private meanings and purposes" would seem to be those which encourage the nurture and implementation of moral intentions.[46] And yet that is precisely what some of the secularist, universalist-hedonistic, or utilitarian school[47] of moralists ask us to do. They ask us to accept "as the foundation of morals . . . the greatest happiness principle."[48] This school of thought is not concerned with "the agent's own greatest happiness, but the greatest amount of happiness altogether." Because "it is unquestionably possible to do without happiness . . . it often has to be done voluntarily by the hero or the martyr." Indeed, we are told, "it is noble to be capable of resigning entirely one's own portion of happiness or chances of it. . . . All honor to those who can abnegate for themselves the personal enjoyment of life, when by such renunciation they contribute worthily to increase the amount of happiness in the world."[49] Nowhere, however, do they tell us why an individual who forgoes his own happiness for the sake of others is to be designated as "noble" rather than "irrational." If there is nothing more important or more precious than happiness here and now, why should someone's or even mankind's happiness be more important to anyone than his own? What rational argument can one offer for commending one who forgoes his own welfare or pleasure in order to advance the welfare and pleasure of any number of other individuals in a world in which the only thing that can possibly have any meaning is physical existence here and now?[50] Shall we offer as a "rational" argument the proposition that moral intentions and their implementation bring one fame and admiration from his contemporaries or descendants, and that these give one the greatest possible pleasure available to man? To the truly noble mind the love of fame is not a noble motivation, and to the rational agnostic spirit, it is not a rational motivation.[51] Insofar as contemporary fame is concerned, anyone with a modicum of understanding soon recognizes how hollow and ephermeral it is at its best.

> When I have fears that I may cease to be
> Before my pen hath gleaned my teeming brain,
> . . . then on the shore
> Of the wide world I stand alone, and think
> Till Love and Fame to nothingness do sink.[52]

As for posthumous fame, what possible significance can it rationally have for a logically consistent secularist or agnostic? What sense does it make to achieve at the expense of one's life, or even of a small fraction of it, a goal which cannot conceivably have any meaning to him who achieves it, when its achievement coincides with his own physical annihilation?[53]

Indeed, it may be cogently argued that our admiration for those who make sacrifices in our behalf is little more than an insidious expression of our self-love. By honoring these "misguided," "self-deluded" idealists we are encouraging them to advance our welfare at their expense and with the least expenditure on our part. The bestowal of admiration or fame is society's cheapest method to advance its own welfare, and only fools fall for it.

Theodor Herzl, after attending his last Zionist Congress, at which he was vilified and denounced as a traitor to his own movement, and being fully aware that he had literally given his all to the movement, noted in his diary: "What a fool I would be if I were to do this for their thanks."[54]

Kant, who is as far removed from utilitarianism as one can be, nevertheless also finds it difficult to include the moral within his philosophy of ethics. Thus he presents the case of one who "is himself flourishing, but he sees others who are struggling with great hardships (and whom he could easily help); and he thinks 'what does it matter to me? Let everyone be as happy as Heaven wills or as he can make himself; I won't deprive him of anything; I won't envy him; only I have no wish to contribute anything to his well being or to his support in distress!' Now admittedly if such an attitude were a universal law of nature, *Mankind could get on perfectly well. . . .* But although *it is possible that a universal law of nature could subsist in harmony with this maxim,* yet it is impossible to *will* that such a principle should hold everywhere as the law of nature. For a will which decided in this way could be in conflict with itself, since many a situation might arise *in which the man needed love and sympathy from others,* and in which, by such a law of nature sprung from his own will, he would rob himself of all hope of the help he wants for himself." What Kant is rationalizing here is not the moral as we have defined it, but the ethical. The doctrine underlying it is not the doctrine of duty as related to the categorical imperative, but a doctrine of down-to-earth prudence.[55]

Hence, it must be obvious that if ethical intentions could not be cogently rationalized within consistently secular terms, then surely moral intentions cannot so be rationalized.

SECTION IV

The Secular Rationalization
of the Unethical

We have defined as unethical an agent's intention to impair the welfare of an object. We are, therefore, not concerned in this inquiry with injuries which were unpremeditated and later regretted. Our concern relates only to the rationalizations offered for consciously avowed intentions to inflict injury upon an object. There is something in man which makes him feel unhappy when he does something to others which he would not have others do to him. Man needs a rationale for his unethical as well as his ethical intentions. That is true not only of individuals, but also of groups. "Exploiting groups seek to cover up in their own eyes, as well as in the minds of the exploited, the fact that they are inflicting misery, and they make the strangest ideological inventions to achieve this purpose."[56]

There are those who believe that an unethical intention can never be satisfactorily rationalized and, therefore, that one ought never to harbor it, much less to implement it. Jesus, in the Sermon on the Mount (Matt. 5:39–40, 44), gave this doctrine its best-known formulation. But for the overwhelming majority of mankind this position is unacceptable.[57] There are too many occasions in the life of every individual when he feels convinced beyond doubt that he is rationally justified in intending to inflict an injury upon another individual.

The consistently logical secularist attempts to rationalize his unethical intentions by basing them upon propositions whose validity appears to him to be self-evident and therefore in no need of further metaphysical grounding. These propositions are usually formulated in a manner that would appear to stress their function as guides for ethical intentions rather than for unethical ones. They are, however, appealed to in practical life, more frequently to justify the kind of ethical intentions which are dependent upon the implementation of subsidiary unethical intentions.

1. *Might makes right.* The oldest of these, which is still very widely practiced and tacitly accepted, though less frequently openly avowed, is the doctrine that might makes right. This doctrine was expounded with unsurpassed clarity by Thucydides, in the answer which he attributes to the Athenians who came to demand that the Melians join them in the war against Sparta or else be utterly annihilated. The Melians plead for justice and then express their hope that, their cause being just, the gods will help them, and that the Lacedaemonians will be "bound, if only for very shame, to come to the aid of their kindred." To this the Athenians are reported to have replied:

When you speak of the favour of the gods, we may as fairly hope for that as yourselves; neither our pretensions nor our conduct being in any way contrary to what men believe of the gods, or practise among themselves. Of the gods we believe, and of men we know, that by a necessary law of their nature they rule wherever they can. And it is not as if we were the first to make this law, or to act upon it when made: we found it existing before us, and shall leave it to exist forever after us; all we do is to make use of it, knowing that you and everybody else, having the same power as we have, would do the same as we do. Thus, as far as the gods are concerned, we have no fear and no reason to fear that we shall be at a disadvantage. But when we come to your notion about the Lacedaemonians, which leads you to believe that shame will make them help you, here we bless your simplicity but do not envy your folly. The Lacedaemonians, when their own interests or their country's laws are in question, are the worthiest men alive; of their conduct towards others much might be said, but no clearer idea of it could be given than by shortly saying that of all the men we know they are most conspicuous in considering what is agreeable—honorable, and what is expedient—just. Such a way of thinking does not promise much for the safety which you now unreasonably count upon.[58]

This doctrine that both the gods and men "by a necessary law of their nature rule wherever they can" found its modern embodiment in "the mainstream of 19th- and early 20th-century ethical interpretations of evolution," which "sang the praises of struggle as the instrument of upward movement. Herbert Spencer's *Social Static* which (as Spencer pointed out later) actually antedated Darwin's *On the Origin of Species* launched the era in which the struggle for existence and the survival of the fittest were to become major slogans of a predatory business ethics. The suffering of the poor, the miseries of the oppressed were seen as by-products of a beneficent evolutionary process in which the able came to the top and the unfit were wiped out. Any interference with this self-propelling upward and onward system of struggle and competition was evil, an absolute violation of nature's moral law."[59]

We should not delude ourselves into thinking that this apotheosis of struggle, of might and of war, which is the ultimate expression of the doctrine that might makes right, is characteristic only of out-spoken militarists, nihilists, or militant revolutionaries. We should recall that it was Hegel who had written that "war has the higher meaning that through it, as I have said elsewhere, 'The ethical health of nations is maintained. . . . just as the motion of the winds keep the seas from the foulness which a constant calm would produce—so war prevents a corruption of nations which a perpetual, let alone an eternal peace would produce.' "[60]

If there are those today who see in the development of nuclear weapons the hope for the ultimate elimination of war from human society, that hope is not based on the proposition that men will, as a matter of principle, reject the dictum that might makes right wherever might can be used, but rather that men will be wise enough to see that as between two equally equipped nuclear powers might cannot function as arbiter. For the moment, the existence of nuclear weapons seems to be man's greatest source of hope, not for a rejection in theory of the proposition that might makes right or for a warless world, but rather for the assumption that nations equally equipped with nuclear weapons will not, if they do not go stark mad, go to war. But it is yet far from certain whether that hope will be realized. Moreover, it may very well be that mankind will prefer to reject the use of nuclear arms in order to be able again to deter-mine who is right in a given dispute by resorting to "conventional arms."[61] Thus far the nuclear-armed powers are doing precious little to discourage those not so armed from using their conventional arms to settle their differences.

2. *The concept of justice.* The second main line of argument for the secular rationalization of the unethical is associated with the concept of justice. The administration of justice almost always in-volves the unethical intention to impair someone's welfare, to punish him because he has violated the requirements of justice.

As secularly conceived, justice is a concept which came into being as a result of the application by man of his increasing intellectual capacities to his daily experiences. It is associated directly or indirectly with some aspect of the Hobbesian theory of a "contract." Hobbes contrasts the *jus naturale,* the right of nature, with the *lex naturale,* the law of nature, "which others confound yet they ought to be distinguished." By the right of nature, Hobbes understands "the liberty of each man to use his own power, as he will himself, for the preservation of . . . his own life; and consequently of doing anything, which in his own judgement and reason, he shall conceive to be the aptest means thereunto."[62] "To this war of every man against every man, this is also consequent: that nothing can be unjust. . . . Where there is no common power, there is no law; where no law, no injustice. Force and fraud are in war the two cardinal virtues. Justice and injustice are none of the faculties neither of the body nor mind."[63] A law of nature for Hobbes "is a precept or general rule, found out by reason, by which a man is forbidden to do that which is destructive of his life or takes away the means of preserving the same. . . ." Hence "it is a precept, or general rule of reason, that every man ought to endeavor peace, as far as he has hope of obtaining it." This Hobbes designates as "the first and fundamental law of nature."

Thus "public benevolence or the regard for the interest of mankind" was not the original motive of justice. It was concern for one's own best interest that led to the conclusion that all members at least of one's family or tribe had as much right as he did to share in the enjoyment of whatever there was to be enjoyed, and that if one wanted to be undisturbed in the enjoyment of his share of it, he had to permit others to remain undisturbed in their enjoyment of their share of it. And that, says Hobbes, "is the law of the Gospel: 'Whatsoever you require that others should do to you, that do ye to them ' "[64] (Matt. 7:12). This law of nature led to "the mutual transfer of right which men call contract," [65] and to the establishment of governments and the formulation of laws and customs to spell out each man's rights. When one felt that his personal right, as defined by these laws and customs, had been violated, he felt "justified" in seeking to inflict injury upon the violator. We continue to feel that way except that in civilized societies the individual is forbidden to take the law into his own hands. We require that the authorities established by the society should inflict the punishment due a violator of justice. For Freud, "this replacement of the power of the individual—which is condemned as 'brute force'—by the power of the community—which is set up as 'right'—constitutes the decisive step of civilization."[66] "But man's natural aggressive instinct, the hostility of each against all, and of all against each, opposes this programme of civilization."[67] Hobbes' *lex naturale* has not abdicated.

The administration of justice thus conceived is to serve two readily comprehended purposes. (a) It is to serve as a deterrent, "so that all may hear and fear and not continue to do such an evil thing" (Deut. 13:12), and thus assure to the law-abiding members of the society, the enjoyment of their rights. (b) It sees to it "that the sinner shall not profit by his sin." It justifies the imposition of an injury upon the transgressor which as accurately as possible equals the injury he may have caused to others. Hence, justice is conceived as being relevant only to the affairs of man, and from the long-range point of view it is considered to be the indispensable servant of man's mundane self-interest. We shall discuss later the limitations of this secular concept of justice.[68]

3. *That the benefit exceed the injury.* The third proposition whereby the secularist rationalizes the unethical is that the injury anticipated from the implementation of the subsidiary unethical intention is less than the benefit anticipated from the implementation of the ethical intention.[69]

The human situation being what it is, it is well-nigh impossible always to avoid having recourse to a subsidiary unethical intention in order to implement an ethical intention. This proposition obviously has merit when both the ethical and unethical intentions are directed toward the same object, as when A intends to injure B in order thereby to benefit him. Thus a surgeon removes a limb in order to benefit the patient. A parent punishes a child for the child's own "future good." There may then be reasonable expectation that one could measure the harm against the good with a fair degree

of accuracy. But the harm inflicted always precedes the good anticipated. The harm is certain, the good always uncertain. Hence,
one must be as humanly certain as possible that he cannot achieve
his ethical intention in a way other than via a subsidiary unethical
intention.

4. *The greatest possible good for the greatest possible number.* The problem of measuring benefit against injury becomes infinitely more complicated when the agent's subsidiary unethical
intention and his primary ethical intention are directed toward two
different objects, one or both of which may be either an individual
or a group of people. Thus if the only factor to be considered is
the excess of benefit over injury, then why is it not ethical for A to
inflict injury on B if thereby the benefit accruing to A will exceed
the injury inflicted by him upon B? When thus formulated, it becomes obvious that the excess of benefit over injury cannot in itself
be an adequate standard for gauging ethical intentions.[70] Hence,
the proposition is modified to read that "one should always intend
so to act as to achieve the greatest possible good for the greatest
possible number."[71] Thus formulated it undoubtedly has some virtue
as a rough measuring rod for the practical politician or statesman
whose chief qualification is an intuitive sense for the possible. It has
the additional virtue that it does not presume to define the good,
nor does it assume that even if it were definable one must strive
always to implement it. It implies that its proponents claim to know
only what is the greatest possible good for the greatest possible
number.

Moreover, it is generally assumed that "the greatest possible
number" to which it refers is presently existing. It does not include
generations yet unborn. Nevertheless, I believe it would be nearer
the truth to say that, as employed in the daily affairs of mankind, it
serves as often as not as a linguistically camouflaged version of the
proposition that might makes right. The greatest possible number
have actually or potentially the greatest possible power, and they
are, therefore, by "nature" entitled to the greatest possible good. It
is, moreover, among the chief components of the demagogue's
arsenal of slogans and half-truths, whereby to rationalize his perse-

cution of dissident minorities, whether they be minorities of one or
of a million. It plagues the conscience of the persecuted, who are
directly or indirectly led to feel, or even to believe, that they should
somehow eliminate themselves in order to increase the amount of
happiness in the world.[72]

5. *The good.* There are those who claim to know the good,
the absolute and ultimate good. For them the pursuit of the good
is in no way to be impeded by consideration for the happiness of
the greatest number of their contemporaries. On the contrary, they
usually assume that only a minority of their contemporaries are
either capable of appreciating the good that is being offered them
or worthy of enjoying it. They believe, however, that in the long
run the good they plan to achieve will bring happiness to the greatest possible number, for in that number they include the generations
yet unborn.[73] The most ruthless of subsidiary unethical intentions
and acts are thus rationalized. One need but recall not only the
half-mad racists, but the host of high-minded religionists and political revolutionaries who were so sure they knew not only what the
good was, but also exactly how to achieve it, that they had little
trouble in rationalizing the most inhuman persecutions and exter-
minations of infidels, heretics, and dissidents.[74]

The experience of mankind would seem, by and large, to validate the generalization that the nobler the conception of the good
in which one unquestionably believes, the more ruthless would he
tend to be in pursuing it. It applies equally to religionists and secularists. The appeal to the good as a rationalization for the unethical
intention should therefore always be suspect, both because we cannot possibly know what *the good* is, nor can we ever be certain that
the consequences of the acts by which one seeks to implement the
subsidiary unethical intention will in fact result in the hoped-for
good.

Of the above-listed secular rationalizations of the unethical, the
only one that is cogently related to the agnostic spirit is the proposition that might makes right, that whatever one can do to advance
his own welfare he is rationally justified in doing. In a world which
is meaningless, the only cogent rationale possible for any inten-

tion is that it advances the agent's welfare. Hence the concept of justice, from the secular point of view, is a cogent rationalization of an intention only when thereby the agent's welfare is advanced. But when the administration of justice would impair the agent's welfare, the agnostic spirit, as we shall later indicate,[75] should and does, with cogent logic, urge him to circumvent justice and do what he can do to advance his own interest.

Thus also from an agnostic point of view, A's intention to injure B in order thereby to benefit him may be cogently rationalized only when B's consent is given, or when B for some obvious valid reason is not in a position either to give or withhold his consent. But what, from an agnostic point of view, gives anyone the right to decide what would be the greatest possible good for the greatest possible number, or what is the absolute good, and then on the basis of that decision to rationalize acts which inflict injury on anyone?

The fact remains, however, that these rationalizations of the ethical and the moral and the unethical have been formulated and defended by secular rationalists of the greatest intellectual distinction. If these rationalizations are as illogical as the foregoing presentation maintains, how explain their failure to take note of it? The truth of the matter seems to be that wittingly or unwittingly they did take note of it, and that the ultimate rationalizations of their positions rest upon grounds that are more akin to the religious than to the secular. Whether knowingly or inadvertently, they introduce into their rationalizations components which are not accessible to the senses and which cannot be fully comprehended by reason. Hence, in accordance with our definition of a religious rationalization, these are in essence religious in nature.[76]

SECTION V

The Religious Component in the Secular Rationalization of the Moral and the Ethical

Secular rationalizations of the ethical and the moral infringe upon the religious in a number of aspects:

1. In the tacit or explicit assumption that the universe, or the human component of it, is so constituted that the ethical and the moral coincide with the self-interest of the agent.[77] As we indicated above,[78] this assumption is not subject to empirical validation. It calls for as vigorous an act of faith as the biblical assurance that "if you obey the commandments that I enjoin upon you this day . . . you shall gather in your new grain and wine and oil . . . thus you shall eat your fill" (Deut. 11:13–15).

2. The tacit or explicit assumption that one should identify his self with his so-called higher self—that is, with his soul,[79] or his reason,[80] or his intellect,[81] rather than with his physical being. It is the interests or the welfare of this higher self that the moral and the ethical are to advance. On the basis of this dualistic conception of the human person, a distinction is made between the lower and the higher pleasures and pains, the former associated with the body, the latter with the soul or reason or intellect. Moreover, without offering any convincing evidence, it is apodictically assumed that those who have experienced both kinds of pleasures overwhelmingly prefer the higher to the lower.[82]

However, the division between higher and lower pleasures has been challenged, not by crass sensualists, but by sensitive and discriminating individuals. W. H. Auden maintains that "it is nonsense to speak of higher and lower pleasures. All pleasures are equally good."[83] Bentham categorically affirms that "quantity of pleasure being equal, 'push-pin' is as good as poetry." [84] For Freud "There is only one pleasure; it is biological and undifferentiated. Following his biological model, Freud refuses to define pleasure in other than quantitative terms. There is no diversity of pleasure, such as pleasure of friendship or of creating, but only more or less pleasure. . . . Pleasure is the diminution of the needs derived from the instincts and displeasure is a heightening of those needs."[85]

But whether challenged by others or not, on what logical basis can the secularist ask A to be guided by the experience of B in an area so completely subjective as pleasure and pain? Human experience, it seems, has established beyond doubt that the so-called lower pleasures are preferred by the overwhelming proportion of mankind, and that very large numbers do not have either the natural inclination or the necessary training to enjoy the so-called higher pleasures.

Be that as it may, one thing is clear. No one can empirically prove that the soul, reason, or the intellect have any reality outside the reality of the body with which they are associated and through which association we come to know them. If so, the proposition that the welfare or pleasures of the intellect or the spirit should take precedence over the welfare or pleasures of the body constitutes a radical reversal of the order of things as conceived by any consistently logical, modern, evolutionary, secular view of the place of man and mind in the universe. The mind, or soul, or reason, we are told by evolutionists, evolved as the servant of the body, as the most efficient tool thus far developed by any animal in its struggle to exist. From the secularist-evolutionary point of view, a human being who knowingly permits his mind to dominate his body, to the point of sacrificing the pleasures or welfare of the body for the pleasure or welfare of the mind or the soul, has failed to learn the most important lesson science is supposed to teach us. There are, to be sure, those who maintain that in evolving the human brain, the blind evolutionary process has produced a phenomenon which is, or can be if it so decides, independent of the process which brought it forth, and can decide its own future course until such a time as the earth and all thereon would be utterly in ruin. But in order to achieve that, the mind would have to take full control over the body and all its primitive heritage of greed, aggressiveness, sexual indulgence, hate, and so forth. Man's so-called animal heritage would have to be fully subservient to his "higher" endowments.[86] It does not require too much acumen to note the analogy between the mind's revolt against the blind evolutionary process, which is said to have accidentally brought it forth, and man's revolt against God, who created him out of His love. In the Bible man seeks to unseat God and occupy His throne (Gen. 11:4, Isa. 14:3–14). In secularist ethical thinking, mind should, so to speak, unseat natural evolution and take control of the process. Nothing in man's experience thus far would indicate that an intellect which is the product of a blind evolutionary force has any greater chance of success in its revolt against its forebear than man had in his revolt against God.

Nay more. From the secular point of view, one can make out a good case for the proposition that the appearance of mind has been a misfortune to its possessor. Instead of limiting itself to the task of serving the body, the mind has become self-serving at the expense of the welfare of the body, and often motivates the body to deeds that result in the impairment of its own welfare. Sub-human creatures are, as far as we know, not tortured by feelings of guilt, or ambition, or pride, or jealousy. Nor are they prone to risk their lives for the sake of their "honor" or in order to win the applause of their fellow creatures. Nor are they subject to moods of despair and futility leading to suicide. If the achievement of happy mundane existence, which is the secularist's rationally inescapable and ultimate synonym for self-interest, is the touchstone for human behavior, then the self-serving mind can hardly be considered man's greatest asset. Indeed, the skeptic of the Bible can be said to have been much more logically consistent than the modern secularist. He drew the conclusion which man's historical experience seems to validate—namely, that "in much wisdom there is much vexation; and he that increaseth knowledge, increaseth sorrow" (Eccles. 1:18). Hence, the cogency of the admonition, "Be not righteous overmuch, and do not make yourself overwise; why should you destroy yourself?" (ibid., 7:16).

One of the paradoxical consequences of the secularist's emphasis upon the supremacy of the pleasures of the higher faculties results from the fact that when taken to its logical conclusion, it leads to almost as severe an asceticism as ever was associated with religion. Epicurus is said to have contented himself with water and brown bread. "A Christian sermon could not scoff at the love of sensory voluptuousness with the harshness of Lucretius,"[87] the most famous of the disciples of Epicurus. But such ascetic implementation of the secular higher-pleasure doctrine was and is, understandably, a rarity. It usually finds its expression in an "enlightened" or a not so enlightened self-abandonment to the "impulses of nature" or in a philosophy of non-involvement. "Who has not met, even today, a practical sage, unknowingly epicurean, moderated in tastes, virtuous without great moral ambition, anxious to live well? He aims to keep body and spirit and soul healthy; he only indulges in pleasures which leave no regrets, in opinions which are undisturbing; he watches his own passions and flees those of others. If he does not allow himself to be tempted by positions and honors, it is due to fear of taking a risk or of being beaten in a contest. . . . he disposes his life with a timid prudence, and does not go abroad among men, except in the circle of his friends where he can enjoy the sentiments which he inspires and those which he approves."[88] He takes no advantage of his fellow man because he has disciplined himself to disdain the objects that such advantage might bring to him. But he feels no duty to exert himself to help his fellow man.

3. Secular philosophers also posit a metaphysic for their ethical systems. The inescapable fact seems to be that every philosophy of human behavior worthy of consideration must, in the final analysis, be grounded in metaphysics, even as every system of metaphysics, of necessity, has implications for the ethical and the moral.[89]

Kant distinguishes between a metaphysics of nature and a metaphysics of morals, nature being identified with the sensibly accessible universe, and morals, with the rationally incomprehensible realm of freedom.[90]

In his metaphysics of nature Kant has no room, and finds no need whatsoever, for God. In his metaphysics of morals, however, he finds it necessary to posit both God—even though he cannot prove that God exists[91]—and the immortality of the soul.[92]

The metaphysic which underlies the ethical thought of the secular moralists of our day consists of the "scientific" view of the origin and nature of the universe. The relationship between this metaphysic and ethics has been passionately rather than persuasively formulated by Bertrand Russell in his essay "A Free Man's Worship," written in 1902, long before the term *existentialism* came into vogue.[93]

A strange mystery it is that Nature, omnipotent but blind, in the revolutions of her secular hurryings through the abysses of space, has brought forth at last a child, subject still to her power, but gifted with sight, with knowledge of good and evil, with the capacity of judging all the works of his unthinking Mother. In spite of Death, the mark and seal of the parental control, Man is yet free, during his brief years, to examine, to criticize, to know, and in imagination to create. To him alone, in the world with which he is acquainted, this freedom belongs; and in this lies his superiority to the resistless forces that control his outward life. . . .[94]

To defy with Promethean constancy a hostile universe, to keep its evil always in view, always actively hated, to refuse no pain that the malice of Power can invent, appears to be the duty of all who will not bow before the inevitable.[95]

To abandon the struggle for private happiness, to expel all eagerness of temporary desire, to burn with passion for eternal things— this is emancipation, and this is the free man's worship. . . .

One by one, as they march, our comrades vanish from our sight. . . . Very brief is the time in which we can help them, in which their happiness or misery is decided. Be it ours to shed sunshine on their path, to lighten their sorrows by the balm of sympathy, to give them the pure joy of a never-tiring affection, to strengthen failing courage, to instil faith in hours of despair. . . .[96]

The two disparate components of this eloquent secular rationalization of the moral and the ethical constitute a patent *non-sequitur*. After positing a metaphysic which cannot be empirically validated, we are asked to believe, nay to stake our lives upon the proposition, that this blind, thoughtless universe could by "secular hurryings through the abysses of space bring forth a child . . . with the capacity of judging all the works of his unthinking Mother." No religion has ever required a greater act of faith from its followers. Then, overwhelmed by the sense of tragedy and despair induced by this metaphysic, Russell counsels men to "abandon the struggle for private happiness" and to give to our comrades "the pure joy of a never-tiring affection."

Neither Russell nor the modern existentialists were the first to posit a metaphysic which declared that human existence was meaningless and that "all is vanity and a striving after wind" (Eccles. 1:1–14). But the consequences for human behavior which the author of Ecclesiastes drew from this metaphysic were at least logically related to it.

> Wherefore I praised the dead which are already dead more than the living which are yet alive. Yea, better is he than both they, which hath not yet been, who hath not seen the evil work that is done under the sun. (Eccles. 4:2–3).

However, having been born, "There is nothing better for a man than that he should eat and drink and find enjoyment in his toil" (ibid. 2:24).

It makes sense "to prompt men to ethical action by the sublime assumption that the universe is itself ethical in its ultimate nature, whatever data to the contrary the immediate and obvious scene may reveal."[97] But what sense does it make to call upon men to opt for the ethical and the moral while simultaneously stressing the utter doom that awaits us and that there is no power in the cosmos that in any way sustains and validates the ethical and the moral?

Hazel Barnes, despite her existentialist position, makes a valiant effort to ascribe some meaning to the life of man. But she finds it necessary to appeal ultimately to a faith as transcendental, as utterly beyond the human mind to comprehend or human experience to validate, as any ever proposed by the most imaginative of religionists. She rejects Russell's position because it "implicitly adopts an unproved hypothesis about man—that the human condition will not essentially change. If we wanted to quibble, we might point out that even in this assumption, we do not necessarily link man's demise and the death of our planet or even of the solar system. The scientific view of man includes faith in the continued growth of his technology. The possibility of his moving to other planets and systems exists, and there is a reasonable hope that he will be allowed the time he needs in order to work out the difficulties of getting there." Moreover, the existentialist dogma "that man is free and self-transcending" implies for her the belief "that man has the possibility of becoming something quite different from what he has been —and this, not just socially and technologically. To say that he will do so is to make a statement of faith that man will live up to his potentialities. Humanistic existentialism too recognizes that faith is a necessary ingredient, perhaps even an ontological structure of the human being."[98]

No greater faith was ever asked of man. Moreover, the vision Hazel Barnes sets before us in no way helps us to answer the question why in the meantime we, who are given some three-score years and ten upon this planet, should exert any effort in behalf of any cause or individual which does not directly and patently help us to enjoy every moment of those years. In the future of mankind as here envisioned, no one now on this planet has any conceivable role. Nor is there anything that anyone now alive can knowingly do in order to hasten the appearance of the biological mutation that will enable man to biologically "become something quite different from what he has been."

SECTION VI

The Religious Component in the Secular Rationalization of the Unethical

1. *The doctrine that might makes right.* This doctrine is identified with the secularist position, for the obvious reason that we can see and feel its functioning.

The Athenian exposition of this proposition (see page 22) clearly indicates, however, that it is not a purely secular doctrine. It has very obvious metaphysical overtones. Might is apotheosized. To do what one can do is of the essence of the nature of "the gods and of men." Nor is Spinoza's god in this respect very different from the gods of the Athenians. "Spinoza's god is simply beyond good and evil. God's might is His right, and therefore the power of every being is as such its right. Spinoza lifts Machiavellianism to theological heights. Good and evil differ only from a merely human point of view: theologically the distinction is meaningless.[99] The modern secularist, having eliminated God from the universe, replaces Him by the "forces of nature" and attributes to them what the Athenians are said to have attributed to their gods—that by "a necessary law of their nature they rule where they can." Hence, the widespread apotheosis of violence and of power. Might thus conceived is a metaphysical concept, despite its apparent validation by so much readily accessible, sensible data, because it makes a judgment about the universe which cannot possibly be empirically proved. On the contrary, the evidences of the presence of love, justice, freedom, and other ethical qualities in the life of man which are as readily accessible to the senses as are the evidences of might, cannot be adequately accounted for by the doctrine of might. Hence, the assumption that might is the ultimate arbiter of the universe requires an act of faith, which for some may not be as great an effort as is involved in believing that love and justice are of the essence of the universe. But for others, who experience the reality of love and freedom, to believe that might is the ultimate arbiter in the universe involves an even greater effort.

The religious quality of the doctrine that might makes right is reflected in Russell's statement that "Carlyle and Nietzsche and the creed of Militarism have accustomed us" to "the worship of Force," and in his question, "Shall we worship Force, or shall we worship goodness?"[100] But as we have seen earlier, on the purely metaphysical level Russell himself attributes much more reality, much more permanence, to force than to goodness. According to him, the one belongs to the very essence of the universe, the other is only an accidental offshot which "must inevitably be buried beneath the débris of a universe in ruins." This metaphysical structure is accepted by the secularist as being "if not quite beyond dispute, yet so nearly certain, that no philosophy which rejects it can hope to stand."[101] To that apodictic pronouncement one can with greater validity respond that no "scientific" or secularist view of the universe offers ground upon which an ethical or moral system can hope to stand. This scientific, secularist view of the universe is obviously far more persuasive as a rationalization of the unethical, as expounded by the Athenians and their later disciples, than of the ethical and moral, as presented by Russell and his predecessors and followers.

2. *The religious component in the secular concept of justice.* We noted above that justice as secularly conceived serves man's enlightened self-interest. But as such it is useful only to equals or to the weak. The cogency of the secular rationalization of justice as between equals in power seems adequately convincing. Two equally powerful individuals or groups, intelligent enough to recognize that might cannot serve as an arbiter between them, appeal to justice. It is not convincing when related to unequals in power. A hungry lion facing a lamb is not inclined to listen to appeals to justice. In such a confrontation justice serves only the enlightened self-interest of the lamb. It is the lamb's medicated dart whereby he seeks to paralyze the lion's claws and fangs.[102] Hence, to rationalize the application of justice to human affairs one must posit the equality of all human beings.

That is what Hobbes did. "Nature hath made men so equal, in the faculties of the body and mind as that, though there be found one man sometimes manifestly stronger in body or quicker in mind than another, yet when all is reckoned together, the difference between man and man is not so considerable, as that one man can thereupon claim to himself any benefit, to which another may not pretend as well as he."[103] He defends his thesis in some detail, attacking Aristotle, who "for a foundation of his doctrine, maketh men by nature some more worthy to command . . . others to serve." He declares this to be "not only against reason, but also against experience." Nevertheless, Hobbes has some hesitation about the "natural" equality of men, adding, "or if nature have made men unequal; yet because men that think themselves equal, will not enter into conditions of peace, but upon equal terms, such equality must be admitted."[104]

Locke's position on the subject of natural equality as the basis for justice is almost verbally identical with that of Hobbes, though he quotes "the judicious Hooker"[105] rather than Hobbes, probably because his (Locke's) overall view of the role of civil government differs so radically from that of Hobbes. But while the doctrine that "nature hath made all men equal" may be valid as regards entire races or nations, it obviously is not valid when applied to individuals even within any given race or nation.

> Since nature has not read very carefully the American Declaration of Independence or the French Declaration of the Rights of Man, we are all born unfree and unequal; subject to our physical and psychological heredity, diversely endowed in health and strength, in mental capacity and qualities of character. Inequality is not only natural, it grows with the complexity of civilization. . . . Nature smiles at the union of freedom and equality in our utopias. For freedom and equality are sworn and everlasting enemies and when one prevails the other dies.[106]

Secularists have therefore advanced the argument that even the lion facing the lamb should be concerned with justice because everyone at some point in his experience will find "himself nearer the bottom than the top." That would be convincing "if all men were losers. . . . Faith in equality would then everywhere prevail. But there are winners as well as losers, and most winners are satisfied with the doctrine of inequality. . ."[107] The validation of the concept of justice therefore involves the search for a principle beyond that of equality.

That principle finds expression in the concept of *rights* which are natural and unalienable.[108] The concept "unalienable" is indispensable since certain originally "natural" rights had been "alienated," so to speak, from the individual when he supposedly willingly surrendered them to the state. However, "there are certain rights possessed by each individual American citizen which in his compact with the others he has never surrendered. Some of them, indeed, he is unable to surrender, being in the language of our system unalienable. . . . These precious principles . . . the American citizen derives from no charter granted by his fellow man. He claims them because he is himself a man, fashioned by the same Almighty hand as the rest of his species and entitled to a full share of the blessings with which He has endowed them."[109] Hence, while Hobbes argues that a king may do "all that is done by virtue of his power," a sovereign cannot command a man to kill himself or to incriminate himself because a sovereign is subject to the laws of nature, and by the laws of nature no man has the right to surrender to the king his right of life.[110]

Locke adds that "men being all the workmanship of one omnipotent and infinitely wise Maker . . . they are His property and being furnished with faculties . . . there cannot be supposed any such subordination among us, that may authorize us to destroy one another . . . or impair the life, or what tends to the preservation of the life, the liberty, the health, limb, or goods of another.[111] . . . Upon this is grounded that great law of nature 'Whoso sheddeth man's blood by man shall his blood be shed' " (Gen. 9:6). Note that Locke does not quote the second half of the verse: "For in the image of God was man created." For Locke, nature and God are to all intents synonymous.[112]

Thus the authors of the American Declaration of Independence found it necessary to attribute to the "Creator" not only the power to create, but also the power to endow his creatures with "certain unalienable rights." In the absence of the concept of a Creator who has endowed man with unalienable rights, "there are no natural rights, for from the bare proposition that 'A' is a man nothing follows about 'A''s rights. . . ." And where there are no unalienable rights, the concept of justice as secularly conceived, does not apply to the weak.

"It is an inescapable consequence of the thesis presented in these pages," Grice writes, "that certain classes cannot have natural rights: animals, human embryo, future generations, lunatics and children under the age of ten. . . . When we speak of the rights of children we must be understood as speaking of rights which mature peoples have in regard to the treatment of them by other mature people . . . nor are they [rights] bestowed upon them at the moment of conception; they grow into the possession of natural rights . . . as they come to understand the notion of a contract and come to understand what it is to be under an obligation to other people."[113] Locke also does not quite know what to do about children. "Children, I confess, are not born in this full state of equality, though they are born to it." It is only "age and reason" which, according to Locke, "loosen the bonds of this subjection" of children to parents.[114]

The inadequacies of a consistently secular concept of justice, which must seek its validation exclusively in the principle of a mundane enlightened self-interest, are then obvious. But when one associates with justice, the concepts "equality," "unalienable rights," and "creator," he obviously reaches out beyond the secular and scientific. He has recourse to concepts whose substantive content is not objectively observable and which deal, not with "material, natural relationships between physically observable phenomena," but rather with intangible moral and ethical relationships between man and his fellow man and the universe.

3. *The religious component in the relativistic or the absolute concept of the "good."* We noted above that one of the secular rationalizations of the unethical involves the concept of the "good." For the purpose immediately before us—namely, that of establishing the encroachment of this apparently secular rationalization upon the religious—the distinction between the relativistic and absolute concepts of the "good" is irrelevant. For whether one speaks of the good in absolute terms or in the relativistic terms of "the greatest good for the greatest number," the fact is that the concept of the "good" or the "greatest good" cannot be defined in terms that would be generally acceptable to either science, philosophy, or religion. If it is to be specifically assigned to any one of the three realms, its most likely place is in the realm of religion, for its chief concern is

that of guiding man in his relation to himself and his fellow man. The secularist who employs his own definition of this concept to rationalize his ethical philosophy, and more particularly to rationalize the unethical, is, whether wittingly or unwittingly, playing God.

SECTION VII

Judaism and the Ethical
Some Preliminary Remarks

As was noted above (page 16), André Malraux states that "for a religious spirit the [Nazi concentration] camps, like the torture of an innocent child by a brute, pose the supreme riddle." The religious spirit manifests itself in a variety of tangible forms and literary formulations. There is only one characteristic which is common to all its manifestations, and that is its ceaseless striving to reach out to realms not accessible to the senses, and its insistence upon defining proper human behavior either in terms of dictates believed to emanate from those realms, or in terms of the behavior logically implied by one's conception of the character of those realms.

The torture of an innocent child does *not* pose "the supreme riddle" for *all* expressions of the religious spirit. We know that the religious spirit has manifested itself in human sacrifice, and in the most brutal persecutions of heretics and non-believers. While all the enlightened religions, both eastern and western deplore "the torture of an innocent child by a brute," the presence of evil in the world does not pose an equally insoluble riddle for all of them. For some the solution is found in a denial of the reality of evil;[115] for others it is found in some form of the Zoroastrian concept of the dual government of the universe, one the source of evil, the other the source of good.[116] The torture of the innocent child poses the supreme riddle primarily to the religious spirit that manifests itself in the monotheistic teaching of the Hebrew Bible, to which the unknown prophet of the exile gave its most uncompromising expression: "I

am the Lord, and there is none else, there is no God beside Me; . . .
I form the light, and create darkness; I make peace, and create
evil; I the Lord do all these things" (Isa. 45:5–7).

The basic sources of Judaism are the Hebrew Bible, the Babylonian Talmud and the Jerusalem Talmud, the tannaitic and later
rabbinic Midrashim. The chief concern of this vast literature is the
problem of human behavior, and it encompasses an elaborate legal
system touching every aspect of human activity. Though these
sources do not constitute a theological or philosophic system, they
are permeated by a large number of intricately and organically
related value concepts related to human behavior.[117] Hence, a comprehensive study of the ethics of Judaism would require an analysis
of each of them. The purpose of this inquiry is more modest. We
are concerned only with the manner in which Biblical-Rabbinic
thought related to the rationalization of the ethical, the unethical,
and the moral.

Because there is no systematically arranged theology or ethics
in the sources indicated, and because these sources are replete with
differences of opinion among the Rabbis, it is important to note here
that such statements as "the Rabbis teach, or say, or comment" or
"the Midrash states," etc., used in the course of this inquiry, should
not be taken to represent a unanimous opinion. Many of the opinions are attributed in the sources to one or more individuals; many
are stated anonymously. Some are stated specifically as minority
opinions. When we use such expressions as "the Rabbis say," our
intention is to indicate that the statement referred to had sufficiently
widespread acceptance among the builders of the Biblical-Rabbinic
tradition to warrant our treating it as an authentic expression of
what George Foote Moore called "the authoritative tradition of
normative Judaism."[118]

Two Categories of Mizvot

In the Mishnah of tractate *Yoma*,[119] the transgressions that one can
commit are divided into two categories.

1. Transgressions involving the relationship between man and man.
2. Transgressions involving the relationship between man and God.

Maimonides employs the same categories, but for classifying the *mizvot,* the virtuous deeds which we are enjoined to perform.[120] Thus there are:

1. *Mizvot sheben adam lahavero, mizvot* regulating relations between man and man.
2. *Mizvot sheben adam lamakom, mizvot* regulating the relations between man and God.

The first category includes ethical and moral law,[121] the second category, ritual and ceremonial law. While the primary concern of this inquiry is the question of the rationalization of the first group of *mizvot,* these categories are not conceived of in Judaism as being sealed off one from the other. As we shall see, God is very much involved in the *mizvot* of the first category, and man's relationship to man is involved in the second category of *mizvot.*[122]

It was widely assumed by Christian and Jewish theologians that the laws of the first category are the laws of "nature" and can therefore be rationalized in purely secular terms.[123] Theoretically, therefore, man should not require God's special intervention in the promulgation of these laws. His own intelligence is adequate to the task of discovering and formulating the natural laws. The ritual laws, however, are not all subject to comprehension. There are ritual laws in Scripture whose relationship to the purpose they are intended to serve is impervious to human reason. Hence their origin had to be attributed to a divine source.[124]

The peculiarly Biblical-Rabbinic doctrine that both categories of law, the moral and ethical as well as the ritual, were divinely ordained and revealed at Sinai,[125] presented a difficult problem to both Jewish and non-Jewish theologians, who were hard-pressed to explain why God had to descend from heaven to command Israelites not to kill, steal, or bear false witness. Could not the Israelites have arrived at these precepts by applying their reasoning powers, even as the gentile philosophers had done?[126] To that question there were those who responded that God had descended from heaven in order to provide mankind with a "shortcut" to a knowledge of Himself and of proper behavior, since "human reason proceeds gradually and does not reach its aim until the end of the process. In the meantime, one is left without a guide. Besides, not everybody's reason is adequate to discover truth."[127] This "philosophic" solution constitutes a misrepresentation of the core of the Jewish tradition. It explains the presence of the ethical and moral in the Sinaitic revelation as being little more than a concession to the intellectually deprived or indolent.

Why Revelation

That a merciful God should act in behalf of his intellectually deprived and indolent children is understandable. But in the Jewish tradition, the Torah was revealed not only to the slow-witted and the mental sluggards, but to the whole people—the tribal heads, the elders, the officials, all the men of Israel, as well as the children, the wives, the woodchopper and waterdrawer (Deut. 29:9). Moreover, until Saadiah Gaon (d. 942), no Rabbi, as far as is known, felt the need to write a systematic theology or ethics. Nor can we attribute this to lack of intellectual capacity or to ignorance of Greek philosophic thought. Certainly, after Alexander's conquest of the Near East, the Rabbis knew a good deal about Greek life and thought. That they were influenced by it in their legal thinking and daily life has been established beyond doubt.[128] Moreover, their capacity for systematic thought is demonstrated in the imposing legal system they erected.

Hence, we may reasonably assume that their failure to create a systematic theology of ethics was due not to intellectual incapacity, but rather to an awareness that human reason alone cannot be the source of the moral or the ethical. The ethical and the moral require what appears to be the utterly unreasonable, or at least the non-reasonable. They have to be rooted, therefore, in the religious, in the transcendental, in the revealed. That is the reason Jewish medieval philosophy, despite its great contribution to the enrichment of the Jewish intellectual experience, proved abortive religiously and ethically, and has remained peripheral to the Biblical-Rabbinic tradition.[129]

The Rabbis do not, to the best of my knowledge, ever state that human reason by itself cannot arrive at the ethical and the moral. Nor do they specifically raise the question of why God found it necessary to reveal the moral and the ethical. But as in other areas of rabbinic thought, the presence of "answers" may be viewed as a reflection of an intuitive or cognitive awareness of a question. To the rabbinically unasked "question," why God found it necessary to reveal the moral and ethical law at Sinai, rabbinic sources offer a number of possible "answers."

1. *Gadol hamezuve ve'oseh, yoter mimi she'ayno mezuve ve'oseh,* "One who acts [properly] because [he believes] God commanded him so to act is more virtuous than one who acts properly even though he was not (or does not believe that he was) commanded by God so to act."[130] What is there in this paradoxical dictum which is valid and which gives it its prominent place in rabbinic thought?

One of the doctrines of the Biblical-Rabbinic tradition is the proposition that though God revealed in the Torah the path of life we should follow, it is we who make the decision to follow or not to follow that path. God does not make that decision for us. It is our divinely imposed, inescapable responsibility.[131] A measure of self-assertiveness is therefore inevitable. But the fact that we have the responsibility to choose between alternatives does not mean that the commandments of the Torah are the products of our wisdom. What is called for, then, is a synthesis between self-assertiveness and humility: self-assertiveness in making a decision, and humility in regard to the motivation behind our decision.

The religiously motivated individual is one who says: "God does not compel me to believe in Him or in His Torah. I have of my own free will decided to do X, and I have so decided because I believe God commanded me to do so. Moreover, because He commanded it, I believe it to be for my best welfare."[132] There is a vast difference between such a one and one who says: "I have of my own free will and on the basis of my own good judgment decided to do thus and so because I believe it to be for my own welfare." Both may harbor the same ethical intentions, but one has made himself "the measure of all things," thereby committing the ultimate sin of self-deification. The other reaches out beyond himself and seeks to identify his will with what he believes to be the will of God.[133]

Because man has the capacity to recognize and appreciate the goodness that inheres in the Law, he falls prey to the sin of believing himself to be the author of the Law. Hence, Rabbi Akiba taught that God's love for Israel was evidenced as much by His having made Himself known as the giver of the Law as by the act of giving it. "Beloved are Israel, for unto them was given the desirable instrument [the Torah]; but it was by a special love that it was made known to them that that desirable instrument, through which the world was created, was given to them," as it is said (Prov. 4:2), "For I give you good doctrine; forsake ye not my Law."[134] God, so to speak, thus did all He could to help us resist the arrogance which claims authorship of the Law, but He did not altogether succeed. One of the purposes of the Sinaitic revelation, therefore, was the curbing of the cardinal sin of human arrogance, of man setting himself up as God.

2. Moreover, neither man's reason nor his inclinations or impulses are stable and consistent. "The heart is deceitful above all things, and it is exceeding weak, who can know it?" (Jer. 17:9). The heart, in biblical times, was believed to be the seat of both reason and emotion. Insofar as reason is concerned, its "deceitfulness," its ability to make the poorer cause appear to be the better, is demonstrated constantly not only in the public forum but in the

life of the average individual. If reason knows only itself as the legislator of the moral and the ethical, it has little difficulty in finding good cause either for annulling its own "laws," or for declaring them inapplicable to any given situation. We know how readily reason becomes the handmaiden of the passion of the moment.

And insofar as our emotions are concerned, how "weak" the heart is, how volatile and capricious it can be! Our impulses, instincts, and emotions, therefore, cannot be depended upon as guides to the moral and ethical life. To be sure, even if one believes that the moral and ethical are divinely commanded, he may yet not have the necessary spiritual resources to obey them. But he will at least know he is violating what he should obey. He will not be among those who "are wise in their eyes . . . who call evil good and good evil" (Isa. 5:20–21). On the contrary, he will be "constantly striving to subdue his own inclination and to fulfill the commands of his Creator."[135]

3. Above all, the Rabbis saw evidence of God's love for man in the fact that He revealed to man laws which man could have arrived at by the power of reason which God had bestowed upon him.

"Rabbi Ḥananya, the son of Akashya said, the Holy One, blessed be He, was pleased to make Israel worthy [*lezakot;* lit. to make it possible for Israel to acquire merit]. Therefore he gave them a copious Torah and many commandments; as it is said, 'It pleased the Lord, for His righteousness' sake, to magnify the Torah and make it honorable [Isa. 42:21].' "[136] Rabbi Ḥananya is saying that the Almighty desired to give Israel a maximum number of opportunities to act in a manner that would make them worthy of His approbation and His reward.[137] He therefore multiplied the number of acts which could be motivated and rationalized by them as acts performed in obedience to His will.

Because the commandments of the Torah are so all-inclusive, any ethical intention can be religiously motivated. Hence Proverbs (3:6) could admonish us to "know God in all that you do,"[138] and Rabbi Yose could urge us always to act "for the sake of heaven."[139]

That is what makes the psalmist's statement, "I have set the Lord always before me" (Ps. 16:8) an authentic alternative for the Jew, and not merely a rhetorical flourish.[140]

On the Religious and the Secular in Judaism

The oft-repeated opinion that in Judaism "there is no absolute bifurcation between the religious and the secular" is not to be understood as implying that the Rabbis were not aware of, or denied the existence of, the secular in contrast to the religious. The element of truth embodied in this statement can be recognized only if we remember that the terms *secular* and *religious* apply to the rationalizations of the intentions that result in acts, rather than to the acts themselves. Because Judaism attributes divine origin to all its commandments, and because its commandments touch upon every aspect of life, it can ask its adherents to rationalize the intentions motivating all their acts religiously. Every act should be motivated by the intention to do God's will.

> One who conducts himself in accordance with the laws of good health, if his purpose is merely that of preserving his physical health, and that he should have sons who do his work and labor for his needs, is following a path that is not good. But his purpose should be to keep his body healthy and strong so that his soul may be sound to know the Lord, for it is impossible for one to study when he is hungry or sick, or when in pain. . . . One who acts thus is constantly serving the Lord, even while he is conducting his business affairs or having sexual intercourse, . . . and even while he sleeps if he has in mind that by sleeping he rests physically and intellectually so that he should not become sick and be unable to serve God. . . . And this is what the Sages had in mind when they said, "Let all thy actions be for the sake of Heaven," and what Solomon in his wisdom said, "In all thy ways acknowledge Him and He will direct thy paths" (Prov. 3:6).[141]

Hence one who deals honestly because he believes that it will redound to his own mundane advantage, or observes the dietary laws of Judaism because "they are good for one's health," is performing acts approved by Judaism; but since they are not religiously motivated, they are not in any significant sense religious acts.

In the realm of rationalization, therefore, the Rabbis do recognize a significant bifurcation. They were conscious not only of the existence of the secular rationalization of the ethical but of its great seductive powers. Since the days of the Greeks, secular, philosophic rationalization of the ethical has been the most ominous threat to the religious rationalization of the ethical. The Rabbis seem to have intuitively recognized, though they never explicitly stated it, that if the religious rationalization for the ethical is dispensable, then the heart of religion, as represented in the Torah, is dispensable.[142] This is true for us today as it was for them.

The religious rationalization of an intention transforms the resulting act into a religious act, and the agent into a religious personality. It adds a dimension to his being which, though it be ineffable, is evident and edifying. It is said that we are what we do. We suggest that the manner in which one rationalizes his intentions plays as great a role in the molding of his personality as do the acts to which the intentions lead.

An act performed in order to implement a religiously rationalized intention, that is, to fulfill a divine commandment, the Rabbis designated as an act performed *lishmah*. An act performed for any reason other than the intention of serving God, they designated as *shelo lishmah*. One can perform an *averah*, a transgression, *lishmah*, with the intention of serving God, thus indicating that in that instance the agent believes that it is God who commands him to perform the *averah*. And one can perform a *mizvah*, a divine commandment, *shelo lishmah*, for a reason other than that God commanded it. In the first instance the deed remains an *averah* even if one believes it to be divinely commanded. In the second instance it remains a *mizvah* even though it is not performed in obedience to God's command.

The Rabbis make bold to say that an *averah* performed *lishmah* is greater than, or at least as great as, a *mizvah* performed *shelo lishmah.*[143] Maimonides, in one passage in his Code, attributes little virtue to a *mizvah* performed *shelo lishmah.* He maintains that it is not enough for a gentile to observe the seven Noahide laws in order to become worthy of a share in *olam haba,* the world to come. He must observe them because he believes that he is thus commanded by God and not out of natural inclination or because he considers them as necessary for his physical or social welfare.[144]

The Talmud records a number of opinions that if one studies Torah or observes its commandments *shelo lishmah,* not because God commanded them but because he wants to boast of his knowledge or because he desires some other mundane benefit, it were better that he had not been born at all.[145] It may even be a "death potion" for him.[146] On the other hand, the diametrically opposite opinion is also expressed, namely, that it is better for one to obey the law regardless of the reason than not to obey at all. Commenting on the verse "Why is the land ruined and laid waste like a wilderness . . . The Lord says: Because they have forsaken My Law . . ." (Jer. 9:12–13), the Rabbis say, "God, as it were, is saying, would that they abandoned Me if only they would observe my teachings."[147]

The following discussion is recorded in the Talmud.

> The prophet says: "For the ways of the Lord are right, and the just do walk in them; but the transgressors do stumble therein" (Hos. 14:10). Rabba Bar Hana said in the name of Rabbi Yohanan . . . This may be applied to two men both of whom roasted their paschal lambs. One of them ate it with the intention of performing the commandment while the other ate his merely to enjoy a substantial (or gluttonous) meal. To him who ate it with the intention of performing the commandment "the just do walk in them" applies, while to him who ate it merely to enjoy a substantial meal, "but transgressors do stumble in them" applies. Said Resh Lakish to him: "Do you call him wicked? Granted he has not performed the commandment to perfection, has he not however eaten of the paschal lamb?" [148]

We may safely venture the opinion that most Rabbis agreed with

Resh Lakish that such a one is not to be called "wicked." They would probably also agree with the great Babylonian Amora, Rav, who would even encourage those who study or observe the *miẓvot shelo lishmah* to continue to do so, for eventually the light which is in the Torah[149] would open their eyes, their hearts, and their minds, so that ultimately they would reach the stage where they would be studying Torah and obeying its commandments *lishmah*.[150]

Section VIII

Judaism and the Unethical Preliminary Remarks

As we have previously noted, it is the monotheistic doctrine of Judaism which declared God to be both "merciful and gracious" as well as "the Creator of evil," hence the ultimate source of the unethical, which "poses the supreme riddle" for the Jewish theologian. There are various aspects to this riddle:

1. Man's inhumanity to man.
2. The suffering of the righteous and the prosperity of the wicked.
3. The great natural catastrophes—floods, earthquakes, hurricanes, etc.—which indiscriminately work havoc with the lives of both the sinner and the righteous, the infant and the adult. Since all the forces of nature and the laws that govern them are the servants of the Lord (Pss. 104:4, 119:90-91), they implement His unethical intentions.
4. The unethical intentions of God directed against individuals whom even He is believed to have considered as being pure and innocent, as in the case of Job (1:8) and of the binding of Isaac (Gen. 22).
5. The commandments in the Torah which direct men to implement unethical intentions against other men, such as the laws enjoining man-inflicted punishment for a variety

of ritual, civil, and criminal transgressions (Exod. 21:12–25); the laws permitting war (Deut. 10) and enjoining the conquest of Canaan and the extermination of its inhabitants (Deut. 20:10–18). It is some of these laws that make it possible for "the devil to quote Scripture."[151]

From the point of view of biblically rooted theology, the solution to this "supreme riddle" belongs to the category of "the hidden things known to God" (Deut. 29:28). Nevertheless, many impressive attempts have been made by Jewish and non-Jewish theologians to cope with these questions.[152] Important as each one of the aspects of the "riddle" unquestionably is to Jewish thought, our immediate concern is only with the fifth aspect, namely, the rationalization of the commandments of the Torah which *permit* or enjoin man to harbor and implement unethical intentions against a fellow man. This will involve our exploring the extent to which Judaism is congenial to the secular rationalizations of the unethical which we have previously discussed, and wherein it departs from them.

1. *Judaism and the principle that might makes right.* There is a faint echo of the principle that might makes right in the rabbinic dictum *kol d'alim gvar.*[153] In cases where no party can lay valid claim to the ownership of an object, possession of it establishes ownership. But this principle does not justify injuring an innocent party for one's own advantage merely because one has the power to injure him.

While the prophets envisioned a warless world at the end of days (Isa. 2:14, Mic. 4:1–5), biblical law and narrative imply the legitimacy not only of wars of defense but even of conquest (Deut. 20; 2 Sam. 11:1). The Rabbis discuss this as if it were a legitimate activity of an unredeemed humanity. They distinguish between *milḥemet reshut,* a war of conquest decided upon by the civil authorities, and *milḥemet miẓvah,* a war of self-defense or the wars Joshua fought at the command of God.[154]

Obviously all war involves the harboring of unethical intentions against other human beings. The only kind of war which, from the point of view of the Biblical-Rabbinic tradition, can be rationalized today is a war of self-defense. Judaism does not advocate a doctrine of absolute pacifism. The rabbinic dictum that if you are certain that someone is planning to kill you, even though you are innocent, you are not only permitted but required to forestall his intentions even if it involves killing him, has universal acceptance in rabbinic literature.[155] The rationalization for this dictum will be discussed later.[156]

The attitude to wars other than in self-defense is far from clear. In this regard, we can unhesitatingly say, *Makom hinikhu lanu avotenu lehitgader boh.*[157] Our fathers tilled this field only partially. Much more tilling is required. It offers us the opportunity to prove our own spiritual mettle.

2. *Judaism and the unethical which is subservient to the ethical.* Judaism is congenial to the rationalization of the unethical when it is clearly subservient and indispensable to the ethical, in cases where both the ethical and the unethical are directed toward the same object. Thus there is nothing in the Jewish tradition which prohibits the surgeon from amputating a man's limb in order to save his life. When, however, the two intentions are directed toward two different individuals, as in the case of removing a kidney from one individual who has healthy kidneys in order to implant it in another whose kidneys do not function, the question becomes more complicated. No one may be forced, nor is he religiously obligated, to give up a healthy kidney to save another's life. One may even question whether, from the point of view of the Biblical-Rabbinic tradition, he may volunteer to do so.[158] However, the tradition does not censure one who does.

3. *Judaism and the principle of the greatest good for the greatest number.* The position of Judaism is clear when an unethical intention is directed against the physical existence of an innocent minority, while the ethical intention it is to subserve is directed toward a majority. Thus, in the case of a beleaguered city, the law forbids the residents to save their lives by handing over one of their innocent members for execution by the enemy. Thus, also, "if a

group of Jewish women are threatened that they will all be violated unless they agree to send one of their members out to be violated, they should rather all be violated than make one of them a sacrifice for the rest."[159]

Judaism's rationalization of these laws is rooted in the rabbinic teaching that in the beginning God created only one man in order to teach us that "he who destroys one human being, it is as if he had destroyed a world full of human beings."[160] In the eyes of God one innocent human being is equal to a world full of human beings. Hence the death of one innocent human being may not be rationalized or justified by any amount of benefit that a world full of human beings may be expected to derive therefrom.[161]

This Biblical-Rabbinic teaching is probably the underlying rationalization for the biblical prohibition of human sacrifice. The "natural"abhorrence to the act of killing another human being is in itself not sufficient to explain that prohibition at a time when the practice was still widespread and appeared to "make sense." It made, and continues to make, sense for those who hold the following assumptions: (1) the more precious the gift offered to the gods, the greater the probability of having one's request granted, and (2) an act which advances the greatest good of the greatest number is self-evidently justified.

On the basis of those assumptions, Agamemnon's sacrifice of Iphigenia to assure a safe crossing for his army on the way to Troy makes sense, as does the sacrifice by the king of Moab of his eldest son in order to affect the fortunes of battle (2 Kings 3:27). In both instances the intention is to serve the greatest good of the greatest number. Although we no longer sacrifice human beings to the gods, we do sacrifice them for *raison d'état,* and for the advancement of some utopian apocalyptic vision.

There can be no doubt about Judaism's position on the question of sacrificing innocent lives for the advancement of the welfare of a greater number. It nevertheless remains true that the welfare of the community as a whole will, from time to time, inevitably involve inflicting some injury of an economic or psychological nature upon some of its innocent members.

However, the general tendency, or what Dr. Kadushin has so felicitously designated as the "emphatic trend,"[162] in Judaism is to be very wary of applying this principle. An ethically sensitive community will make every effort to compensate the individual involved so that its action will accord as much as is humanly possible with the requirements of justice and mercy and the principle of unalienable human rights, rather than depend upon the principle of the greatest good for the greatest number. The less one depends on this principle, the closer does he come to the Biblical-Rabbinic concept of the sanctity of the individual and the inviolability of his personality.[163]

4. *Judaism and the concept of justice.* Both Judaism and the secularists make use of the concept of justice for the rationalization of the unethical. However, Judaism's conception of the nature of justice and the manner of its implementation differs radically from that of the secularist.

As we have previously noted, the secularist limits the concept of justice to interhuman affairs. Its origin is attributed to enlightened self-interest, and its concretizations reflect a compromise between the enlightened self-interest of the individual and of the group. For Judaism, justice is not the product of human intelligence applied to human experience; human intelligence and experience merely play a role in its implementation. Justice is a principle that governs the whole of the universe, for "justice and righteousness are the foundations of God's throne" (Ps. 89:15).[164]

Justice is present in the affairs of men. Men have been endowed by God with the ability to become conscious of its presence and to apply it to their affairs. But the concept of justice reaches far beyond the human. The existence of the whole of creation, not only of an enlightened human society, is dependent upon the preservation of "the foundations of God's throne." One of the fundamental doctrines, therefore, of the Biblical-Rabbinic tradition is that man's violation of justice affects the whole universe. "He turneth rivers into a wilderness, and the watersprings into dry ground;

a fruitful land into barrenness, for the wickedness of them that dwell therein" (Ps. 107:33–34). It was man's unethically motivated acts that brought on the flood (Gen. 6:11) and the transformation of "the well-watered plain of the Jordan which was like the Garden of Eden" (ibid., 13:10) into a wilderness (ibid., 19:13–25).[165] God Himself is concerned with preserving the foundations of His throne, and the viability of His creation.

The implementation of justice in human affairs places a two-fold responsibility upon man:

(a) To harbor and implement the ethical intention to treat one's fellow man justly. One is called upon to do this as a matter of divinely enlightened self-interest. A self-interest which is secularly rooted may, as we have pointed out, counsel one to act unjustly; but a self-interest enlightened by faith that God is concerned with the implementation of justice can never counsel even temporary violation of justice.[166]

(b) To harbor and implement intentions to curb those who act unjustly. Such intentions must on occasion be unethical, since they involve subjecting the wrongdoer to restraints or punishments which are not intended for his welfare, but primarily for the welfare of society as a whole or of the individual who had been wronged.

The Rabbis described the honest judge as "a co-creator of the Universe,"[167] for the "work of creation is daily renewed."[168] The "foundations of God's throne," justice and righteousness, are in need of daily renewal. The courtroom is not the only place where the concept of justice is to be concretized in the affairs of men, nor are judges the only ones charged with that responsibility. Everyone, regardless of his position in society, has the priceless privilege of being God's partner in the daily renewal of the work of creation through his own dealings with his fellow men.

Since nations and individuals fail to fulfill this responsibility, God Himself tends to the "foundations of His throne." Thus God may harbor unethical intentions against His creatures, and He has an infinite number of agencies at His disposal for implementing His intentions. "He maketh the winds His messengers; the flames of fire

His ministers" (Ps. 104:4). Indeed man himself, often unbeknown to himself and despite himself, may be that agent. "O Asshur, the rod of Mine anger, in whose hand as a staff is Mine indignation! I do send him against an ungodly nation, and against the people of My wrath do I give him a charge, to take the spoil, and to take the prey, and to tread them down like the mire of the streets" (Isa. 10:5–6).

The very group or individuals who violate justice may become God's instrument for administering their punishment. "Thine own wickedness shall correct thee. And thy backslidings shall reprove thee" (Jer. 2:19). Abraham Lincoln was able to lead the Northern states during the hard, cruel years of the Civil War under the banner of fighting for the preservation of the Union; the majority of the Northerners would not have fought four long years to free the slaves. Toward the end of the merciless ordeal Lincoln had the courage to share with his bereaved countrymen an insight that had grown upon him during his ceaseless wrestling with the problem of the utter irrationality of the Civil War:

> The Almighty has His own purposes. "Woe unto the world because of offenses; for it must needs be that offenses come; but woe to that man by whom the offense cometh." If we shall suppose that American slavery is one of those offenses which, in the providence of God, must needs come, but which, having continued through His appointed time, He now wills to remove, and that He gives to both North and South this terrible war as the woe due to those by whom the offense came, shall we discern therein any departure from those divine attributes which the believers in a living God always ascribe to Him? Fondly do we hope, fervently do we pray, that this mighty scourge of war may speedily pass away. Yet if God wills that it continue until all the wealth piled up by the bondmen's two hundred and fifty years of unrequited toil shall be sunk, and until every drop of blood drawn with the lash shall be paid by another drawn with the sword; as was said three thousand years ago, so still it must be said, "The judgments of the Lord are true and righteous altogether." [169]

Being the partner of God in daily recreating the universe by acting justly and correcting the violation of justice by others has its dangers as well as its opportunities. The self-confident are in danger of becoming self-righteously arrogant and exercising power for their own aggrandizement. "Howbeit he meaneth not so, neither doth his heart think so; but it is his heart to destroy and cut off nations not a few" (Isa. 10:7). The humble, on the other hand, are constantly beset by doubts regarding their ability to judge what justice may require of them. As safeguard against both pitfalls, humility and arrogance, Judaism teaches that God has given us the Torah, "whose statutes and commandments" are righteous (Deut. 4:8). However, no safeguard is safe against man's willfulness, folly, or ignorance. Moreover, serious stumbling blocks are found in the "safeguard" itself.

In the first place there are laws in the Torah whose literal meaning is clear, but whose ethical intention appears to be equivocal. Such, for example, are the laws regarding the treatment of the population who inhabited Canaan before Israel's conquest (Deut. 7:1–5), and the punishments to be inflicted upon violators of the ritual laws (Lev. 24:13, Num. 15:32). Moreover, the laws of the Torah, like all laws, must be interpreted, and differences arise among the interpreters.

To some aspects of the problem raised by the misuse of the Torah as a rationalization for the unethical, there is no final and unquestionable solution. I have dealt elsewhere with some aspects of the problem.[170] Here I shall discuss only the manner in which Judaism coped with the problem of the unethical associated with the conquest of Canaan and the annihilation of the native population. According to Scripture both were not only abetted, but commanded, by God.[171]

Judaism's Rationalization of Israel's Conquest of Canaan

The ethical sensitivity attained by the people of Israel very early in its history is reflected most significantly in the manner in which the national conscience wrestled with the ethical problem raised by Israel's conquest of Canaan, the destruction of its population, and the rationalization whereby this spiritual struggle found its dénouement.[172] One may find fault with the rationalization, but one can hardly find fault with the state of mind that felt the need for a rationalization of a people's conquest of a territory, a rationalization quite different from that offered by the Athenians for the destruction of Melos.

At the core of the tradition regarding the conquest of the promised land is the doctrine that it was not achieved by the might of Israel's armies. "For not by their own sword did they get the land in possession, neither did their own arm save them; but Thy right hand, and Thine arm, and the light of Thy countenance, because Thou wast favorable unto them" (Ps. 44:4). This in itself, however, only sharpens the ethical issue. How can one reconcile the concept of a universal God who is just and merciful with the command to conquer a land and destroy its inhabitants? Two considerations made this reconciliation possible.

1. "The earth is the Lord's and the fullness thereof" (Ps. 24:1). "And the land shall not be sold in perpetuity; for the land is Mine; for ye are strangers and settlers with Me" (Lev. 25:23). God alone decides how it should be distributed among men. "The Most High gave nations their homes and set the divisions of man . . ." (Deut. 32:8).[173]

2. No people has an unalienable right to inhabit a land. They inhabit it only as long as they prove worthy in the sight of God. The God who made it possible for Israel to conquer Canaan was the same God who had made it possible for the Canaanites to occupy the land in the first place. If Israel proves unworthy of occupying the land, it too will be dispossessed.

According to the tradition, a few hundred years elapsed between the time that God promised Abraham that his descendants would possess the land of Canaan and their actual possession of it. God informed Abraham that this would be so when the promise was made. At the same time He explained the reason for it. "Know well that your offspring shall be strangers in a land not theirs, and they shall be enslaved and oppressed four hundred years. . . . And they shall return here in the fourth generation, for the iniquity of the Amorites will not be fulfilled until then" (Gen. 15:13, 16). As long as the Amorites remain worthy of possessing their land, they will not be dispossessed.[174]

The tradition repeatedly admonishes: "It is not because of your virtues and your rectitude that you will be able to occupy their country, but because of the wickedness of those nations the Lord your God is dispossessing them before you, and in order to fulfill the oath that the Lord made to your fathers, Abraham, Isaac, and Jacob" (Deut. 9:5). In the case of Canaan, Israel was the "rod of God's anger." It was chosen for this sad task not because of the virtue of the generation that served as the "rod" but because of the virtues of its patriarchs.

But why prefer this apparently "self-deceptive" religious rationalization of the unethical involved in the conquest of Canaan to the "honest" Athenian rationalization of wars of conquest? Wherein can it be said to be superior?

In the biblical rationalization of Israel's conquest of Canaan there are a number of ethical implications.

(a) It rejects the self-glorification of the conqueror, the spirit of "My power and the might of mine own hand has given me all this" (Deut. 8:17).

(b) It sets up an objective standard equally applicable to all. Israel was ultimately rationally compelled to apply to itself what it believed to be a divinely ordained principle. God, who permitted and even commanded Israel to dispossess the Canaanites, could summon others to exile Israel if it sank to the spiritual level of the inhabitants it replaced. "Do not defile yourselves in any of those ways, for it is by such that the nations which I am casting out before you defiled themselves . . . and the land spewed out its inhabitants . . . so let not the land spew you out for defiling it, as it spewed out the nation that came before you" (Lev. 18:24–28).

Israel applied the same measuring rod to itself when it was

expelled from the land first by the Babylonians and later by the Romans. On every Sabbath and Festival the synagogue liturgy reminds Jews that it was not the power of the Babylonian or Roman armies which deprived them of their homeland, but their own sins.[175] They failed in their responsibility to do their share as God's partners in maintaining the integrity of the foundations of His throne, and He acted through His appointed messengers to compensate for their failure.

(c) This religious rationalization of the unethical implies the paradox that only God can command its implementation.[176] No one may feel justified in harboring an unethical intention, no matter how slight an injury will be inflicted upon another, unless he feels or "knows" in every fibre of his being that God commands him to do so. He must know or feel that what he intends involves the very integrity of the "foundations of God's throne." The "casting out" of Hagar and Ishmael (Gen. 21:9–12) was no less unethical than the binding of Isaac (Gen. 22:1–19). Abraham did both things, not because he felt like it, or because he thought he would thus please his wife or God, but because he believed himself to be so commanded by God.

Moreover, each instance of the unethical commanded by God is *sui generis,* and the act implementing it may not serve as a precedent to be followed by someone else. Each individual must himself believe that he is divinely commanded to perform the unethical act.

In 1926 a delegation of three rabbis who had just come from the USSR solicited help for colleagues whom they had left behind. One of the three had once spoken to Trotsky, and I asked about the conversation.

"I asked him," he said, "why he is killing so many innocent people merely because they owned some property."

"And what did he answer?"

"He said he was following the example set by Joshua, who exterminated the inhabitants of Canaan so that the Israelites should not learn their evil ways."

"And what did you say to that?" I asked.

"What do you mean what did I say to him?" he answered with some heat. "Joshua was commanded by God to do what he did, but who commanded Trotsky?"

At the time this response troubled me, because of its seeming indifference to the ethical quality of the command attributed to God. The tone of his voice, however, indicated that he was surprised, either at the lack of piety implied in my question, or at my ignorance of the rabbinic teaching that an unethical act performed by an individual at the specific command of God *may not be used by another individual as a precedent in what appears to be a similar situation.*

Thus, in a discussion regarding an animal bought from a gentile under conditions prohibited by rabbinic law, the Rabbis say that such an animal is to be hamstrung. The question is raised whether this would not constitute a violation of the biblical prohibition of cruelty to animals. To counter that argument Abbaye quotes the verse in which God commands Joshua, on the eve of battle, "to hamstring the animals" of the foe (Josh. 11:6), implying that what God had commanded Joshua to do may be used as a precedent for a later rabbinic enactment. One of the great rabbinic authorities of the Middle Ages finds Abbaye's response to be valid only if the prohibition against cruelty to animals is rabbinic not biblical. Under such circumstances the Rabbis may make exceptions to their own enactments. But if the prohibition of cruelty to animals is biblical, Joshua's action of hamstringing the animals cannot be used as a precedent, for Joshua could not violate a biblical commandment except "at the direct command of God,"[177] and such violations may not be used as precedents by anyone not so commanded.[178] Thus when Samuel tells Saul to exterminate the Amalekites, he does not tell him to do to Amalek what Joshua did to the "seven nations" of Canaan. Nor does he call upon him to fulfill the biblical commandment to exterminate Amalek (Deut. 25:19). He enjoins Saul on the basis of a specific divine communication (1 Sam. 15:2–3).

"Only as one stands in an absolute relation to the absolute" can one experience God as the sanction for unethical intention. "That for the particular individual this paradox may easily be mistaken for a temptation (*Anfechtung*) is indeed true."[179] We may doubt his claim, even as the ecclesiastical court which condemned Joan of Arc denied her claim that it was God who commanded her to lead the armies of the Dauphin against the English. An individual's action, however, has some semblance of rationality when it is subordinated to a concept or a principle or a reality whose transcendence the agent acknowledges. He does not cast himself in the irrational role of being his own "measure of all things," of being God. Hence the secularist, who rationalizes his unethical purpose and acts by appealing to a precedent set by a religiously oriented individual, is acting hypocritically, since he does not believe in God or in any transcendent power which exercises sanctions over man.

The paradox that only a just and merciful God can command the unethical is the counterpart of the proposition that only a just and merciful God can command the ethical and the moral. For the ethical occasionally, and the moral always, requires the agent to act unethically toward himself when he causes injury to himself, while the unethical intention involves injury to an object. Just as there is no cogent secular rationalization for the ethical and the moral, so there is no cogent secular rationalization for the unethical, except the proposition that might makes right.

The individual who feels that a given situation requires him to act unethically feels a greater need for a transcendent sanction than when called upon to act ethically or morally. The latter challenges his self-interest. The former presents a challenge to his conscience, to his ideal image of himself. Hence, one who intends the unethical and does not simultaneously experience "inner pangs of conscience" must conceive of himself as "the measure of all things," of being in fact God. They are those "who said, 'Our tongue will we make mighty; Our lips are with us; who is Lord over us?' " (Ps. 12:5). There are and have been such men in every generation. To Nazi, Fascist, and Communist dictators of the twentieth century, one may appropriately apply the words spoken by the prophet with regard to the rulers of Babylon: "And thou saidst in thy heart: 'I will ascend into heaven, above the stars of God will I exalt my throne; and I will sit upon the mount of meeting, in the uttermost parts of the north; I will ascend above the heights of the clouds; I will be like the Most High' " (Isa. 14:13–14).

Lincoln is probably the best example of the ethically sensitive individual confronted with a situation which, in his opinion, required him to act unethically. The possibility that he would make war on the South roused profound turmoil in Lincoln's innermost being. He was to ask young men to kill and be killed when there was the alternative of permitting the Southern states to secede. Who gave him that right? In his First Inaugural, after a masterful presentation of the secular rationalization for his intention to accept war if necessary, he concludes, speaking to the South: "You have no oath registered in Heaven to destroy the government, while I shall have the most solemn one to preserve, protect and defend it." In the case of other men, his statement might be interpreted as nothing more than a rhetorical flourish. It cannot be so interpreted in the case of Lincoln. There is altogether too much evidence bearing on his continuous wrestling with the ethical, religious, and metaphysical problems raised by the war. It is recorded in a great number of his private notations and public remarks.[180] It bursts forth with well-nigh prophetic power in the Second Inaugural. What Lincoln was saying, therefore, was that all his logically formulated arguments might perhaps be counterbalanced by other equally well formulated arguments. But over and above all of these was the divinely enjoined responsibility placed upon him by the solemn oath which he had taken upon assuming the duties of the presidency. It was the belief that he had "an oath registered in heaven" that served as the ultimate sanction of his determination to be "firm in the right" as God gave him to see the right. Only one who experiences what Lincoln experienced may act as he did. One may not merely imitate Lincoln or use him as a precedent.

There is no human sanction for the unethical. Hence, one cannot justify his unethically motivated act by the plea that another human being ordered him to do it. Therefore, while ordinarily a man is held responsible for the acts performed by his appointed messenger if he acts in accordance with his instructions, in the case of unethically motivated acts, Jewish law does not hold one responsible for the actions of his messenger even if the messenger had acted in accordance with his instructions.[181] The only religious sanction by which one may try to rationalize his unethical act, whether he be a judge sentencing a convicted criminal, or a general ordering men into battle, or a parent punishing a child, is the firm conviction that in some significant manner God had commanded him to do so. Those who believe that he who speaks to them in the name of some transcendent power was actually the recipient of such a message and therefore follow him, are, in a measure, direct recipients of the message. The soldiers who responded to Lincoln's call to save the Union were to some extent directly affected by the "mystique of the Union";[182] they too had heard "the voice" that had spoken to him.

There is no foolproof barrier that can be erected against self-delusion. Nor does the fact that one feels divinely commanded to perform the unethical free him from responsibility for the consequences of his acts in the eyes of the civil law. In the eyes of many of his contemporaries, John Brown was a self-deluded, half-mad fanatic, and they hanged him for what he had done. But Emerson and many of his colleagues, and less sophisticated Americans and non-Americans in vast numbers, joined in proclaiming that while John Brown's body was "amoldering in the dust, his soul goes marching on." [183]

The Rabbis set up a formidable barrier against the danger of self-delusion or of being deluded by others who claim that God had spoken to them. They declared that with the destruction of the Temple the era of prophecy ended in Israel, and that the sage was superior to the prophet.[184] No longer could a man claim that God had spoken to him as He spoke to Moses or Joshua or Amos.[185] Since Malachi, God speaks to all Israel only through the Torah and its interpreters. Heavenly "voices" are no longer to be decisive.[186] These and other rabbinic precautions have limited, but have not eliminated, the appearance of "prophets" and "messiahs" who come with "messages from the Lord." There is no safeguard within Judaism, or anywhere else, against the self-deluded and their power to win followers. All we can do, after exercising whatever rational powers are at our disposal, is to pray that the "right" in which we determine to be firm is the right which God has given us to see.

SECTION IX

Judaism and the Moral
Introductory Remarks

It is generally assumed that the "religious spirit," manifest in all the major religions and philosophies of mankind, uniformly bestows its highest praises upon the moral intention and its implementation. That is not so.[187] Two concepts in particular have challenged the moral for the position of supremacy in the life of man: asceticism and intellectual contemplation.

Asceticism appears superficially to be almost synonymous with the moral, because it too stresses "injury to the agent," in that it requires self-denial. But the self-denial of asceticism per se is not necessarily associated with the welfare of anyone but the ascetic.[188] With the exception of egoistic hedonism, none of the known significant religions or philosophies of man advocates self-indulgence. All, even Epicureanism as propounded by its founder,[189] advocate a measure of self-restraint verging on the ascetic. But the motivating idea of philosophic asceticism is the achievement of inner peace, of freedom from the importunities of the instincts and from the vainglories associated with the possession of mundane goods and power. "The Hellenic pursuit of knowledge culminates in a preparation for ecstasy, and the Hellenic idealization of man's natural life ends in a settled antipathy to the body and its works."[190]

For some, asceticism was the surest path to personal salvation and redemption. It never gave "peace of mind" to the religious, because one was never sure that he had gone far enough in self-denial, in withdrawal from the affairs of society and the satisfactions of this world, to be worthy of redemption.

> Since the characteristics of the evangelical ethic were self-denial, . . . as though everything which was difficult, self-denying, and contrary to nature were a service to God demanded by the Gospel . . . the exercises which were meant to aid in religious concentration, and the preservation of morality were made an end in themselves. . . . the "good works" of mortification and humiliation . . . served the ends of salvation of the soul and the deliverance from the final judgment. Mortification—as well as the ideal of "virginity"—became the most peculiar and most frequent form of Christian asceticism.[191]

This did not mean that the philosophically or religiously oriented ascetics did not care to see their fellow men happy. Like the Buddha, who is "the most venerable being for the Buddhist," they too "can not be charged with cruelty." But like him they too are at best "the embodiment of insight and a peculiarly detached compassion."[192] It was a "compassion" for those who were foolish enough to permit themselves to become involved in the pursuit of mundane pleasures, in their fleeting satisfactions and consequent tragedies. It was "detached" in that it did not encourage going out of one's way to help others. It preferred, rather, that one should concentrate his energies upon keeping himself free from mundane pursuits. This emphasis upon the futility of worldly pleasures and upon one's own salvation underlay the quietistic tendencies not only in Buddhism, but also in Stoicism[193] and Christianity.[194]

The other major challenge to the moral derives from the awe and reverence which man experiences toward his intellect, his ability to think. For Aristotle and the many who followed him, man's noblest achievement is to contemplate and dwell upon the highest or noblest thoughts of which he is capable. That is what being godlike means to Aristotle.

> The activity of God which surpasses all others in blessedness must

be contemplative; and of human activity therefore that which is
most akin to this must be most of the nature of happiness. . . .
He who exercises his reason and cultivates it seems to be both
in the best state of mind and most dear to the gods. For if the gods
have any care of human affairs as they are thought to have, it would
be reasonable both that they should delight in that which is best
and most akin to them [i.e., reason] and that they should reward
those who love and honor this most. . . . And that all these attributes belong most of all to the philosopher is most manifest. He
therefore is dearest to the gods. And he who is that will presumably also be happiest.[195]

For Spinoza too, "the highest good of the mind is the knowledge of
God, and the highest virtue of the mind is to know God."[196] "Insofar
as we understand that He is eternal" do we achieve "the intellectual
love of God," and "from this kind of knowledge arises the highest
possible peace of mind, the highest joy."[197]

This emphasis upon the intellect was expressed for the Rabbis
by Yoḥanan ben Zakkai's statement that "if you have studied much
Torah, claim no credit for yourself, for that is the purpose for which
you were born."[198] A great number of other rabbinic statements set
the study of Torah above all the other virtues. But like almost everything else in the rabbinic tradition, this judgment does not go unchallenged. The sages gathered in Lud once debated the question,
What is greater, study or deeds? Rabbi Tarfon responded that deeds
were greater, Rabbi Akiba, that study was greater. They finally
agreed that study was greater, because study leads to deeds.[199] But
this conclusion, which apparently gives precedence to study, in
reality subordinates study to deeds.[200] Rabbi Simeon bar Yoḥai, a
contemporary of Rabbi Akiba and Rabbi Tarfon, resolves the controversy by attributing equal status to study and the performance
of deeds.[201] Hence, great as was and is the emphasis in Judaism
upon the pursuit of knowledge and study of Torah, it is not an end
in itself. If it does not stimulate ethical and moral intentions which
culminate in deeds of loving-kindness, of concern for the welfare
of one's fellow man, it is a futile and sterile pursuit.[202]

Ethical and moral excellence is incompatible with "detached compassion." It demands involvement of one's whole personality in a profound concern for the welfare of one's fellowman. The religious spirit, which sets "concerned involvement" rather than "detached compassion" as its highest goal, finds its highest expression in the moral injunctions of the Torah and in the preachment of the prophets of Israel. Hence before we discuss Judaism's rationalization of the moral, we shall present its concept of the moral.

The Moral Component in Judaism

The primary source of the moral component in Judaism is the nineteenth chapter of Leviticus. In the opinion of the Rabbis, this chapter includes the whole of the Torah.[203] It reaches out beyond the Ten Commandments. They are included in the chapter, but its law of holiness, of charity, and of love is not included in them. The intermingling of the ethical, the moral, and the ritual in this chapter reflects not only the scope of Judaism, but also its insistence upon the interdependence of the three components. Our discussion of the moral in Judaism will, therefore, center around passages in this chapter which deal with the moral, and with other relevant passages from rabbinic literature.

1. *To share one's physical possessions with the needy.* The most frequently encountered expression of the moral intent is the act of sharing one's possessions with the needy. Every act of charity entails a deprivation to the agent. One would have to use a sensitive instrument indeed to measure the deprivation suffered by a Rockefeller or a Rothschild in giving a dime to a beggar. But even such small deprivations should not be disregarded when dealing with the spiritual. Science has taught us to think in terms of the infinitely small even in the realm of the physical.[204]

Parting with a valued possession is a painful act to a miser. It requires a conscious decision-making effort on the part of everyone. We do not consider the compulsive miser or the compulsive squanderer as normal human beings, but the tendency to hold on to what one has is more deeply rooted in our biological inheritance than the tendency to part with it. Sharing one's possessions with the needy may give one a gratifying sense of power and self-importance. It may be a satisfying response to the emotion of pity, or serve as a warrant against a time when one may himself be in need of a fellow man's generosity. But these psychological and sociological considerations do not make the act of charity so "natural" and commonplace as not to require frequent encouragement and evoke admiration and commendation. Hence all religions, and many secular philosophies,[205] are generous in their praise of the virtue of charity.

To the best of my knowledge, Judaism broke new ground when it integrated the act of sharing one's possessions with the needy into its ritual and civil law. The giving of charity is not considered to be merely the exercise of another virtue, like courage, prudence, or self-control. It is an integral part of the Law, like the commandment to offer sacrifices, or not to steal or swear falsely. The commandment enjoining the sharing of one's possessions with "the poor and the stranger" is sandwiched between a ritual law regarding animal sacrifice and a civil law forbidding deceitful dealing with one another.

"When you reap the harvest of your land, you shall not reap all the way to the edges of your field, or gather the gleanings of your harvest. You shall not pick your vineyard bare, or gather the fallen fruit of your vineyard; you shall leave them for the poor and the stranger. I am the Lord" (Lev. 19:9–10). A large tractate of the Mishnah and the Jerusalem Talmud[206] are devoted to the elaboration of these verses. They form the basis for the law of *zedakah*, of sharing one's material possessions with the less fortunate. This occupies a prominent place in every major code of Jewish Law.[207]

The legal aspect of the law of charity is further reflected in the fact that "the edges of the field, the gleanings of the harvest, the fallen fruit," and the other categories established by the Torah are considered to be the property of the poor and the stranger as of right, and not because of the kind-heartedness of the owner of the field or vineyard. He has no right to choose the poor to whom these

should be given. All poor and all strangers have an equal right to
them.

Does converting the giving of charity into a legal responsibility
rob it of its moral significance? We do not identify that part of the
income tax which the government uses to help the needy as charity
given by the citizen. We have previously discussed this question.[208]
Moreover, the commandment does not deprive the owner of the
vineyard of all exercise of choice. The Torah does not specify the
size of the edges of the field, or the quantity of the gleaning that is
to be left to the poor. To guide the owner, the Rabbis later indicate
what would be considered niggardly, fair, and generous gifts,[209] but
the final decision is the owner's. Nor was the obligation to leave the
indicated portion for the poor and the stranger limited to the wealthy.
The portions were not to be given merely from surplus, from what
one did not need. Everyone who had a field to harvest or a vineyard to glean was obligated by this law whether or not he had
enough for his own needs. Even those who were recipients of charity
were morally, though not legally, obligated to give charity.[210]

These injunctions to the landowner are supplemented by the
commandment to share one's financial resources with the needy.
"If there be among you a needy man, one of thy brethren, within
any of thy gates, in thy land which the Lord thy God giveth thee,
thou shalt not harden thy heart, nor shut thy hand from thy needy
brother; but thou shalt surely open thy hand unto him, and shalt
surely lend him sufficient for his needs in that which he wanteth"
(Deut. 15:7–8).

How much economic help is one obligated to give to his fellow
man? Commenting on the passage "Thou shalt *surely* open thy
hand," the Rabbis say, "Open thy hand even a hundred times." They
interpret the words "sufficient for his needs" to mean that a man's
needs are relative to his station in life. Hillel is said to have provided an impoverished descendant of a once prosperous family with
a horse on which to take his exercise and a servant to attend him.[211]
When Hillel could provide no servant for him, he himself "ran in
front of him for three miles."[212]

Sharing one's possessions with others is not associated in Judaism, as it is in other religions and philosophies, with any denigration of the possession of wealth. Sin does not inhere in affluence, nor virtue in poverty. The Rabbis, however, do not recommend the accumulation of wealth as a goal of life and frequently stress the pitfalls which surround the affluent. Hillel warned his students that "the more property, the more anxiety."[213] Those desirous of acquiring Torah are advised: "A morsel of bread with salt thou must eat, and water by measure thou must drink; thou must sleep upon the ground, and live a life of trouble while thou toilest in the Torah."[214] There are also stories without number of Jewish saints, both ancient and modern, who lived lives of the utmost frugality and austerity. However, the Jewish tradition does not commend such generosity as would reduce one to indigence and mendicancy, as is apparently urged by Jesus[215] and is practiced by religious orders both in the West and the East.

On the contrary, the Rabbis taught that one should not distribute in charitable gifts more than twenty percent of his resources at any one time.[216] The Rabbis do not permit one to dedicate all of his possessions even to God, and if he has done so, it is not to be accepted.[217] The rationalization of this and other limitations placed by Judaism on the implementation of the moral we shall discuss later.[218]

2. *Not to take advantage of the defenseless.* "You shall not wrong a stranger or oppress him . . . you shall not mistreat any widow or orphan" (Exod. 22:20–21). The admonition is repeated some thirty-six times in the Torah.[219] Obviously, the orphan, the widow, and the stranger are not the only ones who are not to be wronged or mistreated. They are singled out merely because they are the most defenseless members of society. The same is true of the admonition "not to insult the deaf or place a stumbling block before the blind" (Lev. 19:14). They cannot protect themselves by responding in kind. They do not even know who wronged them. Resisting the temptation to take advantage of a fellow man when

one can do it with impunity, verges, as we have previously pointed out, more on the moral than on the ethical.

But the Torah goes beyond merely forbidding such abuse of the weak. It commands that provision be made that "they rejoice with you." "Thou shalt keep the feast of tabernacles seven days, after that thou has gathered in from thy threshing-floor and from thy winepress. And thou shalt rejoice in thy feast, thou, and thy son, and thy daughter, and thy man-servant, and thy maid-servant, and the Levite, and the stranger, and the fatherless, and the widow . . . within thy gates" (Deut. 16:13–14).

3. *The obligation to perform acts of mercy.* "By mercy and truth, iniquity is expiated" (Prov. 16:6). "He that followeth after righteousness and mercy findeth life, prosperity, and honor" (ibid., 21:21). The Hebrew word which is here translated as "mercy" is *ḥesed.* An extensive literature is devoted to the various meanings of *ḥesed.* While the studies dealing with this concept vary, there is general consensus that *"ḥesed* involves an element of moral obligation, the recognition of a social bond which demands mutual helpfulness even beyond the requirements of justice . . . beyond that which one normally had the right to expect, beyond that which was deserved."[220]

The Rabbis identify this biblical concept with their concept of *gemilut ḥasadim,* acts of mercy or loving-kindness.[221] They distinguish *gemilut ḥasadim* from *zedakah* in three ways. *Zedakah* is an act implementing a moral intent whose object is a human being in need of material help, and its performance requires the sacrifice on the part of the agent of some of his material goods. *Gemilut ḥesed* is an act whose object may be either a living or a dead individual, rich or poor, and does not necessarily involve the giving of one's material goods. It can be performed by giving of one's time, as in burying the dead or visiting the sick or performing any act expressing concern for another's physical or spiritual welfare.[222] The Rabbis designate as *gemilut ḥesed shel emet* an "unquestionable act of loving kindness," an act performed in behalf of the dead,[223] especially an unidentified person, for under those circumstances one cannot expect any favor in return.

Utopians foresee the day when the *mizvah* of *zedakah* will be obsolete since no one will be in need of financial aid from his fellow man. The Pentateuch is ambivalent on the subject (Deut. 15:4, 11). The prophet is more sanguine (Mic. 4:4). However, there will never be a time when men will not be in need of *gemilut hasadim,* acts of loving-kindness. This fact alone bestows upon the religious element in human life a longevity equal to that of mankind, for acts of loving-kindness can be rationalized only religiously, and men will always need a rationalization for what they do.

4. *Obligation to one's enemies.* "When you encounter your enemy's ox or ass wandering, you must take it back to him. When you see the ass of your enemy prostrate under its burden and would refrain from raising it, you must nevertheless raise it with him" (Exod. 23:4–5).

5. *Remaining true to a commitment.* "That which is gone out of thy lips thou shalt keep and perform; even a freewill offering, according as thou has vowed unto the Lord thy God, which thou hast promised with thy mouth" (Deut. 23:24). "O Lord, who shall sojourn in Thy tent? . . . He who . . . swears to his own hurt and changeth not" (Ps. 15:1, 4).

The question of whether a pledge may ever be honorably violated is one which is discussed frequently.[224] Obviously, a pledge implies that it will be honored even when it may involve considerable loss or discomfort, and even when it can be violated with impunity. The psalmist does not praise the man who merely fulfills a pledge. He praises one who does so when it is to his hurt, and when presumably he could have avoided fulfilling it. Such an act belongs in our category of the moral.

6. *Acting as the conscience of society.* "Thou shalt surely rebuke thy neighbor, and not bear sin because of him" (Lev. 19:17). On the basis of this verse and the rabbinic interpretations of it, Maimonides concludes that one is to rebuke a sinner even a hundred times until the sinner either repents or is so angered that he is ready

to strike the rebuker.[225] The Rabbis are ambivalent about this commandment.[226] There are those who question whether there is anyone of sufficient stature to rebuke others and who knows how to do it without public insult, for to rebuke to the point of public humiliation is sinful. The discussion indicates how sensitive the Rabbis were to the possible pitfalls in fulfilling this commandment. However, one feels that the majority believe that one who does not rebuke a sinner when he has the opportunity to do it, partakes of his sin.[227] The Talmud records the opinion that Jerusalem was destroyed, the righteous perishing with the wicked, because the righteous did not rebuke the transgressors.[228] This commandment seems to encourage the individual who meddles in other people's affairs. It has probably often so served. But it is the underlying motivation of all prophetic activity. The prophet is one who cannot be a silent witness to an injustice or impiety and who feels the irrepressible need to warn, to rebuke, and to denounce even though he knows he will pay heavily for his meddlesomeness.[229]

It is this commandment, and the exhortations and personal example of the prophets, that has been the seed, the soil, and the climate to which we can perhaps attribute the presence of so disproportionately large a number of Jewish leaders and workers in the ranks of so many movements aiming to reform or overthrow unjust and oppressive social orders.

Something of this quality of meddlesomeness inheres in the commandments regarding justice and peace. Most commandments of the Torah are to be fulfilled when the occasion naturally arises for their fulfillment. Righteousness and peace, however, are to be "pursued," that is, one is not to wait until the opportunity to do righteousness and to establish peace comes to him. "Righteousness, righteousness shalt thou pursue" (Deut. 16:20). "Turn from evil and do good. Seek peace and pursue it" (Ps. 34:15). And Job says, "I was a father to the needy; and the cause of him that I knew not I searched out" (Job 20:16).[230]

7. *The obligation to risk limb and life in behalf of a fellow man.* The rather obscure verse "Do not stand upon the blood of

your neighbor" (Lev. 19:16) is interpreted by the Rabbis to mean that if one has information that can benefit his neighbor in a lawsuit, he is obligated to testify even though it may involve great risk or inconvenience. And if one sees a man drowning or being attacked by robbers or beasts, or being pursued by a murderer, he is bound to come to his aid even at great risk to his own possessions or to his limb and life.[231] Though the Rabbis taught that one must be prepared to risk one's life in behalf of an endangered fellow man, they do not teach, as Jesus is said to have taught, that the ultimate test of friendship is "that a man lay down his life for his friends" (John 15:12–13).[232]

The Rabbis discuss the hypothetical case of two men lost in the desert, one of whom has sufficient water to save himself. If he shares it, neither one would survive. Ben Petura taught, "Both should drink and perish." Rabbi Akiba, however, taught that the owner of the water should drink it and save his life, for "one's own life takes precedence over that of one's fellow man."[233]

8. *Love thy neighbor as thyself.* The moral law of Judaism is climaxed in the commandments: "Love your neighbor as yourself" (Lev. 19:18); "The stranger who resides with you shall be to you as one of your citizens; you shall love him as yourself" (ibid., v. 34). The Rabbis do not specify whether this commandment implies additional obligations toward one's fellow man, or is merely a summary of all that preceded, implying that if one does all that he is there commanded, he will act as one who loves his neighbor as himself. This is one of the few verses designated by the Rabbis, in this instance by Rabbi Akiba, as *klal gadol,* a biblical teaching of "surpassing importance." Ben Azzai preferred the verse "This is the book of the generations of man (Gen. 5:1).[234] But Hillel, some two centuries before Rabbi Akiba, said to a prospective convert who wanted to be taught the whole Torah while standing on one foot, "What is hateful to you do not unto others. This is the whole Torah. All the rest is commentary. Go and study it."[235]

We had occasion earlier in this essay to make extended comments on this verse,[236] whose intention is obvious though its literal meaning may be subject to questioning. Coming as a climax to a series of injunctions, it urges upon man a concern for the welfare of his fellow man that approaches the depth and consistency of concern that a normal, spiritually healthy human being has for his own welfare.

9. *Kindness to animals.* The Torah imposes moral obligations even toward animals. Their welfare is to be taken into consideration even when it involves an injury to the owner. Three passages in the Pentateuch specifically enjoin consideration for the welfare of animals.[237] One is part of the fourth commandment. On the Sabbath day, not only are old and young, male and female, free and slave, stranger and citizen to rest, but beasts of burden may also not be worked (Exod. 20:10, Deut. 5:14). Hence a Jew is not permitted to sell or hire out his animal to anyone who is known to work his animals on the Sabbath.[238] The Torah also commands that one shall not team an ox with a donkey when plowing (Deut. 22:10). As the human laborer is permitted to eat from the crop he was gathering,[239] so is the animal (ibid., 25:4). Animals are to be treated humanely, and their slaughter for food or Temple sacrifice is to be accomplished in a manner that inflicts the minimum of pain.[240] The ancient Greeks and Romans had no sympathy with these laws, which involved economic sacrifices. Spinoza is of the opinion that "the law against killing animals is based upon an empty superstition and womanish tenderness, rather than upon sound wisdom."[241]

Limitation of the Scope of the Moral

We have previously noted the two instances in which Judaism places limits on the moral intention:

1. One is not obligated to lay down his life for one or more other individuals.

2. One should not be generous to the point of indigence.

These limitations derive from the fundamental premise that one's life is not his own to do with as he sees fit. Each man's life is a gift entrusted to him by God, and he is responsible for its well-being.[242] Just as one has no right to assume that his life is more precious than the life of his fellow man, so he has no right to assume that his life is less precious.

This rationale is explicitly articulated in a rabbinic discussion in regard to the three situations in which a Jew is obligated to accept martyrdom rather than violate a biblical commandment; namely, when he is required to worship an idol in the presence of other Jews, to commit adultery, or to kill an innocent human being. For the first two instances specific biblical warrant is offered. There is, however, no biblical passage to support the third situation. Whereupon the Talmud says: "It stands to reason. Even as one who came before Rabba and said to him, 'The governor of my town has ordered me, go and kill so and so, if not I will slay thee.' He [Rabba] answered him, 'Let him rather slay you than that you should commit murder; who knows that your blood is redder? Perhaps his blood is redder.' "[243] In commenting on the passage, Rashi explains: "Who knows whether his own life is more precious in the eyes of his Creator than the life of his fellow man?" Just as one is not obligated to save his fellow man's life at the expense of his own, so is he forbidden to save his own life at the expense of the life of his fellow man.

The same considerations explain the limits Judaism places upon generosity. The Rabbis list the poor among the three classes of people who, though physically alive, are not really living.[244] They go so far as to compare them to the dead.[245] One is therefore not obligated to impoverish himself through generosity to others.

We turn now to the question of how Judaism rationalized the ethical and the moral.

SECTION X

Judaism's Rationalization of the Ethical and the Moral

We noted previously that the ethical or moral quality of an intention does not depend upon the consequences of the act that implements it or upon the rationalization offered to justify it. It depends exclusively upon the nature of the effect the agent expects to have upon an object and/or upon himself as a result of his implementation of his intention. We did, however, note that the character of the agent is affected by the rationalization of his intention. Secular and religious rationalizations will result in different kinds of personalities. But even within the framework of the religious rationalization there is room for diverse personality development. Assuming that man lives a moral and ethical life because he believes he is so commanded by God, do we ascribe the same virtue to one who obeys God's commandments out of fear of punishment or hope for reward as to one who obeys the commandments out of love for God?[246]

This question is raised by the teaching of Antigonos of Sokho, who flourished in the first half of the third century B.C.E.: "Be not like slaves who serve their master for their daily rations; be like those who serve their master without regard to emoluments, and let the fear of God be upon you."[247]

The opinion of later Rabbis regarding this teaching of Antigonos is reflected in the tradition that "Antigonos of Sokho had two disciples who used to study his words. They taught them to their disciples, and these to their disciples. These proceeded to examine the words closely and demanded: 'Why did our ancestors see fit to say this thing? Is it possible that a laborer should do his work all day and not take his reward in the evening? If our ancestors, forsooth, had known that there is another world and that there will be a resurrection of the dead, they would not have spoken in this manner.' So they arose and withdrew from the Torah and split into two sects, the Sadducees and the Boethusians: Sadducees named after Zadok, Boethusians, after Boethus. And they used silver vessels and gold vessels all their lives, not because they were ostentatious; but the Sadducees said, 'It is a tradition amongst the Pharisees to afflict themselves in this world; yet in the world to come they will have nothing.' "[248] Let us examine this teaching of Antigonos and the comments upon it of the later Rabbis.

1. *Love of God vs. Fear of God.*[249] After admonishing his students not to serve God for a reward, Antigonos urges them so to live as to reflect an attitude of *mora* of heaven.[250] The term *mora* is usually translated as "fear." This implies that the slave should expect punishment for failure to perform his services, otherwise why should he fear his master? This means that God only punishes but never rewards, and that one should set his heart on avoiding punishment rather than on expecting reward. If we interpret *mora* as fear, Antigonos' maxim contradicts itself, because the concepts of punishment and reward constitute an inevitable polarity. Non-punishment, when punishment is feared, is also a "reward."[251] Hence others maintain that the term *mora* is to be taken as equivalent to *ahavah,* "love."[252] Antigonos is thus admonishing his students to serve God not in expectation of reward or in fear of punishment but purely out of love.

While Antigonos may have used the word *mora* as an absolute synonym of *ahavah,* of love, it was not thus generally understood by later generations. It has been identified with fear in its most literal sense, as it is used in God's blessing of Noah and his sons: *Umoraakhem*—"And the fear of you and the dread of you shall be upon every beast of the earth" (Gen. 9:2).

When *mora* and its equivalent, *yirah,* became identified with fear and hence contrasted with *ahavah,* love, the question of the relative merits of love and fear of God arose. Though serving God out of love seems, on the face of it, to be superior to serving Him out of fear, Scripture and some rabbinic sources use the two terms indiscriminately when speaking of what man's attitude should be toward God. Thus, commenting on the verse "And thou shalt fear the Lord," the Midrash says: "Be like those three of whom it is written that they feared the Lord. Be like Abraham (Gen. 22:12), Joseph (Gen. 42:18), and Job" (Job 1:1).[253]

On the other hand, Rabbi Simeon ben Elazar (second half of second century C.E.) quotes Scripture to prove that "he who serves God out of love is superior to one who serves God out of fear, for Scripture ascribes a greater reward to him."[254] Thus also we are led to believe that Rabban Yoḥanan ben Zakkai was unhappy at the thought that Job served God out of fear rather than out of love.[255]

Rabbi Meir, too, seems to have been uneasy about describing men like Abraham and Job as God-fearing men, for he quotes Scripture to prove that the word *yareh* in the case of Abraham is to be understood as synonymous with love. Hence, since the same word is used in the case of Job, it means love there also. If this is true of these two cases, why not of all cases where it is used to describe individuals of whom Scripture approves? This attempt to make *yirah*, fear, synonymous with *ahavah*, love, in the case of the heroes of the tradition reflects the opinion that he who serves God out of love is superior to one who serves Him out of fear. However, the very same passage in the Talmud ends with the story of Rabba, two of whose students told him that verses of Scripture appeared to them in their dreams. The one saw the verse "Oh how great is Thy goodness, which Thou has laid up for them that *fear* Thee" (Ps. 31:20); the other, the verse "Let them also that *love* Thy name be joyful in Thee" (Ps. 5:12). Whereupon he said to them, "Both of you are altogether completely righteous individuals, one out of love, the other out of fear."[256]

Three propositions seem to underlie discussions on the relative merits of love and fear as motives for serving God. (1) Love and fear constitute a polarity. (2) To serve God out of fear implies that you are serving Him for a reward, while if you serve Him out of love you do not expect a reward. (3) One who serves God out of fear expects a reward not only in some future world but here on this earth, and conceives of that reward, if not exclusively then at least primarily, in materialistic terms. Let us turn our attention to these propositions.

Is the polarity between fear and love as clear as we generally assume it to be? To be sure we can distinguish between the sentiment of love and that of fear. Fear of a master need have no admixture of love or respect for him. However, love has a component of fear in it, for to love an object implies a sense of fear of losing or impairing it. The greater the love, the greater the fear.

Thus "people of superior refinement and of active disposition identify happiness with honor. Such people can be said to love honor,
and the more one loves honor, the more he will fear disgrace. . . . For
to fear some things is ever right and noble, and it is base not to fear
them. For example, disgrace: he who fears this is good and modest
and he who does not is shameless."[257] Thus, also, to love a human
being implies vigilance to do nothing that may physically or psychologically harm that person. He who loves most also fears most the
possibility that he may do injury to the beloved. The punishment
that is feared is not inflicted by the beloved object but by something
within oneself.[258] To the sensitive individual, the disappointment
which he experiences in himself, and the disappointment in him
which he feels he might have roused in the beloved object, constitute the greatest punishment which can be inflicted upon him. Serving God out of fear and serving God out of love do not therefore ·
constitute a polarity. They may just as often constitute a compound.

In the Hebrew Bible there is no polarity between love and fear
in the service of God. Equal emphasis is placed on both. The
author of the 119th Psalm surely loved God and His Torah. Yet he
says, "My flesh trembleth for fear of Thee; and I am afraid of Thy
judgments" (v. 120). Preceding the injunction "And you shall
love the Lord your God with all your heart, with all your soul, and
with all your might" (Deut. 6:5), is the statement "Now this is the
commandment, the statute, and the ordinance, which the Lord your
God commanded to teach you . . . that thou mightest fear the Lord
thy God . . . and that thy days may be prolonged." (Deut. 6:
1–2). And following it is the admonition, "Thou shalt fear the
Lord thy God . . ." (Deut. 6:13).[259]

Hence, while the Biblical-Rabbinic tradition knows the difference between love of God and fear of God, and the rabbinic
tradition inclines toward setting love above fear, serving God out
of fear is not disparaged.[260] It all depends on what one fears and
what one loves. Yohanan ben Zakkai's fear of meeting his Creator
was not due to fear of being physically hurt. It was rooted in a sense
of his own inadequacy to fulfill what he believed God had the right

to expect of him. He was a lover who feared to disappoint his beloved, a fear that sprang from and was permeated by love.[261]

2. *On expecting a reward.* As indicated before, the rabbinic tradition records that the disciples of Antigonos found a logical flaw in their teacher's admonition. They asked, "Is it possible that a laborer would do his work all day and not take his reward in the evening?" To serve God as Antigonos expected them to, involved the rejection of many desirable mundane pleasures. What did he offer in return? Nothing; either in this world or in any other world. A rational human being cannot but expect some "reward," some benefit commensurate with the "injury" resulting from an act of self-sacrifice. "A specific ethic must make the individual feel and believe that this way of life offers the highest degree of value experience open to him. Otherwise there is no reason at all for him to choose the ethical."[262] A "selfish" component must be part of any rationalization of the moral or the ethical.

Having been offered nothing by Antigonos but fear or love of a master, his pupils decided to use their "silver and gold vessels," not because they were ostentatious, but because in the light of their master's teaching that was the only course that seemed to them to make sense.[263]

Antigonos did what utopian idealists before and after him have done. He set up a goal for human conduct whose achievement required a denial of both reason and instinct. The superficial reaction to demands so extreme and so irrational is all too often that of the ancient Sadducees. The Biblical-Rabbinic tradition preserved Antigonos' aphorism not merely out of reverence for one who must have been both saint and sage, but also because it rejected the Sadducean interpretation of it.[264]

While the logical flaw which the disciples of Antigonos are said to have discovered in their teacher's position is real, the course their reaction to it took was not the only one available to them. The teaching of Antigonos does not constitute the whole of the Torah. On the contrary, it is but a very small fraction of the whole Torah, and obviously diametrically contradicts the main body of the tradition. There is, in the first place, the very clear and oft-repeated bib-lical promise of mundane reward for obedience to God and of punishment for failure to obey. "If you walk in My statutes, and keep My commandments and do them . . . ye shalt eat your bread until ye have enough and dwell in your land safely. And I will give peace in the land, and ye shall lie down, and none shall make you afraid" (Lev. 26:3–6). "But if you will not hearken unto Me . . . and if ye shall reject My statutes . . . I will appoint terror over you . . . you shall sow your seed in vain, for your enemies shall eat it . . . they that hate you shall rule over you; and ye shall flee when none pursueth you" (ibid., 14–17).

We noted previously that the secular moralist also implies that there is a relationship between ethical action and mundane wel-fare.[265] From the days of the prophets to our own day, no teacher of Judaism has ascribed efficacy to ritual acts divorced from ethical behavior. The God of the Biblical-Rabbinic tradition "cannot endure iniquity along with the solemn assembly" (Isa. 1:13). "Will you steal, murder, and commit adultery, and swear falsely, and offer unto Baal, and walk after other gods whom ye have not known, and come and stand before Me in this house, whereupon My name is called and say: 'We are delivered,' that ye may do all these abom-inations? Is this house, whereupon My name is called, become a den of robbers in your eyes?" (Jer. 7:9–11).

Like all men of religious faith, however, the Rabbis believed that the biblical promise of mundane prosperity as a consequence of man's observance of the moral, ethical, and ritual law is largely valid not only for mankind as a whole, but also for any organized group, or for an individual. Hence, "He who says I give this coin for charity so that [or with the hope that] my sick son shall recover, or that I may have a share in the world to come, is a *zaddik gamur,* a wholly righteous man" (his act is *zedakah gmura,* a perfect act of charity).[266] He is a wholly righteous man because he has faith in a world order in which an ethical act can influence the course of events beneficially. But he is perfectly righteous only if the granting of the request is not made a condition of the gift, and if the gift is not regretted if the request is not granted.[267] The act of charity or the ritual act is not a magical formula to compel God to grant a request. To believe that man can compel God to do his will by prayer or charity or in any other way is to view these acts as magical formulae and to subordinate God to magic.

The subordination of the gods to magic is a universal characteristic of paganism. "Pagan religion even in its highest manifestation, is amenable to belief in magic" because there is "the ever present assumption of a realm of forces apart from the gods." Magical rites that supposedly have access to these forces "are viewed as automatically effective, or even capable of coercing the gods to do the will of the practitioner."[268] The Biblical-Rabbinic tradition is unequivocally opposed to magic. "There shall not be found among you anyone that makes his son or his daughter to pass through the fire, one that uses divination, a soothsayer, or an enchanter, or a sorcerer, or a charmer, or one that consults a ghost or a familiar spirit, or a necromancer. For whosoever does these things is an abomination unto the Lord; and because of these abominations the Lord thy God is driving them out from before thee" (Deut. 18:10–12). Few things so clearly distinguish Judaism from all forms of paganism as Judaism's insistence that God is in no way subject to magic or coercion of any kind.[269]

The wholly righteous man ever bears in mind that God owes man nothing. On the verse in Job "Who has preceded Me, so that I should be in debt to him? All that is under the Heavens is Mine" (Job 41:3), the Rabbis comment: "Who ever gave charity before I gave him treasure? Who ever helped the blind before I gave him sight?"[270] As David said, "But who am I, and what is my people, that we should be able to offer so willingly after this sort? For all things come of Thee and of Thine own have we given Thee" (1 Chron. 29:14).

A man's character is ultimately tested by how he acts if, while living the ethical and moral life, he is not rewarded with mundane goods.[271] He does not necessarily conclude that there are no rewards at all. He may have faith that there is another realm of existence in which the irrationalities of the human experience upon this earth will be rationalized.[272] Since Antigonos made no reference to a future world, his disciples had good ground for concluding that he did not believe in its existence. But that conclusion does not necessarily follow from what Antigonos taught. The fact that he does not mention a future world does not necessarily imply that he did not believe in its existence. He may have taught that even though there is a future world one should not serve God in order thereby to gain a portion in it.

There are many stories told of the righteous who expressed regret that the Jewish tradition included faith in the existence of the *olam haba,* for that precluded the possibility of their serving God with absolute certainty that they would not be rewarded. But since faith in the *olam haba* was an integral part of their religious outlook, the only way they could achieve their religious ideal was by denying a basic doctrine of the Biblical-Rabbinic tradition. And just as Kant had to admit that no human being can ever be sure that he acts purely out of a sense of duty,[273] the saintliest among the followers of the Biblical-Rabbinic tradition cannot be sure that they would have served God as wholeheartedly as they do if the concept of *olam haba* were not integral to that tradition. The righteous man's regret that the tradition includes *olam haba* is as ambivalent as Abraham's statement might have been, if after Isaac was restored to him, he would have said he regretted that God did not permit him to prove beyond doubt that he was ready to forgo being the father of the people of Israel in order to obey His commandment.

Assuming that the pupils of Antigonos were right in thinking that their master did not believe in a future world or in the resurrection of the dead, and therefore that they too were on sound ground in repudiating this doctrine, the conclusion that there is therefore no reward and that Antigonos so believed did not follow. There was another alternative available to them. Mundane physical welfare and life in a future world are not the only rewards known to Judaism. There are rewards available upon this earth in addition to those of good health, long life, and economic well-being which are at least as desirable and, in the opinion of some, even more desirable. Those rewards are repeatedly stressed by the psalmists and the Rabbis.

The psalmist tells us that his first reaction to the contrast between the well-being of the wicked and his own poverty and suffering was to say, "Surely in vain have I cleansed my heart, and washed my hands in innocency" (73:13). But he did not cease searching for an answer, even though he tells us that "when I pondered how I might know this, it was wearisome in mine eyes" (v. 16). He finally found his answer when he "entered into the sanctuary of God" (v. 17). There he discovered that "the nearness of God is my good" (v. 28). The psalm does not end, as does the Book of Job, by telling us that the psalmist was rewarded with a two-fold increase in his worldly possessions. It ends by proclaiming the proposition that the moral life of man finds its greatest reward in the experience of being "near to God."[274]

Ben Azzai's dictum *"skhar mizvah, mizvah"*[275] is usually explained as "the reward for doing a *mizvah* is that one is thereby disposed to do another *mizvah*." Urbach, however, interprets it to mean that "the reward for the *mizvah* inheres in the very doing of it.[276] This interpretation is but another formulation of the psalmist's pronouncement that "nearness to God" is in itself the greatest reward available to man in this world or the future world. The "nearness to God" which the psalmist experienced when he entered "the sanctuary of God" (Ps. 73:17), Ben Azzai experienced when he performed a *mizvah*.

The crux of the difference between the Sadducean interpretation of the statement of Antigonos and the way it was understood by the Rabbis who preserved it, consists, therefore, not in whether the good life is rewarded but rather in the nature of the reward that one should reasonably expect and desire. And this in turn depends upon the answer one gives to the question, Who am I? The answer to this question, in turn, depends upon one's view of the universe in which man finds himself. The consistently logical secularist view sees the universe as a conglomerate of blind, amoral forces aim-

lessly and endlessly producing an infinite variety of transient phenomena, one of which is man. This view of the universe leads
logically to a concept of the human self as that which is contained
within the skin of one's body, and nothing more. At the end of a
period of time this "self" disintegrates into the elements from which
it was composed. In the light of such a conception, the Sadducean
conclusion "to use silver and gold dishes all the days of their lives"
is rational and well-nigh inescapable. Judaism rejected this Sadducean conclusion because it had rejected the secular concept of the
universe and the concept of man which is integrally related to it.

SECTION XI

*Judaism's Conception of the
Universe and of Man*

A comprehensive fomulation of Judaism's teachings regarding the
nature of the universe and of man's place within it would take us
far beyond the limits set for this inquiry.[277] We shall therefore con-
fine ourselves to those aspects which have direct bearing upon the
problem before us. Judaism teaches that:

   1. "In the beginning God created heaven and earth" (Gen.
1:1).
   2. "In His goodness the world of creation is continually renewed day by day."[278]
   3. "And God created man in His image, in the image of God
created He man" (Gen. 1:27).
   Rabbi Akiba said, "Beloved is man, for he was created in the
image of God; but it was by a special love that it was made known
to him that he was created in the image of God; as it is said 'For in
the image of God made He man' " (Gen. 9:6).[279]
   The idea that man was created in the image of God is found
not only in the Hebrew Bible. As previously noted, philosophers
who step beyond the ultimate limits of the secular and infringe on

the realm of the religious, also speak of the likeness between man and God.[280] The fundamental difference between Judaism and the philosophers lies rather in the concept of the God in whose image man was created.

With the possible exception of Plato, "who has given us two conceptions of the nature of deity that are mutually exclusive and contradictory," the philosophers' concept of God makes him out to be "a changeless, metaphysical unity, with no relation or a very tenuous relation with anything that lives."[281] He is in essence self-centered, like the God of Aristotle "contemplating" Himself, or like the God of Spinoza "loving" Himself.[282]

The God of Judaism is neither aloof nor self-centered. He is very much involved in the world which He created.[283] The nature of that involvement, insofar as it bears upon the behavior of man, is subsumed under the concept of holiness. Because God is holy (Isa. 6:3), and because man was created in His image, "the utmost virtue of man is to become like unto Him, may He be exalted, as far as he is able; which means that we should make our actions like unto His, as the Sages make clear when interpreting the verse 'Ye shall be holy' (Lev. 19:2). They said 'He is gracious, so you too be gracious; He is merciful, so you too be merciful'" (Sifre, Deut. 10:12).[284] We noted above that Scripture spelled out in considerable detail what being "holy" required of man in terms of his behavior toward his fellow man.[285] The Rabbis point out that God does not ask man to do anything which He Himself, as it were, does not do.

Man is commanded not to afflict the stranger, the widow, and the orphan (Exod. 22:20–21), and is warned that if he does afflict them and they cry unto the Lord, God will "hear their cry" and will take up their cause (ibid., 21–23), because God is "the father of the orphans and the pleader in behalf of widows" (Ps. 68:6). Man is commanded "not to seek revenge nor to bear a grudge" (Lev. 19:18), even as God forgives those who transgress against Him— "The Lord God, merciful and gracious, long-suffering and abundant in goodness and truth" (Exod. 34:6). Man is commanded, "Ye shall do no unrighteousness in judgment; thou shalt not respect the person of the poor, nor honor the person of the mighty; but in righteousness shalt thou judge thy neighbor" (Lev. 19:15), even as God "regardeth not persons nor taketh reward. He executes justice for the fatherless and widow and loves the stranger" (Deut. 10: 17–18).

God asks man to "walk humbly" (Mic. 6:8), even as humility is of the essence of God's greatness. Rabbi Yoḥanan (d. 279) said, "In every passage where you find the greatness of God mentioned, there also you find His humility." This is written in the Torah (Deut. 10:17–18), repeated in the Prophets (Isa. 57:15), and stated in the Writings (Ps. 68:5–6).[286]

"Rabbi Ḥama the son of Rabbi Ḥanina taught: It is written 'follow none but the Lord your God' (Deut. 13:5). Is it possible for man to "follow" the Lord who is "a consuming fire"? (Deut. 4:24). What it means, therefore, is that we should follow His virtues. Just as He clothed the naked, as it is written 'And the Lord God made for Adam and his wife garments of skins and He clothed them' (Gen. 3:21), so you too clothe the naked. Just as the Holy One, blessed be He, visited the sick, as it is written 'The Lord appeared to him by the terebinths of Mamre' (Gen. 18:1),[287] so you too visit the sick. The Holy one, blessed be He, comforts the mourners, as it is written 'After the death of Abraham, God blessed his son Isaac' (Gen. 25:11), so you too comfort the mourners. Just as the Holy One, blessed be He, buried the dead, as it is written 'He buried him [Moses] in the valley' (Deut. 34:6), so you too bury the dead." [288]

Hence, the divine commandments merely serve as our guides. It is our being, in the image of God, that obligates us and should determine our intentions and acts.[289]

In the light of these postulates, Judaism may be said to offer the following syllogism in place of that offered by the secularist:

Major premise: It is every man's responsibility and privilege to seek his own best interests.

Minor premise: It is man's best interest to act in accordance with those of his capacities which reflect the "image of God" with which he has been endowed.

Conclusion: Therefore every man should harbor and implement those intentions which are in accord with his God-like capacities.

The postulates that God is holy, in the Biblical-Rabbinic sense, and that man is created in God's image, constitute the rationalization of the ethical and the moral. Given these postulates the mind cannot rationally challenge the conclusion of the syllogism.

It make sense to ask one who believes in the "scientific" view of man and the universe why he should be either ethical or moral, because it is rational to ask why one should be expected to be something which he believes to be contrary to his nature. But it does not make sense to ask one who believes that there is a just and merciful God, and that man was created in God's image, why he should strive to live in harmony with his nature. It is this ultimate conception of the self which rationalizes our being "selfish" and, indeed, obligates us to be so.[290]

The extent to which man achieves his God-like potentialities depends upon what he does during his sojourn, brief or lengthy, upon this earth. It is the belief that our ultimate self-fulfillment depends upon what we do with our lives that gives meaning to our physical existence and obligates us to do all we can in order to lengthen our days upon this earth. Nowhere is the rabbinic concept of the significance of our physical existence upon this earth more profoundly formulated than in the statement of Rabbi Jacob that "one hour of repentance and good deeds in this world is to be preferred to all of one's life in the future world."[291] Despite all the wonderful things awaiting the righteous in the future world, no Jewish saint ever expressed impatience at the delay in getting there, because the future world cannot offer its inhabitants the opportunity "to repent and to perform good deeds." That can be done only upon this earth.

No greater estimate can be placed upon the significance of man's physical endowments than that placed upon them in this rabbinic statement. Just as man's greatest distinction lies in his having been created in the image of God, so the greatest distinction of man's physical endowments lies in the fact that they can be of service to his divine potential.

To seek fulfillment of our divine image is our primary duty to ourselves. The happiness that inheres in the striving and the achievement is the reward which a rational being will experience upon this earth and for which, Jewish tradition teaches, he will be eternally and infinitely rewarded in the world to come. "The performance of the following commandments brings both immediate reward and everlasting bliss in time to come: honoring parents; deeds of loving-kindness; prompt attendance at the house of study, morning and evening; hospitality to strangers; visiting the sick; dowering the needy bride; attending the dead; devotion in prayer; and effecting peace between men. But the study of Torah is basic to them all." [292]

The rationalization which Judaism offers for the ethical and the moral is related to man's mundane welfare. But its chief distinction lies in its recognition that mundane welfare per se cannot cogently rationalize any aspect of the moral, and only a limited area of the ethical, since these require man to forgo his mundane welfare.

Epilogue

It is not my purpose here to prove that Judaism's conception of the universe is "objectively" or "scientifically" more correct, or more in accord with the phenomena available to our senses, than the secularist's or anyone else's conception. We are long past the time when any thoughtful person will presume to say that we shall ever know the ultimate nature of the universe. As long as we do not know with certainty whence we came and whither we are going, we cannot, with certainty, decide in favor of the Hebrew prophets against the Athenian delegates to Melos. We are not searching in this inquiry for an answer to the question of man's origin and destiny. All that we are here seeking is a conception of the universe and of man that most cogently rationalizes man's ethical and moral intentions.

Judaism's rationalization of the moral and the ethical may therefore be viewed as its response to man's greatest of all needs, his need to preserve his rationality, which is the indispensable component of his sanity.[293] Civilized man fears insanity far more than he fears death. Men have in overwhelming numbers preferred life with physical pain to death, but no sane person would willingly choose a life of irrationality or insanity to death. One conscious of the ethical and moral stirrings within him cannot but feel a sense of awe and wonder at their presence. He cannot but feel that they above all bestow upon him a sense of ineffable dignity. They set him above the beast. He must come to terms with them because they make demands upon him which run counter to his biological instincts and impulses. He must decide either to curb his moral and ethical stirrings so that they conform to his instincts, or to curb his instincts to conform to his moral and ethical sentiments. The first alternative offers no challenge to his rationality. The second does.

We do not challenge the rationality of one condemned to death who tries to flee from prison, nor that of Josephus currying the favor of the Romans. We understand fully the rationality of these actions. But Socrates preferring to drink the hemlock, and Akiba exposing himself to martyrdom, seem to be acting irrationally. We challenge their sanity, and they feel the need to justify their acts. Each could have responded with the statement that he acted as he did because his "character decreed it,"[294] because that is the way they felt. But each explained his action in a way that made it rationally cogent for him,[295] and each hoped that the questioners, too, would find the answers rationally persuasive.

Of all the reasons formulated by theologians and philosophers to "prove" that this universe was brought into being and is sustained by a just and merciful God, none is more cogent than the proposition that in the alternative, so-called scientific conception of the universe, all moral intentions, and a high proportion of our ethical intentions, make no sense. The alternatives before us are, therefore, rather clear and simple. We must either posit a scientifically conceived universe and regard our moral and ethical promptings as aberrations from our physical needs and pleasures, or we must posit a religiously conceived universe to which our ethical and moral promptings are related and therefore are to be nurtured and implemented.[296]

If those who choose the second alternative are to preserve their rational integrity, they must posit a loving and just Creator and acknowledge that the greatest blessing He bestowed upon man was His having created him in His own image.[297] Indeed, man must do more than "posit" such a God. "You could not get much comfort from postulating the existence of God so long as you remembered that you were postulating it in order to give yourself comfort."[298] Man must believe in God with a perfect faith.[299]

2.

ETHICS AND LAW IN THE AMERICAN TRADITION

Introductory Remarks

What Does It Mean to Be an American?

THE CONCEPT "AN AMERICAN" came into being as the result of a long series of historical events. The meaning of these events for the individuals who initiated or participated in them was recorded not only in deeds, but in carefully worded documents. Only these documents, which are the direct product of the events that led to the establishment and preservation of the government of the United States, and which were later, by public act, adopted by its citizens, can authentically guide us in our search for an answer to the question of what it means to be an American.

The Declaration of Independence and the Constitution

Two documents constitute what might be called the "sacred texts" of the American people—the Declaration of Independence and the

95

Constitution of the United States.[1] It was not always thus. Before the adoption of the Thirteenth, Fourteenth, and Fifteenth Amendments, abolitionists, and others who were among the most highly respected Americans, publicly denounced the Constitution as "a covenant with death," an "agreement with hell" (Isa. 28:15),[2] while others dismissed the opening paragraphs of the Declaration as a conglomeration of high-sounding phrases intended for immediate propagandistic purposes, but whose substantive content was scientifically and philosophically untenable and socially inapplicable.[3] It was a long and at times tragedy-laden history that bestowed their present quality of sanctity upon them for the overwhelming majority of Americans.

It is in these two documents that the answer to the question—What does it mean to be an American?—inheres.

Each of the documents has its own unique distinctions. Thus, there is no way whereby a word or even a comma can legitimately be added to or subtracted from the Declaration. The Constitution provides a method whereby it can be amended. The Declaration has no legal status. It bestows no legally defensible privileges and immunities nor any legally enforceable obligations upon an American. The Constitution, and all local, state, and national legislative bodies functioning under its authority, does. The police forces functioning under the various governmental units can compel a citizen to fulfill his legal obligations and are enjoined to defend him in the exercise of his privileges and immunities. They cannot, however, compel him to exercise his privileges. An American cannot be compelled to vote or to express his opinion. Nor can he be compelled to hold as self-evident truths the propositions "that all men are created equal, that they are endowed by their Creator with certain unalienable Rights, that among these are Life, Liberty and the pursuit of Happiness. That to secure these rights, Governments are instituted among Men, deriving their just powers from the consent of the governed."

The concepts and ideas expressed in these propositions did not originate with the authors of the Declaration. They had been previously propounded and expounded by European philosophers.[4] But this was the first time in human history that they were pronounced to be self-evident truths in accordance with which a people was to set up a government for themselves. Moreover, the momentous, historically determinative occasions on which the Founding Fathers of America first formulated these propositions and pledged their "lives, their fortunes and their sacred honor" to uphold them, and then attempted to embody them in the provisions of the Constitution, served as inviolable warrant that they will forever after be inextricably intertwined with the destiny and fortunes of the American people. The only other documents which are about equally revered by most Americans are Lincoln's Gettysburg Address[5] and his Second Inaugural. The inspiring, felicitious terms in which they epitomize the spiritual essence of the most tragically traumatic experience in American history made and make it possible for the American people to think of those four years of self-immolation, not as an explosion of a masochistic drive which gripped the whole nation, but rather as "costly a sacrifice" as any people ever "laid upon the altar of Freedom," and as committing them forever, therefore, to the advancement of the cause for which that sacrifice was made. The American people inscribed both of them in full on the walls of a monument which, of all monuments they have thus far built, comes closest to being a religious shrine.

The Declaration and the Constitution were composed by men who were rare masters of words. They represent a supreme effort to achieve clarity and conciseness in expression. Nevertheless, there has never been a time when there was unanimous agreement among Americans on their literal or implied meaning. Hence, there are probably no two Americans who, when they turn to these documents in search of an answer to the question what it means to be an American, find exactly the same answer. Each one finds his own distinctive answer. *But insofar as one's attitudes, intentions, and acts are consciously motivated by his honest understanding of the contents of the Constitution and the Declaration,* they constitute his answer to the question of what it means to be an American.

Many of the attitudes and acts of an American are unquestionably motivated by his religious or philosophic convictions or ethnic
loyalties, or by the transient popular whims and fashions of thought
and act that from time to time sweep through the country. These
convictions, loyalties, whims, and fashions are in and of themselves
not of the essence of what it means to be an American. However,
the fact that one feels free to harbor and implement those whims,
loyalties, and convictions, and can, within very broad and generous
limits, do so with impunity as an American, is a primary component of the meaning that being an American has for him.

There has never been any doubt that being an American means
to be *legally* obligated to obey the provisions of the Constitution and
of *all* laws enacted under its authority. There have, however, always
been profound differences of opinion whether being an American
means that under all conditions one is *morally* obligated to obey
them. Many Americans in every generation have felt that when a
law is in conflict with one's religious convictions or with one's conscience—however he chooses to define his conscience—he is in duty
bound to disobey the law.[6] The *general,* abstract problem of what
one ought to do in case of a conflict between his legal and moral
obligations does not concern us at this point in our inquiry. What
concerns us is the *peculiarly American aspect* of the conflict between
one's legal and moral obligations.

For many thoughtful Americans that conflict did not and does
not arise from a difference between one's religious or ethnic loyalties
or one's conscience and his American loyalties. It arose and arises
within the framework of one's purely American loyalties, of loyalty
on the one hand to the Declaration and on the other hand to the
Constitution. That was and is due to the difference between the
spirit which emanates from the literal meaning of the opening
words of the Declaration and that which emanates from the literal
meaning of a number of passages in the Constitution.

The opening paragraphs of the Declaration both consciously
and subconsciously served the spiritually more sensitive members
of the American people as the Higher Law to which they appealed

as Americans against some of the provisions of the Constitution as it came from the Convention which had written it, or against laws later enacted under its authority.[7] *The uniquely American aspect of the spiritual history of America, as it is reflected in the American historical experience, can be viewed as the repeated attempts of the American people to translate the "self-evident" truths into legally enforceable enactments.* Issues of all kinds—economic, political, social, and religious—have divided American citizens into contending parties from the very founding of the United States. But if one took the trouble to trace the publicly avowed arguments in behalf of one or the other side of any significant issue to their ideological or conceptual roots, one would most likely find that these consist of basically different attitudes toward and understandings of, the "truths" of the Declaration.

Americans have from the very beginning related themselves to the substantive content of the Declaration in one of the following ways:

1. It is a statement that had the specific limited "purpose of justifying the colonists in the eyes of the civilized world in withdrawing their allegiance from the British crown, and dissolving their connection with the mother country." [8] That purpose "having been effected, . . . the Declaration is of no practical use now—mere rubbish—old wadding left to rot on the battlefield after the victory is won."[9] It had no message for later generations and was in no sense obligatory upon them.

2. There were those who accepted the validity of the "self-evident" truths of the Declaration, but understood them as applying "to the white population alone . . . and to the British subjects on this continent being equal to British subjects born and residing in Great Britain."[10]

3. And there were those who chose to view the statements of the Declaration as what one could designate as "prophetic pronouncements," whose substantive content had obvious and immediate relevance to the circumstances which occasioned them, but were couched in language capable of infinite growth in meaning

and therefore in applicability to circumstances totally unforseen by the authors of the pronouncements.[11]

> That's a hard mystery of Jefferson's.
> What did he mean? Of course the easy way
> Is to decide it simply isn't true.
> It may not be. I heard a fellow say so.
> But never mind the Welshman got it planted
> Where it will trouble us a thousand years.
> Each age will have to reconsider it.[12]

One can safely assume that as long as the American people continue to enshrine the Declaration, its truths will continue in various guises to be the ultimate source of the most fundamental differences that agitate the American body politic.

Hence, when for an extended period of time the "self-evident" truths of the Declaration are not directly or indirectly the subject of lively interest and debate in the public arena, the chances are that America has lost hold of its own unique character. And, conversely, whenever those truths are in one form or another found at the center of public discussion, we may assume that America is engaged in a soul-searching effort to define in deeds its essential being, and is hopefully on the way toward "a new birth of freedom."

We cannot within the scope of this inquiry follow in detail the role of the "self-evident" truths in all the great public debates that have agitated the American people during the well-nigh two centuries of their national history. But neither can we intelligently discuss what it means to be an American without referring in some detail to at least three periods during which those truths were at the very core of the lively public discussions then in progress.

1. The period between the signing of the peace treaty of 1783 with England and the adoption of the first ten amendments (1791).

2. The period between the passage of the Kansas-Nebraska Bill (1854) and the enactment of the fifteenth amendment (1870).

3. The period between the Supreme Court's decision in the *Slaughter House* cases (1873) and the passage of the Civil Rights Act of 1965.

The Period Between 1783 and 1791

The purpose that dominated the thoughts of the colonists in setting up a government to administer their joint affairs was to take every possible precaution against the possibility of its exercising tyrannical powers. That aim they achieved in the Articles of Confederation (1781). But the government set up under the Articles proved incapable not only of becoming a tyranny but also of governing effectively. The second attempt (1787) produced the document by which the American people have governed themselves now for almost two hundred years.

The Preamble to the Constitution reformulates some of the basic principles of the Declaration.

1. The Declaration declares that governments are established and govern by "the consent of those governed." The Preamble states that it is "We, the people" who established the government of the United States and who "ordained" the Constitution by which that government shall be guided.

2. The Declaration declares that "liberty" is an unalienable right of all men. The Preamble states that it is the purpose of the government to be established "to secure the blessings of liberty to ourselves and our posterity."

3. The Declaration declares that the "pursuit of happiness" is an unalienable right. The Preamble states that it shall be the purpose of the government to "promote the general welfare."

"To preclude the exercise of arbitrary power," three coordinate branches of government were created. "The purpose was, not to avoid friction, but, by means of the inevitable friction incident to the distribution of the governmental powers among three departments, to save the people from autocracy."[13]

No one of the three branches was granted sufficient power to govern without the cooperation of the other two. No branch of the government could on its own ascribe powers to itself. Its powers were specified as clearly as possible in the Constitution, which could be amended only by a process which involved the active participation of the whole body politic. Its ultimate meaning could be interpreted only by the Supreme Court.[14]

To implement and concretize the proposition that the governors derived their powers from those whom they govern, the members of the more numerous branch of the national legislature were to be periodically elected directly by the people. But neither the members of the Senate nor the President nor the members of the Supreme Court were to be thus elected. This limitation upon the people's right to choose their governors clearly indicated that the authors of the Constitution were as wary of the possible tyranny of the "mob" as they were of the tyranny of the "elite." They did not have an "absolute faith" in the virtue of the common man,[15] no more than they had an absolute faith in the virtue of the elite.

There have been many critical moments of high tension among the three coordinate branches of the government, and from time to time adjustments had to be made. The Constitution itself had to be amended. But in essence the structure created by the authors of the Constitution has remained intact. The history of the country, which thus far has been governed by that Constitution, has testified far more eloquently than even they could have anticipated to the wisdom of the machinery of government they had established.

There were, however, two things of major importance the Constitution failed to do. (1) It did not abolish human slavery. It thus ignored, neglected, or radically limited the meaning of the phrases "all men are created equal" and "We, the people." (2) It inadequately spelled out the implications of the term *liberty,* which the Declaration declared to be an unalienable right, and which the Preamble said was to be preserved for posterity. On the first item there was no significant agitation among the colonists who were to adopt or reject the Constitution. There was widespread recognition that if the union were to come into being at all, the compromise on that question which had been arrived at by the members of the Constitutional Convention was the most that could then be achieved.[16]

On the second issue, however, there was overwhelming agreement. The people insisted that the implications of the term *liberty* must be far more fully spelled out and made an integral part of the basic law. "Serious fears were extensively entertained that those powers which the patriot statesmen . . . deemed essential to union . . . might be exercised in a manner dangerous to liberty. In almost every convention by which the Constitution was adopted amendments to guard against the abuse of power were recommended. The Constitution would most likely not have been adopted had there not been a widely accepted gentleman's agreement that immediately after its adoption a series of amendments would be added to it, which specified those rights."[17]

The first ten amendments, known as the Bill of Rights (proposed in 1789, adopted in 1791), spelled out what the average American at the end of the eighteenth century meant when he spoke of the unalienable right to liberty. The full implications of the amendments, and the scope of their applicability, have been immeasurably enlarged over the decades by scores of Supreme Court decisions.[18] We shall have occasion to refer to these in the course of this inquiry. Here we shall merely note that judging by the contents of the first ten amendments, the people had nothing to offer regarding a constitutional provision positively "promoting" the individual's right to the pursuit of happiness. The notion that the government has some *positive* responsibilities in this area was, generally speaking, foreign to the dominant American political thought of the eighteenth century and most of the nineteenth.[19]

The Period Between 1854 and 1869

The greatest of the public controversies which engaged the minds and the hearts of the American people during the first "four score and seven years" of its career centered around the meaning of the phrases "We, the people" in the Preamble and "all men" in the Declaration. The controversy ultimately developed so much heat, acrimony, and violence as to come within a hair's breadth of the destruction of the whole political fabric built upon the foundations of the two documents.

The implication of "We, the people" became a subject of serious controversy early in American history since it involved the question of the source whence the Constitution derives its authority.

The first and most authoritative statement on this question was made by Chief Justice John Marshall in his opinion in *McCulloch* v. *Maryland,* rendered in 1819. It is generally regarded as his greatest state paper.   The case involved, among other things, the contention that each state has the power to nullify a decision of Congress.

> Counsel for the State of Maryland consider that instrument [the Constitution] not as emanating from the people but as the act of sovereign and independent States. The powers of the general government, it has been said, are delegated by the States, who alone are truly sovereign; and must be exercised in subordination to the States, who alone possess supreme dominion. It would be difficult to sustain this proposition. The convention which framed the Constitution . . . reported to the then existing Congress of the United States with a request that it might "be submitted to a convention of delegates, chosen in each state by the people thereof." They (the people) assembled in their several states, and where else should they have assembled? No political dreamer was ever wild enough to think of breaking down the lines which separate the States and of compounding the American people into one common mass. Of consequence, when they act, they act in their States. But the measures they adopt do not on that account cease to be measures of the people themselves, or become the measure of State governments. . . . The government proceeds directly from the people. . . . The Constitution when thus adopted was of complete obligation, and bound the State sovereignties.[20]

The proposition that the Constitution is a compact among sovereign states rather than among the people of the United States was to become the formal legal argument to justify secession.[21]

The Civil War gave the definitive answer to that aspect of the argument. No state has the legal right to secede. The Constitution is not the creation of the states, but of the people of the United States.

But the question of the People vs. the States as the source of the Constitution's authority was but one aspect of a far profounder problem which agitated the soul of America. Who constitutes the "people" to which the Preamble refers. More particularly, who are the "men" to whom the Declaration refers when it speaks of "all men." The ongoing smoldering public controversy around these questions was kindled anew by the passage in 1854 of the Kansas-Nebraska bill, probably "the greatest error ever committed by the Congress of the United States." It was brought to a white heat by the Supreme Court's *Dred Scott* decision of 1857. Between 1854 and 1870, when the Fifteenth Amendment to the Constitution was adopted, the American people engaged in the most passionate, the most soul-searching debate regarding the essential meaning of America and of being an American in which they have ever engaged, before or since. Two fundamental issues surfaced in the course of the debate: (1) the rightness or wrongness of slavery; (2) the meaning of "men" in the Declaration and "people" in the Preamble.

Well-nigh every thoughtful and articulate American took some part in this debate. The protagonists on the national level who attracted the widest attention, and who epitomized three basically different approaches, were Senator Stephen A. Douglas, the "little giant" from Illinois, Chief Justice Taney, and Abraham Lincoln.

To Douglas neither of the two issues seemed important. For him the only issue was the right of the majority in any territory or state to decide whether slavery be or not be permitted. He personally did not care whether it was "voted up or down" in the territories or anywhere else.[22] Moreover, it was obvious to him that "men" and "people" did not include blacks. He believed that "no man can vindicate the character, motives and conduct of the signers of the Declaration of Independence, except upon the hypothesis that they referred to the white race alone, and not to the African, when they declared all men to have been created equal."[23]

The matter was not quite that simple to Chief Justice Taney. He did care whether slavery was "voted up or down." He wanted to have it voted "up." In addition, he had a profound reverence for the men who wrote the Preamble and the Declaration. He was, therefore, troubled by the use of these documents as testimony that their authors were uneasy about slavery and its legitimization by the Constitution.

With skill and erudition worthy of a better cause, Taney set about mustering data to prove what was obvious to Douglas—that neither the authors of the Declaration when they spoke of "all men," nor the framers of the Preamble when they referred to "We, the people," included, or intended ever to include, even the free Negroes then resident in the colonies. Blacks were neither "men" nor "people."

After quoting the opening statements of the Declaration, the Chief Justice went on to say:

> The general words above quoted would *seem to embrace the whole human family, and if they were used in a similar instrument at this day, would be so understood* [emphasis added]. But it is too clear for dispute, that the enslaved African race were not intended to be included, and formed no part of the people who framed and adopted this Declaration; for if the language, as understood in that day would embrace them, the conduct of the distinguished men who framed the Declaration of Independence would have been utterly and flagrantly inconsistent with the principles they asserted; and instead of the sympathy of mankind, to which they so confidently appealed, they would have deserved and received universal rebuke and reprobation. Yet the men who framed this Declaration were great men—high in literary acquirements—high in their sense of honor, and incapable of asserting principles inconsistent with those on which they were acting. They perfectly understood the meaning of the language they used and how it would be understood by others. . . . They spoke and acted according to the

then established doctrines and principles, and in the ordinary language of the day, and no one misunderstood them.

As for the phrase "We, the people":

It declares that it is formed by the people of the United States: That is to say, by those who were members of the different political communities in the several states. . . . It speaks in general terms of the people of the United States, and of citizens of the several States. . . . It does not define what description of persons are intended to be included under these terms, or who shall be regarded as a citizen and one of the people. It uses them as terms so well understood that no further description or definition was necessary. But there are two clauses in the Constitution which point directly and specifically to the Negro race as a separate class of persons, and show clearly that they were not regarded as a portion of the people or citizens of the government then formed.[24]

The Constitution never refers to "slaves" or "slavery." It refers merely to "all other persons." The Chief Justice therefore assumes that the framers of the Constitution thought of them as "a separate class of *persons*."

The protagonist of the "prophetic character" of the Declaration was Abraham Lincoln. It is not that he expressed thoughts that were entirely new. On the contrary. Even as Jefferson in the Declaration sought primarily to speak the hearts and minds of the noblest sons of his generation,[25] so Lincoln "took, and made his own, the thought and spirit of those phases of the epoch which he has since come to symbolize, in such a manner that, though others spoke before him and others have spoken since, today one can scarcely think of the common matter of his argument except as matter that is particularly and peculiarly his."[26]   Even as the addresses of Winston Churchill, during the fateful years of World War II, were as veritable regiments in the winning of that conflict, so were the speeches which Lincoln delivered, between 1854 and the day of his death, the greatest single spiritual and intellectual force sustaining America in her heroic, tragic struggle to recapture, in a decisive era of her history, the pristine spirit of liberty and equality which attended her birth as a nation. Hence, in our search for at least a working definition of Americanism, and for a partial answer to the question what it means to be an American, we can engage in no labor more rewarding than that of studying these speeches. I know nothing written on this subject before or after which continues to be intellectually as cogent and emotionally as compelling.[27]

In regard to his own intellectual and emotional relation to the Declaration, Lincoln said in an address delivered in Independence Hall on February 22, 1861:

> . . . all the political sentiments I entertain have been drawn, so far as I have been able to draw them, from the sentiments which originated and were given to the world from this hall. I have never had a feeling politically that did not spring from the sentiments embodied in the Declaration of Independence. . . . I have often inquired of myself what great principle or idea it was that kept this Confederacy so long together. It was not the mere matter of the separation of the Colonies from the Motherland; but that sentiment in the Declaration of Independence which gave liberty, not alone to the people of this country, but, I hope, to the world, for all future time. It was that which gave promise that in due time the weight would be lifted from the shoulders of all men. This is a sentiment embodied in the Declaration of Independence. Now, my friends, can this country be saved upon that basis? If it can, I will consider myself one of the happiest men in the world, if I can help to save it. . . . But if this country cannot be saved without giving up that principle, I was about to say I would rather be assassinated on this spot than surrender it.[28]

Among the greatest services Lincoln performed for America during the fateful years preceding the Civil War was that of pinpointing and formulating the fundamental issues before the country. For some years before the passage of the Kansas-Nebraska Bill he had withdrawn from active participation in public affairs. The passage of the bill brought him back into the fray. He tells us why. "I have always hated it [slavery], but I have always been quiet about it until this new era of the introduction of the Nebraska Bill began. I always believed that *everybody* [emphasis added] was against it, and that it was in the course of ultimate extinction."[29]

To Lincoln, to be an American meant to be against slavery But Douglas, who was reputedly a good American, asserted repeatedly that he did not care whether slavery was voted up or down. Lincoln saw *that* as the ultimate issue before America. He came finally to realize that the protagonists of slavery would not be satisfied until all Americans would, voluntarily or under the compulsion of the law, "cease to call slavery *wrong,* and join them in calling it *right.* And this must be done thoroughly—done in *acts* as well as in words. Silence will not be tolerated—we must place ourselves avowedly with them. . . . Holding, as they do, that slavery is morally right, and socially elevating, they cannot cease to demand a full national recognition of it, as a legal right, and a social blessing. . . . Nor can we justifiably withhold this, on any ground save our conviction that slavery is wrong. . . . All they ask we could readily grant, if we thought slavery right; all we ask, they could as readily grant, if they thought it wrong. Their thinking it right and our thinking it wrong, is the precise fact upon which depends the whole controversy."[30]

Note that Lincoln does not think that he can present a logically convincing argument against slavery. He knew how many attempts had been made to prove that slavery was not only morally wrong but economically disastrous.[31] They all failed to change the opinions of the slaveholders. Hence, the note of well-nigh tragic despair in his statement: "Nor can we justifiably withhold this, *on any ground save our conviction* that slavery is wrong." He had formulated the same position somewhat differently a few years earlier. "Repeal the Missouri Compromise—repeal all compromises—repeal the Declaration of Independence—repeal all past history, you still cannot repeal human nature. It will be the abundance of man's heart, that slavery extension is wrong, and out of the abundance of his heart, his mouth will continue to speak."[32]

But Lincoln was not satisfied with leaving the rightness or wrongness of human slavery merely to "human nature" and "man's heart." The slaveholders could lay equal claim to "human nature" and "man's heart." *Their mouths* presumably spoke out of the abundance of *their hearts*. Was there no other source to which one could appeal at least to buttress, if not to definitely validate, his conviction on this subject. There were only two significant sources of moral authority to which American antagonists on the question could appeal. The one was the religious tradition to which most Americans were presumably committed. The other was the historical experience—the Declaration and the Constitution—which brought the American people into being.

To the everlasting injury of religion, the leaders of the organized religious communities, Jewish as well as Christian, did not speak with one unequivocal voice. Scripture was quoted by respected religious leaders in defense of both positions. Nor did the American historical experience, as it found expression in its two most revered documents, the Declaration and the Constitution, speak with one clear, unequivocal voice. Each of the two documents, when read by itself, seems to take a rather clear and unmistakable position on the issue of slavery. But the two documents quite obviously appear diametrically to contradict one another. The Constitution not only did not condemn slavery, it was not even neutral. On the contrary, it seemed to be weighted in its favor. It sanctioned its existence, and permitted the passage of legislation whose avowed purpose it was not only to perpetuate the institution wherever it existed, but also to provide for the expansion of the area into which it could legally be brought. Allegiance to the Constitution as such did not therefore necessitate the condemnation of slavery. Against the legal authority of the Constitution, the anti-slavery men set the moral authority of the Declaration. Hence, in order "to aid in making the bondage of the Negro universal and eternal, it [the Declaration] is assailed and sneezed at, and construed, and hawked at, and torn; till, if its framers could rise from their graves, they would not at all recognize it."[33]

Lincoln did not feel it incumbent upon him to take up the banner of religion on this issue. He did not feel himself either adequately committed to any organized religious group or adequately equipped intellectually to wrestle with the religious aspect of the problem at that time, though we know how profoundly religious a personality he was, and how pointed and accurate were the arrows he directed at religious teachings that sanctioned or condoned slavery.[34] His central concern was with himself as an American and with the meaning of his American heritage. If being an American meant that one could be unconcerned whether slavery was voted up or down, if the Declaration could be made to read "all men are created equal *except negroes"*—and if the Know-Nothings got control, "all men are created equal, except negroes, *and foreigners and Catholics"*—then he, Lincoln, "should prefer emigrating to some country where they make no pretense of loving liberty—to Russia, for instance, where despotism can be taken pure, and without the base alloy of hypocrisy."[35]

Once he became fully aware of the ultimate implications of what was happening in America, Lincoln became obsessed with the need to expound the prophetic character of the Declaration and to defend it and those who authored and signed it, not only against their ignorant and ribald detractors, but more especially against those among them who were erudite and sophisticated. For if the detractors were right, then the Declaration was "shorn of its vitality and practical value and left without the *germ* or even the *suggestion* of the individual rights of man in it . . . and was no more at most than an interesting memorial of the dead past."[36]

Lincoln passionately maintained, therefore, that in the opening statements of the Declaration the authors

> meant to set up a standard maxim for free society, which could be familiar to all, and revered by all; constantly looked to, constantly labored for, and even though never perfectly attained, constantly approximated, and thereby constantly spreading and deepening its influence, and augmenting the happiness and value of life to all

people of all colors everywhere. The assertion that "all men are created equal" was of no practical use in effecting our separation from Great Britain—and it was placed in the Declaration, not for that, but for future use. Its authors meant it to be, thank God, it is now proving itself, a stumbling block to those who in after times might seek to turn a free people back into the hateful paths of despotism. They knew the proneness of prosperity to breed tyrants, and they meant when such should re-appear in this fair land and commence their vocation, they should find left for them at least one hard nut to crack.[37]

In addition to this role of conscience of America which the Declaration was to play, it was to be the "electric cord" binding the millions of men and women coming from all climes and all kinds of different ethnic, cultural, and religious backgrounds into one people, enabling them to feel an essential kinship as Americans, not only with their contemporaries, but also with the Founding Fathers of America.

If they [the immigrants who came to America after 1783], look back through this history to trace their connection with those days [of the Revolution], by blood, they find they have none. They cannot carry themselves back into that glorious epoch and make themselves feel that they are part of us, but when they look through that old Declaration of Independence, they find that those old men say that "We hold these truths to be self-evident, that all men are created equal," and then they feel that that moral sentiment taught in that day evidences their relation to those men, that it is the father of all moral principle in them, and that they have a right to claim it as though they were blood of the blood, and flesh of the flesh, of the men who wrote that Declaration, and so they are. That is the electric cord in that Declaration that links the hearts of patriotic and liberty-loving men together, that will link those patriotic hearts as long as the love of freedom exists in the minds of men throughout the world . . .[38]

But what of the contradictions between the provisions in the

Constitution regarding slavery and the actions of the authors of the Declaration and the sentiments expressed in the Declaration?

In the course of his gigantic intellectual and spiritual exertions to establish the Declaration as the arbiter of the moral issues facing America, Lincoln also redeemed the authors of the Declaration and the Constitution from the stigma of being hypocrites, or being either favorably disposed or even merely neutral on the question of slavery. He proved, as well as anybody under the circumstances could prove, that the framers of the Constitution did not have in mind any retreat from the high moral ground that was occupied when the Declaration was promulgated.

> Chief Justice Taney, in his opinion in the Dred Scott case, admits that the language of the Declaration is broad enough to include the whole human family, but he and Judge Douglas argue that the authors of that instrument did not intend to include negroes, by the fact that they did not at once, actually place them on an equality with the whites. Now this grave argument comes to just nothing at all, by the other fact that they did not at once, or ever afterwards, actually place all white people on an equality with one another. I think the authors of that notable instrument intended to include all men, but they did not intend to declare all men equal in all respects . . . They defined with tolerable distinctness, in what respects they did consider all men created equal—equal in "certain inalienable rights, among which are life, liberty, and the pursuit of happiness." This they said, and this they meant. They did not mean to assert the obvious untruth, that all were then actually enjoying that equality, nor yet, that they were about to confer it immediately upon them. In fact they had no power to confer such a boon. They meant simply to declare the *right,* so that the *enforcement* of it might follow as fast as circumstances should permit.[39]

It may be argued that there are certain conditions that make necessities and impose them upon us, and to the extent that a necessity is imposed upon a man, he must submit to it. I think that was the condition in which we found ourselves when we established this government. We had slavery among us, we could not get our Constitution unless we permitted them to remain in slavery, we could not secure the good we did secure if we grasped for more, and having by necessity submitted to that much, it does not destroy the principle that is the charter of our liberties. Let that charter stand as our standard.

My friend has said to me that I am a poor hand to quote Scripture. I will try it again. It is said in one of the admonitions of the Lord, "As your Father in heaven is perfect, be ye also perfect." The Saviour, I suppose, did not expect that any human creature could be perfect as the Father in Heaven; but He said, "As your Father in Heaven is perfect, be ye also perfect." He set up that as a standard, and he who did most towards reaching that standard, attained the highest degree of moral perfection. So I say in relation to the principle that all men are created equal, let it be as nearly reached as we can. If we cannot give freedom to every creature, let us do nothing that will impose slavery upon any other creature. Let us then turn this government back into the channel in which the framers of the Constitution originally placed it.[40]

Referring to the biblical proverb, "A word fitly spoken is like apples of gold in settings of silver" (Prov. 25:11), Lincoln went on to say:

The assertion of that principle, that "all men are created equal," at that time, was the word, "fitly spoken" which has proved an "apple of gold" to us. The Union and the Constitution, are the picture[41] of silver, subsequently framed around it. The picture was made, not to conceal or destroy the apple; but to adorn and preserve it. The picture was made for the apple—not the apple for the picture.

So let us act, that neither picture, or apple, shall ever be blurred, or broken.[42]

Thus Lincoln, more than any other single individual, placed the interpretation upon the Declaration, and established the relationship between it and the Constitution, that gives to the Declaration its permanent place as the highest, uniquely American source for defining what it means to be an American.

The Declaration is ever to stand in moral judgment on the Constitution and an all laws enacted under its authority. It is the Constitution which must be ever changed to conform to the standards set for it by the Declaration. The Declaration can never be changed. It shares the awe-inspiring eternity of the everlasting hills.

The Declaration thus formulates the never-to-be-fully achieved but ever-to-be-passionately-sought goal of human political organization. It is the solemn pledge made at the very inception of the United States, morally obligating every American forever after to strive ceaselessly to bring American and all human society ever more closely within sight of this goal. The Declaration thus viewed is a sacred covenant, which the American people, at the beginning of their history, freely and solemnly made, not only among themselves but with mankind and the God of history. Their descendants, by enshrining the Declaration and by teaching it to every physically and spiritually newborn American, declare it to be the duty of every American, to the end of time, to identify himself with the historic moment when the Declaration was first announced to the world, and to see himself as a veritable signer of it, thus joining the original signers in pledging, as they did, his life, his fortune, and his sacred honor to the implementation of the truths that it proclaims.

The military victory won on the battlefields of the Civil War was followed by hard-fought verbal battles in the halls of Congress during the years immediately following. At the time it seemed to many, though not to all, that those who had won the decisive military battles were equally successful on the field of verbal combat. Their legislative victories consisted in the addition of three amendments to the Constitution.

1. The Thirteenth Amendment, adopted in 1865, provided that "neither slavery nor involuntary servitude, except as a punishment for crime whereof the party shall have been duly convicted, shall exist within the United States, or any place subject to their jurisdiction."

2. The Fourteenth Amendment, adopted in 1868, provided in its first section that: "All persons born or naturalized in the

United States, and subject to the jurisdiction thereof, are citizens of the United States and of the State wherein they reside. No State shall make or enforce any law which shall abridge the privileges or immunities of citizens of the United States; nor shall any State deprive any person of life, liberty, or property, without due process of law; nor deny to any person within its jurisdiction the equal protection of the laws."

3. The Fifteenth Amendment, adopted in 1870, in its first section provides that: "The right of the citizens of the United States to vote shall not be denied or abridged by the United States or by any state on account of race, color, or previous condition of servitude."

The addition of these three amendments to the Constitution undoubtedly constituted a glorious victory for those who sought to embody the self-evident truths of the Declaration into enforceable law.

A superficial reading of the texts of the amendments would lead one to believe that all that had to be done to make the Constitution conform fully to the goals of the Declaration had been done, that the high-sounding rhetoric of the Declaration about equality and unalienable rights was at last imbedded in down-to-earth legal language, as enforceable as all the other provisions of the Constitution. The words "men" and "people," about whose meaning there had been so much controversy, were defined as terms that refer to human beings subject to the jurisdiction of the United States. Justice Taney made much of the fact that the Declaration speaks of "men," while the Constitution, in referring to the slaves, speaks of "persons." The Fourteenth Amendment speaks of "all persons born or naturalized in the United States," and ascribes to "any person" the unalienable right to "life, liberty, and property."

The concept that all men are created "equal" was defined to mean that all men have the unalienable right to "equal protection of the law." But many decades were to pass, and many a hard physical and verbal battle was to be fought, before what seemed to be the obvious intent of the Fourteenth Amendment was, on the administrative level, translated into enforceable law.

The Third Period, 1873–1965

The third period in America's never-ending search for a self-definition was characterized by two major issues: (1) the scope of applicability of the Fourteenth Amendment; (2) the role of the national government in "promoting the general welfare," thus helping the individual "to pursue happiness." The two issues frequently overlapped. Decisions regarding the first almost always had direct bearing upon the second. But the second issue was broader in scope than the first. It involved constitutional provisions other than the Fourteenth Amendment and reached out to areas beyond the purely legal.

As Chief Justice Warren wrote in his *Brown* v. *Board of Education* opinion, "The most avid proponents of the post Civil War amendments undoubtedly intended them to remove all legal distinctions among all persons born or naturalized in the United States. Their opponents just as certainly were antagonistic to both the letter and the spirit of the Amendments and wished them to have the most limited effect. What others in congress and the State legislatures had in mind cannot be determined, with any degree of certainty."[43] Of the three post-Civil War amendments, it was Section I of the Fourteenth Amendment which was the subject of the longest and most acrimonious controversy.

Both sides were fully conscious that this amendment represented a compromise satisfactory to neither of them.[44] The profound disappointment felt by those who had hoped to bestow at once maximum equality upon blacks in specific and unmistakable terms was expressed by Thaddeus Stevens just before the Fourteenth Amendment was put to the vote in the House.

> In my youth, in my manhood, in my old age, I had fondly dreamed that when any fortunate chance should have broken up for a while the foundation of our institutions, and released us from

obligations the most tyrannical that ever man imposed in the name of freedom, that the intelligent, pure and just men of this Republic . . . would have so remodeled all our institutions as to have freed them from every vestige of human oppression, of inequality of rights, of the recognized degradation of the poor, and the superior state of the rich. In short, that no distinction would be tolerated in this purified Republic but what arose from merit and conduct. This bright dream has vanished "like the baseless fabric of a vision." I find that we shall be obliged to be content with patching up the worst portions of the ancient edifice. . . . Do you inquire why, holding these views and possessing some will of my own I accept so imperfect a proposition? I answer because I live among men and not among angels.[45]

It was inevitable, therefore, that the meaning of this amendment, in terms of the practical, legal applicability of its provisions, should increasingly become a subject of national controversy. No amendment, indeed no section of the Constitution, has figured as often as it has in the litigation before the Supreme Court during the last century.[46] After some seventy-five years had passed since its adoption, Justice Black noted that "the scope and operation of the Fourteenth Amendment have been fruitful sources of controversy in our Constitutional history."[47] He could refer to them as *fruitful* sources, not merely because of the number of cases in which they were involved, but because no amendment, as finally interpreted by the court, has served the individual citizen as effectively as it has in his efforts to preserve, enjoy, and expand the scope of his inalienable right to life, liberty, and the pursuit of happiness. As Justice Fortas formulated it, "Our understanding and conception of the rights guaranteed to the people by the 'stately admonitions' of the Fourteenth Amendment has deepened, and have resulted in a series of decisions enriching the quality of our democracy."[48]

This did not happen at once. For decades after its adoption, the worst forebodings of the "avid proponents" of black equality, regarding the effectiveness of the post–Civil War amendments, were more fully realized than even they had feared. "There is plenty of evidence to indicate that from the first the freedmen were often denied their civil rights and subjected to discrimination, exclusion and mistreatment by railroads, hotels, inns and places of entertainment generally."[49] But if "from the first" this was done out of force of prejudices and habits inherited from antebellum days, it was not long before these habits were reinforced in the South by state and local laws which segregated the black population from the white in every possible way. The constitutionality of these laws was upheld by the Supreme Court despite the postwar amendments. In the North, social and racial prejudices, plus the universally recognized "right" of private owners of places of public accommodations to exclude whomever they chose to exclude from their premises, achieved a degree of segregation almost equal to that of the South.

The process whereby the Fourteenth Amendment was first "debilitated"[50] and then restored as one of the greatest bulwarks of the privileges and immunities not only of the black citizens of America but of all Americans, occupied the very center of American legal history for a century. A summary of some of the highlights of this long, tiresome, frequently frustrating process is not only germane to our inquiry. We deem it indispensable, for only as one has an acquaintance with some of the significant details of the process can he begin to comprehend the nature of his responsibility as an American who, with Lincoln, believes in the prophetic character of the Declaration.

The Debilitation of the Fourteenth and Fifteenth Amendments

The political conditions which made possible, and even abetted, the debilitation of the Fourteenth and Fifteenth Amendments were set by the compromise of 1877, which included the withdrawal of federal troops from the South and the end of the Reconstruction.[51] The legal process whereby the debilitation was consummated had its origin at the very beginning of American constitutional history. Hamilton's "ingenious argument" in the *Federalist* (84) against the need for a Bill of Rights in the Constitution reflects the fact that "the early statesmen thought of a federal bill of rights only in terms of restrictions on national power" and not on the power of the state governments. That frame of mind is further evidenced in the choice the First Congress made among the seventeen amendments that were proposed by the various state conventions that had ratified the Constitution. One of the proposed amendments provided restrictions upon the power of the states in matters of civil rights. The Congress rejected it. Moreover, by specifically stating in the first amendment that *"Congress* shall make no law, etc.," the intention that these amendments were to be viewed as limitations upon the power of the federal government rather than upon that of the states was clearly indicated.[52]

This intention was explicated by Chief Justice John Marshall in 1833. The case involved a complaint by a citizen against the city of Baltimore for having deprived him of property without the due process of law. He was appealing to the Supreme Court under the terms of the Fifth Amendment. Speaking in behalf of the court, the Chief Justice declared:

> The Constitution was ordained and established by the people of the United States for themselves, for their own government and not for the government of the individual states. Each state established a Constitution for itself. . . . If these propositions be correct, the Fifth Amendment must be understood as restraining the power of the general government, not as applicable to the states. . . . In almost every convention by which the Constitution was adopted, amendments to guard against the abuse of power were recommended. These amendments demanded security against the apprehended encroachments of the general government, not those of the local governments.[53]

The only recourse, therefore, that a citizen had against the invasion of his civil rights by the laws of the state in which he resided was that of using the machinery afforded by the republican form of government, which the federal government guaranteed for each state, to change those laws. But that was a recourse which, as a matter of fact, could not be invoked by minorities who were deprived by the laws of the state of the power to change those laws.

What Justice Marshall had said regarding the Fifth Amendment, and by implication regarding all the provisions of the Bill of Rights, a later justice said about the Fourteenth. The "due process" clause of the amendment had been invoked to restrain the governor of Louisiana from creating a monopoly in the slaughtering business in the city of New Orleans.

Because Justice Miller's opinion in this instance had such far-reaching consequences, we shall quote him verbatim at some length.

> The first section of the Fourteenth Amendment . . . opens with a definition of citizenship—not only citizenship of the United States but citizenship of the States. No such definition was previously found in the Constitution nor had any attempt been made to define it by an act of Congress. . . . It had been said by eminent judges that no man was a citizen of the United States except as he was a citizen of one of the States composing the Union. Those, therefore, who had been born and resided always in the District of Columbia or in the territories, though within the United States were not citizens. Whether this proposition was sound or not had never been judicially decided. . . . to establish a clear and comprehensive definition of citizenship which should declare what should constitute citizenship of the United States, and also citizenship of a State, the first clause of the first section [of the Fourteenth Amendment] was framed. . . . The next observation is more important in view of the arguments of counsel in the present case. It is that the distinction between citizenship of the United States and citizenship of a State is clearly recognized and established . . . not only may a man be a citizen of the U.S. without being a citizen of a State, but an important element is necessary to convert the former into the latter. He must reside in a State to make him a citizen of it, but it is only necessary that he should be born or naturalized in the United States to be a citizen of the Union. . . . The next paragraph of this section . . . speaks only of privileges and immunities of citizens of the United States and does not speak of those of citizens of the several States. . . . The language is "no State shall

make or enforce any law which shall abridge the privileges or immunities of citizens of the United States"! It is a little remarkable, if this clause was intended as a protection to the citizen of a State against the legislative power of his own state, that the word citizen of a State should be left out when it is so carefully used, and used in contradiction to citizens of the United States, in the very sentence which precedes it. It is too clear for argument that the change in phraseology was adopted understandingly and with a purpose. Of the privileges and immunities of the citizens of the United States, and of the privileges and immunities of the citizen of the State . . . it is only the former which are placed by this clause under the protection of the federal Constitution, and the latter, whatever they may be, are not intended to have any additional protection by this paragraph of the Amendment. . . . Was it the purpose of the Fourteenth Amendment . . . to transfer the security and protection of all the civil rights which we have mentioned from the states to the federal government? And where it is declared that Congress shall have the power to enforce that article, was it intended to bring within the power of Congress the entire domain of civil rights heretofore belonging exclusively to the States? We are convinced that no such results were intended by the Congress which proposed the amendments nor by the legislature of the states which ratified them.[54]

Thus by one fell swoop many of the civil rights of the blacks, which had been so dearly won on the battlefield, and which the "avid proponents" of the Fourteenth Amendment had hoped were thus legally assured, were now placed at the mercy of the several states. It did not take long for the evil effects of the Miller opinion to be implemented in the laws of the Southern states and in the decisions of the court.

Soon after the Miller decision the court asserted that "the Fifteenth Amendment did not confer the right . . . [to vote] upon anyone," but merely "invested the citizens of the United States with a new constitutional right which is . . . exemption from discrimination in the exercise of the elective franchise on account of race, color, or previous condition of servitude."[55]

The court further held that the equal protection clause of the Fourteenth Amendment is operative only "where there has been involvement of the State or of one acting under the color of its authority. The Equal Protection clause 'does not . . . add anything to the rights which one citizen has under the Constitution' against another."[56] Hence the court declared the Civil Rights Act of 1866, which prohibited all interference with the right to vote, to be unconstitutional. This decision gave free rein to all manner of legal maneuvering and physical intimidation whereby black people were kept from exercising their right to vote.

In 1875 Congress had passed a Civil Rights Bill which prohibited discrimination against blacks in all places of public accommodation, even those privately owned. In 1883 the court declared the law unconstitutional because the Fourteenth Amendment prohibited only the states, but not private citizens, from practicing racial discrimination.[57] In 1920 the court ruled "that the right to reside quietly within the state of one's domicile is not a right which the national government may protect against local mobs."[58] The same basic principle was reaffirmed in 1926, when the court upheld the legality of privately negotiated "restrictive covenants" wherein individuals pledged to one another not to sell certain of their properties to Negroes. The covenants had been made by residents of the District of Columbia and were challenged as a violation of the due process clause of the Fifth Amendment. The court decided that "the Amendment was a limitation only upon the powers of the general government and is not directed against the action of individuals." [59]

Perhaps the most notorious of the court's decisions which resulted in a nullification of whatever high hopes the "avid proponents" of the Fourteenth Amendment may have had for it, was handed down in 1896, when the court held that a statute requiring railroads to provide "equal but separate" accommodations for the white and colored races "did not constitute a denial of the equal protection clause of the Fourteenth Amendment." Such a law was deemed to be a proper exercise of the state's police power to main-

tain law and order. The contention that the "enforced separation
of the two races stamps the colored race with a badge of inferiority"
was dismissed by the court with the observation that "if this be so, it
is not by reason of anything found in the Act, but solely because the
colored race chooses to put the construction upon it."[60] This decision did not go unchallenged. In a minority opinion dissenting
from the doctrine of "separate but equal," Justice Harlan gave voice
to one of the most frequently quoted judicial statements. "Our constitution," he said, "is color blind, and neither knows nor tolerates
classes among citizens. In respect of civil rights, all citizens are
equal before the law."[61] But many years had to pass before this
minority opinion was transformed into enforceable law.

In accord with the spirit of this decision, the court in 1908
upheld the constitutionality of a state law prohibiting desegregated
private schools.[62] As late as 1927 it held valid a law requiring a
Chinese girl to attend a school for colored children in a neighboring
school district rather than be allowed to attend a nearby school for
white children.[63]

"With the passing of the Reconstruction era and the return of
'White man's government' to Southern States, state laws were again
adopted" which "established, and enforced by legal penalties, a system of racial segregation under which members of the Negro and
white races were required to be separated in the enjoyment of public
and semi-public facilities. Separate schools, parks, waiting rooms,
bus and railroad accommodations were required by law to be furnished each race."[64]

Thus, for almost a hundred years after the Civil War, and
after the legal abolition of slavery, America permitted her citizens
and residents to be differentiated legally on the basis of color. For
blacks, the applicability of the provisions of the Bill of Rights and
the Fourteenth and Fifteenth Amendments was reduced to little more
than a symbolic minimum.

In 1949 President Truman appointed a Committee on Civil
Rights "to inquire into and to determine whether and in what respect current law enforcement and measures and the authority and

means possessed by Federal, State and local governments may be strengthened and improved to safeguard the civil rights of the people."[65]

The committee correctly interpreted its task to be not that of assessing "the great progress which the nation has made" but rather to focus exclusively "on the bad side of our record."[66] What it reported shocked every ethically sensitive American who was accustomed to thinking of the American political and social order as a mirror reflecting the sentiments of the Declaration.

The fact that the committee felt moved to give high praise to "the voluntary elimination of racial bans or differentials in employment practices by many business concerns and the employment of negro baseball players in both major leagues" in itself indicates how far the country as a whole was from guaranteeing to its black citizens in particular, but also to members of other minority groups, such as Jews, Catholics, Indians, Mexicans, Japanese, and Filipinos, enjoyment of the "unalienable rights" in equal measure with its white Protestant citizens. Lynchings were the most reprehensible evidence of the violation of civil rights. "This committee has found that in the year 1947 lynching remains one of the most serious threats to the civil rights of America. . . . The decade from 1936 through 1946 saw at least 43 lynchings. No person received the death penalty, and the majority of the guilty persons were not even prosecuted." Between 1937 and 1946, "226 persons were rescued from threatened lynchings. Over 200 of these were negroes."[67] It would serve little purpose to repeat here the depressing statistics regarding black employment, discrimination in employment and higher education against Jews, as well as blacks and other minorities, and the laws and practices which disenfranchised the vast majority of the blacks of the Old South.

Mindful of the court decisions that had debilitated the amendments, the committee, in a series of some eight recommendations, suggested laws that should be enacted in order to assure equal treatment of all by the federal government, and parallel "enactment by the state legislatures" of "fair education" practice laws for public and private educational institutions, "fair health practice statutes," "laws guaranteeing equal access to places of public accommodation, broadly defined for persons of all races, colors, creeds, and national origins," and so forth.

The next two decades saw the legal implementation of practically all the committee's recommendations. But this was made possible by circumventing many of the state legislatures and by rehabilitating or nationalizing[68] the amendments. The role of the Supreme Court in this process was momentous and decisive.

The Rehabilitations of the Amendments

One of the earliest indications that the court was beginning to have second thoughts regarding the solid phalanx of legally protected racial discrimination which it had erected was its increasing insistence upon the literal interpretation of the term *equal* in its "separate but equal," formula.

Thus, while in 1899 the court did not consider the failure of a Southern county to provide a high school for sixty colored children, although it maintained one for white children, a violation of the formula,[69] in 1914 it invalidated a law which allowed railroads to provide sleeping and other special facilities for white passengers without providing such facilities for blacks.[70] The railroads then reserved a table for blacks only in the dining cars, but separated it from the tables reserved for white passengers by a curtain or partition. It was not until 1950 that the court held that such segregation subjected blacks to undue prejudice and disadvantage.[71] Finally, in 1961, a regulation of the Interstate Commerce Commission forbade all interstate motor carriers to discriminate on grounds of race, color, creed, or national origin in the seating of passengers or in the terminal facilities provided for them.[72]

In 1938 the court declared a Missouri law offering to pay the tuition of Missouri blacks studying in out-of-state law schools, rather than to provide equal facilities for them within the state, to be a violation of the separate but equal principle.[73] When Texas offered to build a law school for its blacks instead of admitting them to the existing State University Law School, the court invalidated the proposal because it could not "find substantial equality in the educational opportunities offered white and negro law students by the State."[74]

The court also gradually proceeded to abandon its purely legalistic approach to issues involving the civil rights of blacks. Thus the Constitution provides that those who vote for "the most numerous Branch of the State Legislature shall have the right to vote for members of The House of Representatives." But each state set for itself "the Qualifications requisite for Electors" of the most numerous branch of its legislature.[75] Moreover, while the Fifteenth Amendment stated specifically that "the rights of citizens to vote shall not be denied or abridged by the United States or by any state on account of *race, color,* or *previous condition of servitude,*" it did not require much legalistic ingenuity to set qualifications other than these in order to deny blacks the right to vote.[76] Among these were the infamous "grandfather" clauses, which in one case required that all those who were eligible to vote on January 1, 1866 and their descendants need not pass a literacy test in order to exercise their right to vote. All others had to take what was a formidable literacy test. In 1915 the court invalidated an Oklahoma statute containing such a provision as being in violation of the Fifteenth Amendment even though the law did not mention color or race specifically.[77] The following year Oklahoma attempted to achieve the same end by a more carefully worded statute. It was not until 1939 that the court declared that the "Fifteenth amendment nullifies sophisticated as well as simple-minded modes of discrimination," and voided the statute.[78]

The separate but equal formula itself, however, was not challenged until 1952, when cases involving segregation in the public schools came before the court. The cases were argued at two different sessions of the court. In preparation for reargument the court asked the attorneys to present briefs on the question: "If neither the Congress in submitting nor the states in ratifying the Fourteenth Amendment understood that compliance with it would require the immediate desegregation in public schools, was it nevertheless the understanding of the framers of this Amendment (a) that future Congresses might, in the exercise of their power under Section 5 of the Amendment, abolish such segregation, or (b) that it would be within the judicial power in light of future conditions, to construe the Amendment as abolishing such segregation of its own force?"[79] What the court was asking was whether the Fourteenth Amendment gave only to *Congress* the power to abolish school segregation by enacting specific legislation, or whether it in itself was sufficient to justify a court decision that school segregation was unconstitutional. These questions assume that the Fourteenth Amendment could be applied to the problem of local school segregation, an assumption that Justice Miller's earlier opinion had unequivocally rejected.[80] In 1952 the court was in doubt merely as to whether the power to make that application rested exclusively with Congress or could also be exercised by the court. But there was no longer any doubt that the amendment's guarantee of "equal protection of the law" for all citizens was applicable to school segregation. All that was necessary, then, was for the court to decide whether or not the formula "separate but equal" violated that provision of the amendment.

After a rather lengthy history of the case and of the circumstances that led to the adoption of the Fourteenth Amendment, Chief Justice Warren continued:[81]

> We come then to the question presented: Does segregation of children in the public schools solely on the basis of race, even though the physical facilities and the "tangible" factors are equal, deprive the children of the minority group of education opportunities? We believe it does. . . . Whatever may have been the extent of psychological knowledge at the time of Plessy v. Ferguson, this finding is amply supported by modern authority. Any language in Plessy v. Ferguson contrary to this finding is rejected. . . . Separate educational facilities are inherently unequal. Therefore, we hold that the plaintiffs . . . are, by reason of the segregation complained of, deprived of the equal protection of the laws guaranteed by the Fourteenth Amendment.[81]

The court, therefore, ordered the desegregation of the schools "with all deliberate speed." More than two decades have passed since that court decision was handed down. The sorry story of the attempts to defy or circumvent this court order has not yet ended. But the legal underpinnings of school segregation have been removed, and the evil can no longer claim the protection of the law.

But this legal development would not have been possible had there previously not been a complete reversal of the court's stance regarding the scope of the Fourteenth Amendment. Not only was Justice Miller's position in the *Slaughter House* cases voided,[82] but the amendment was gradually construed as the constitutional instrument through which, in time, practically all the amendments in the Bill of Rights, and all other privileges and immunities guaranteed by the Constitution to the citizen as over against the federal government, were made applicable also over against the states.

It was not until 1939 that Justice Cardozo, speaking in behalf of the court, formulated the *legal vocabulary and concepts* which gave direction to, and hastened, this transformation. Palko, a resident of Connecticut, brought suit against the state, arguing that he was being deprived of the protection against double jeopardy guaranteed by the Fifth Amendment. "In appellant's view, the Fourteenth Amendment is to be taken as embodying the prohibition of the Fifth. His thesis is even broader. Whatever would be a violation of the original Bill of Rights (Am. 1–8) if done by the Federal government is now equally unlawful by force of the Fourteenth Amendment if done by a state. There is no such general rule." Justice Cardozo then cited instances in which the court had held that the provisions, not only of the Fifth but of other amendments, were not held applicable to the states. But he then proceeds to cite instances in which the due process clause of the Fourteenth Amendment was held to make it unlawful for a state to abridge by its statutes the freedom of speech which the First Amendment safeguards against encroachment by Congress. These cases were all decided in the 1930s. "In these and other situations, immunities that are valid against the federal government by force of the specific pledges of particular amendments *have been found to be implicit in the concept of ordered liberty, and thus through the Fourteenth Amendment became valid against the states"* [emphasis added]. Justice Cardozo then asks whether there is "a rationalizing principle which gives to discrete instances a proper order and coherence." He thinks that there is, and he proceeds to formulate it. "Some of the immunities guaranteed by the Bill of Rights have not been *absorbed* [emphasis added] by the Fourteenth Amendment because their abolition would not violate a principle of justice so rooted in the traditions and conscience of our people as to be ranked fundamental." The principles and immunities that are thus "rooted" "have been taken over from the earlier articles of the Federal Bill of Rights and brought within the Fourteenth Amendment by a *process of absorption. . . .* the process of absorption has had its source in the belief that neither liberty nor justice could exist if they were sacrificed. . . . So it has come about that the *domain of liberty withdrawn by the Fourteenth Amendment from encroachment by the states,* has been enlarged by latter-day judgements to include liberty of the mind as well as liberty of action."[83]

The "concept of ordered liberty," "the process of absorption" whereby "a principle of justice so rooted in the traditions and conscience of our people as to be ranked fundamental" was *absorbed* by the Fourteenth Amendment, offered legal minds the vocabulary they required to enable the Fourteenth Amendment to fulfill some of the highest hopes that its "avid proponents" had had for it. From this point on the process of "absorption" was accelerated, though its path was never without stumbling blocks.

In 1940 Justice Black, speaking for the court, said: "In view of its [the Fourteenth Amendment] historical setting and the wrongs which called it into being, the due process provision of the Fourteenth Amendment—just as that of the Fifteenth Amendment—has let few to doubt that it was intended to guarantee procedural standards adequate and appropriate, then and thereafter, to protect at all times, people charged with or suspected of crime by those holding positions of power and authority. . . . This requirement of con-

forming to fundamental standards of procedure in criminal trials
—was made operative against the states by the Fourteenth Amendment."[84] In 1948 the court decided that even though restrictive
covenants may be valid,[85] the state may not enforce them because
of the Fourteenth Amendment, and the District of Columbia may
not enforce them because of the Fifth Amendment.[86]

Equally long and difficult was the legal battle to compel states
and subdivisions of states to apportion representation in legislative
bodies, whether federal, state, or in the subdivision of a state,
on the basis of a reasonable numerical equality of those represented.[87] Illinois had for forty-five years not redrawn the boundaries of the districts that had been set up for purposes of representation in the national or state legislative bodies, even though
vast shifts in population had in the meantime taken place. In 1946
the issue came before the Supreme Court. By a four to three decision the court refused to act in the case, declaring that "due regard
for the effective working of our Government revealed this issue to
be of a peculiarly political nature and therefore not meet for judicial
determination."[88]

The court reversed this decision in 1962, when the question
of reapportionment again came before it. Justice Brennan, speaking
in behalf of a profoundly divided court, said, "We hold today only
(a) that the court possessed jurisdiction of the subject matter (b)
that a justifiable cause of action is stated upon which appellants
would be entitled to appropriate relief. . . . That judicial standards
under the Equal Protection Clause are well-developed and familiar,"
and, therefore, that "the complaint's allegation of a denial of equal
protection presents a justifiable constitutional cause of action upon
which appellants are entitled to a trial and a decision." The right
asserted is within the reach of judicial protection "under the Fourteenth Amendment."[89]

Justices Frankfurter and Harlan each wrote separate, vigorously
dissenting opinions. Justice Frankfurter, in one of his longest
opinions, maintained that "the Court today reverses a uniform
course of decision established by a dozen cases, including one by

which the very claim now sustained was unanimously rejected only five years ago."[90] Justice Harlan could "find nothing in the Equal Protection clause or elsewhere in the Federal Constitution which expressly or impliedly supports the view that state legislatures must be so structured as to reflect with approximate equality the voice of every voter."[91] However, as a consequence of the opinion "that the court possessed jurisdiction of the subject matter," the court, "between March 1962 and June 1964 . . . literally and figuratively changed the map of American politics. In those few years the court held that legislative apportionment was a justifiable issue, that all votes must count equally in elections for statewide offices, and that, so far as practicable, there must be equally populated election districts within a state for members of congress and for both houses of the state legislature," and in "local government units."[92]

There is little doubt that American political and legal history furnish adequate data to support the opinions of Justices Frankfurter and Harlan. And one may even plausibly question the political wisdom or ethical stance of the majority opinion.[93] The Senate of the United States is not made up of members representing approximately numerically equal constituencies. The same was true for many state legislatures and local units of government.

The majority opinions in the reapportionment cases were not based upon historical or legal precedents. Unfortunately, "the Court . . . offered no tenable principle in support of its conclusion that election of governors and other statewide officials by the county-unit method is unconstitutional. Justice Douglas' frustration gave voice to the familiar 'creed' at the highest possible level of abstraction."[94]

The familiar "creed" was formulated by Justice Douglas: "The conception of political equality from the Declaration of Independence, to Lincoln's Gettysburg Address, to the Fifteenth (no racial restrictions in voting), Seventeenth (popular election of Senators) and Nineteenth (women's vote) Amendments can mean only one thing—one person one vote."[95]

The following year Justice Warren again "gave voice to the

familiar creed" when he said that "logically in a society ostensibly grounded on representative government it would seem reasonable to conclude that a majority of the people of a State could elect a majority of that State's legislators. . . . to the extent that a citizen's right to vote is debased, he is that much less a citizen. . . . This is the clear and strong command of our Constitution's Equal Protection clause. . . . This is at the heart of Lincoln's vision of 'government of the people by the people and for the people.' "[96]

Thus, after decades of debate during which "rotten buroughs" were permitted to fester in the body politic of America, the form of government envisioned by the principles of the Declaration of Independence, and Lincoln's Gettysburg Address, served as the ultimate sanction for writing into law the "one man–one vote" formula, giving, as far as it was humanly possible to do so, each person equal weight in electing those by whom he shall be governed on all levels of government

The Right to Privacy

The Fourth Amendment to the Constitution provides that "the right of the people to be secure in their persons, houses, papers, and effects, against unreasonable searches and seizures, shall not be violated, and no Warrants shall issue, but upon probable cause, supported by Oath or affirmation, and particularly describing the place to be searched, and the persons or things to be seized."

While this amendment forbids "unreasonable searches and seizures," it does not forbid the use of evidence so obtained in a court of law against the accused. It was not until 1914 that the court ruled that this amendment forbade use by the federal government against the accused of evidence illegally secured by federal agents.[97] But decades were to pass before the same protection was extended to the citizen in relation to the states. In 1949 Frankfurter, in behalf of the court, took the first hesitant step when he wrote that "the security of one's privacy against arbitrary intrusion by the police—which is at the core of the Fourth Amendment —is basic to a free society. It is therefore implicit in 'the concept of ordered liberty,"[98] and as such enforceable against the states through the Due Process Clause" (of the Fourteenth Amendment).[99] He did not, however, go as far as to say that evidence illegally obtained may not be used against the accused in a state court or in a federal court if not obtained by a federal agent. "Granting that in practice the exclusion of evidence may be an effective way of deterring unreasonable searches, it is not for this Court to condemn as falling below the minimal standards assured by the Due Process Clause a State's reliance upon other methods which, if consistently enforced, would be equally effective."[100]

Twelve more years were to pass before Mr. Justice Clark, delivering the opinion of the court, said in part:

> Today we once again examine Wolf's constitutional documentation of the right to privacy free from unreasonable state intrusion, and after its dozen years on our books, are led by it to close the only court room door remaining open to evidence secured by official lawlessness. . . . we hold that all evidence obtained by searches and seizures in violation of the constitution is, by that same authority, inadmissable in a state court. Since the Fourth Amendment's right to privacy has been declared enforceable against the States through the Due process Clause of the Fourteenth, it is enforceable against them by the same sanction of exclusion as is used against the Federal Government.[101]

Two years later the court closed another "courtroom door" that admitted practices inimical to the accused by declaring that federal constitutional standards of reasonableness of searches are "the same under the Fourth and Fourteenth Amendments."[102]

Another great service performed by the court in behalf of the right of privacy through the application of the Fourteenth Amendment involved the first significant judicial interpretation of the Ninth Amendment. It provides that "the enumeration in the constitution of certain rights shall not be construed to deny or disparage others retained by the people." These "retained rights" had previously never been appealed to, nor had the "right to privacy" ever previously had "the status of an independent right."[103]

In 1965 the constitutionality of a Connecticut law forbidding recommendation of contraceptives was challenged before the court. Justice Douglas delivered the opinion of the court. After indicating that the "specific guarantees in the Bill of Rights have *penumbras*" (emphasis added), he concludes that the first Amendment, which was made applicable to the states by the Fourteenth Amendment, "has a penumbra where privacy is protected from governmental intrusion," and that in the case of marriage, "We deal with a right of privacy older than the Bill of Rights."[104]

While Justice Douglas refers to the Ninth Amendment as but another link in his overall argument, Justice Goldberg makes it central to his opinion and an indispensable handmaiden to the concept of liberty.

> The concept of liberty protects those rights that are fundamental, and is not confined to the specific terms of the Bill of Rights. My conclusion that it embraces the right of marital privacy though that right is not mentioned explicitly in the constitution is supported both by numerous decisions of this Court . . . and by the language and history of the Ninth Amendment. . . . While this Court has had little occasion to interpret the Ninth Amendment, it cannot be presumed that any clause in the Constitution is intended to be without effect. *(Marbury* v. *Madison)* . . . To hold that a right so basic and fundamental and so deep-rooted in our society as the right to privacy in marriage may be infringed because that right is not guaranteed in so many words by the first eight amendments to the Constitution is to ignore the Ninth Amendment and to give it no effect whatsoever . . .

Then, after quoting the amendment, Justice Goldberg proceeds:

> I do not take the position of my brother Black . . . that the entire Bill of Rights is incorporated in the Fourteenth Amendment and I do not mean to imply that the Ninth Amendment is applied

against the States by the Fourteenth. . . . The Ninth Amendment
simply lends strong support to the view that the "liberty" protected
by the Fifth and Fourteenth Amendment from infringement by the
federal government or the States is not restricted to the rights
specifically mentioned in the first eight amendments.[105]

Thus it was that through the first ten amendments and the Fourteenth Amendment, the self-evident truths of the Declaration that
all men are endowed with the unalienable right to life and liberty
were themselves endowed with legal muscle, and the blessings of
liberty for which the founders of the Republic risked their lives has
been at least legally assured for their posterity.

The Pursuit of Happiness and the General Welfare

The unalienable right to the "pursuit of happiness," for the preservation of which, according to the Declaration, governments are
established, is probably as amorphous and indefinable a right as
one could conceive. It is, in fact, a right which to the best of my
knowledge is first formulated in, and remains unique to, the Declaration. It was obviously quite purposefully included since it represents a variation from the then widely used trinity of "life, liberty,
and property."[106] The phrase "the pursuit of happiness" is, to the
best of my knowledge, never appealed to by a justice of the court
in support of a legal opinion, even though it was used in an argument before the court challenging the constitutionality of an act
of Congress.[107] Nor could the reason have been that it is not found
in the Constitution itself. The court did appeal to the phrase "all
men are created equal" to support its decision in the reapportionment cases,[108] even though it does not occur anywhere in the Constitution. The reason would seem to be the fact that happiness is
so subjective a state that no definition could be offered which could
conceivably be endowed with legal status. It is difficult enough to
define legally what a government may or should do to establish
equality among the governed and enable them to enjoy life and
liberty. One could conceivably establish some objective, generally

acceptable criteria for those three concepts. But how could one legally define what a government should do to enable a citizen to pursue so utterly subjective a quality as happiness? And yet there is no reason to doubt that the authors of the Declaration must have had something in mind when they spoke of a government's obligation to assist the governed in their pursuit of happiness, which is distinct from what is expected of it in relation to the concepts of life, liberty, and equality. Does it then seem too farfetched to assume that what they had in mind was later subsumed by the phrase "to promote the general welfare" in the Preamble, and by the phrase "provide for the common Defense and general Welfare of the United States" in Article I, section 8 of the Constitution?

To be sure, the term "general welfare" is itself amorphous enough. But it at least implies some potentially objective standard of judgment. It obviously refers to the observable well-being of the community at large—not necessarily of every single member, but of the overwhelming majority or of a very substantial minority. Yet until the economic crisis of the 1930s, the phrase "promote the general welfare" did not in itself play a significant role in court opinions validating legislation that was avowedly intended to do just that. This was due not merely to the fact that the phrase is, from the legalist's point of view, too indeterminate, and that almost any act of Congress could conceivably be construed as intended to promote the general welfare. The phrase could thus conceivably be used to cancel out all constitutional limitations upon the power of federal or state legislative bodies.[109] It was due in large measure to the fact that the American government came into being as a revolt against governmental constraints. What the people wanted was to be let alone. They were as wary of a paternalistic government as of a tyrannical one. The early American, having a wide open continent before him, felt that he could take care of himself, and that the less the government interfered with his life, the greater his opportunity to "pursue happiness."[110] This mood, which was nurtured and sustained by the presumably endless frontier and its infinite potentialities, was philosophically buttressed by the dominant

economic *laissez-faire* theory of the century, which maintained that
the less the government interferes with the "natural" laws of supply
and demand, the better for everybody, and by the biological theory
that the human race progressed in the past, and will therefore best
progress in the future, if the "unfit" are not "artificially" assisted
in their struggle with the "fit," so that in the future also only the
"fittest" will survive. There is no doubt but that judges, even of the
Supreme Court, being human, could not completely emancipate
themselves from the main currents of thought of their day.

Thus in 1905 the court voided a New York State law which limited the work of bakers to sixty hours per week, reasoning that "the
statute necessarily interferes with the right of contract between the
employer and employee, concerning the number of hours in which
the latter may labor in the bakery of the employer. The general
right to make a contract in relation to his business is part of the
liberty of the individual protected by the Fourteenth Amendment
of the federal constitution. . . . There is no reasonable ground for
interfering with the liberty of person or the right of free contract by
determining the hours of labor in the occupation of a baker. There
is no contention that bakers as a class are not equal in intelligence
and capacity to men in other trades or manual occupations or that
they are not able to assert their rights and care for themselves without the protection of the arm of the state, interfering with their independence of judgment and action. They are in no sense wards of
the state."[111]

Justice Holmes, in a vigorous dissent, declared: "The Fourteenth Amendment does not enact Mr. Herbert Spencer's social
statics. . . . a Constitution is not intended to embody a particular
economic theory, whether of paternalism and the organic relation
of the citizen to the State or of *laissez faire*. . . . General propositions
do not decide concrete cases. The decision will depend on a judgement or intuition more subtle than any articulate major premise."[112]

Nevertheless, though the obvious intent of the New York
State labor law was to promote the general welfare and hence the
individual's pursuit of happiness, in this case, involving particular

bakers, the court refused to validate it because, in the opinion of the court, it ran counter to the constitutional provision guaranteeing the "right of the individual . . . to enter into those contracts in relation to labor which may seem to him appropriate or necessary for the support of himself and his family."[113] Thus it happened that the constitutional provision which, for a long time, proved to be the most fruitful legal source validating legislation promoting the "general welfare," has been the clause granting Congress the power "to regulate commerce with foreign nations and among the several states."[114]

The Commerce Clause and the General Welfare

Perhaps the best-known and most far-reaching judicial use of the commerce clause to implement the proposition that all men are created equal and that all have an equal right to pursue happiness, each in his own way, occurred in the court's decision regarding the constitutionality of the Civil Rights Act of 1964, which, among other things, prohibited discrimination on account of race or color in places of public accommodation even when privately owned. The first such case came before the court in the spring of 1964. Negroes who had "sat in" at a Baltimore restaurant had been prosecuted and sentenced for trespass.[115]

The court upheld the right of the Baltimorian "sit-ins," not on constitutional grounds, but on the "technical ground . . . that there had been a 'significant change' in Maryland law subsequent to the decision of the highest state court which heard *Bell* on appeal below."[116] The question, therefore, whether the Fourteenth Amendment in itself, without further legislation, guaranteed to everyone equal access to places of public accommodation remained unanswered. But by the 1960s the question of equal access by everyone, regardless of race, to all places of public accommodation had to be answered. And the answer had to be affirmative. American public opinion had matured to the point where the overwhelming majority could no longer associate discrimination in places of public accommodation on account of race with their image of what America represented, or should represent, before their own consciences and before the world. Hence, shortly after the noncommital decision of the court in *Bell* v. *Maryland,* Congress, on June 19, 1964, passed the Civil Rights Act of 1964. What the court failed to grant as a constitutional right, Congress, in Title II of the Civil Rights Act of 1964, granted as a statutory right. It prohibits discrimination in public accommodations, defining a public accommodation to include any inn, hotel, motel, or other establishment providing lodgings to transient guests (excepting those which have no more than five rooms for rent and in which the owner also lives), as well as restaurants, lunch counters, gasoline stations, and places of entertainment, and declares that such a public accommodation is subject to this title if "its operations affect commerce, or if discrimination or segregation by it is supported by state action."[117]

Much to the psychological distress of every ethically sensitive American, it was the effect of racial discrimination upon commerce that was used by the government in arguing the act's constitutionality before the Supreme Court. Moreover, the favorable decision of the court is based upon that argument, so that discrimination in public accommodations in America is today legally prohibited not because "all men are created equal," or even because the Constitution guarantees "equal protection of the law" to all citizens, but because Congress has the power to regulate interstate commerce. Since racial discrimination affects commerce, Congress has the power to legislate in regard to it.

That is the purely legalistic aspect of the case, but it is not the whole story. Part of the story is reflected in the following excerpts from the arguments before the Supreme Court on October 6, 1964 on the constitutionality of the Civil Rights Act of 1964. Moreton Rolleston, Jr. of Atlanta represented the Heart of Atlanta Motel, challenging the law. The solicitor general, Archibald Cox, defended the statute.

MR. ROLLESTON: In the [sit-in] case that was decided in this court, handed down on June 22nd of this year, Bell versus Maryland, Mr. Justice Black's decision that was joined in by Mr. Justice White and Mr. Justice Marland you three Justices said in substance that the Constitution, including the Fourteenth Amendment, did not prohibit an individual from practicing racial discrimination unsupported by any state action. . . .

MR. COX: The Civil Rights Act of 1964 is surely the most important legislation enacted in recent decades. It is one of the half-dozen most important laws, I think, enacted in the last century. No legislation within my memory has been debated as widely as long, or as thoroughly. Certainly none has been considered more conscientiously.

Title II, as I shall show, is addressed to a commercial problem of grave national significance.

JUSTICE GOLDBERG: Only commercial, Mr. Solicitor General? Isn't there a moral problem also?

MR. COX: I wish to emphasize and will emphasize repeatedly in my argument that Title II is addressed to a grave commercial problem, grave at the time the Act was enacted and plainly growing.

Nor should we forget, Mr. Justice Goldberg, that Congress in addressing itself to that commercial problem, *was also keeping faith with the proposition declared by the Continental Congress that all men are created equal.* [Emphasis added]

The failure to keep that promise lay heavy on the consciences of the entire nation, North as well as South, East as well as West.

Happily, the difficulty of the constitutional issues here is not equal to their importance. Title II, as we see it, rests upon the powers delegated to Congress to regulate commerce among the several states and upon the power to enact laws that are necessary and proper to effectuate the commerce powers.[118]

The vagaries of legalistic thought required, in the opinion of the majority of the court, a constitutional provision regarding commerce to legalize the enactment of a law further concretizing the implications of the proposition that all men are created equal. Political and social events also undoubtedly played their part in influencing the mental processes that resulted in the court's legally formulated decision. But neither can there be any doubt that the fact the

"Welshman" had placed the proposition where it continues "to lay heavy on the conscience of the nation" played a predominant role in both the action of Congress and the decision of the court.

The intellectual and emotional uneasiness with the legalistic method employed in order to achieve a desirable ethical goal is reflected in the defensive stance taken by Mr. Justice Clark, who spoke in behalf of the court.

> The same interest in protecting interstate commerce which led Congress to deal with segregation in interstate carriers and the white slave traffic had prompted it to extend the exercise of its powers to gambling . . . to criminal enterprise . . . to deceptive practices in sale of products . . . and to racial discrimination by owners and managers of terminal restaurants . . .
>
> That Congress was legislating against moral wrongs in many of these areas rendered its enactment no less valid. . . . given this basis [the commerce clause] for the exercise of its power, Congress was not restricted by the fact that the particular obstruction to interstate commerce with which it was dealing was also deemed a moral and social wrong.[119]

Justice Douglas concurring, said in part:

> Though I join the Court's opinion, I am somewhat reluctant here, as I was in Edwards v. California . . . to rest solely on the Commerce Clause. My reluctance is not due to any conviction that Congress lacks power to regulate commerce in the interests of human rights. It is my belief rather that the right of people to be free of state action that discriminates against them because of race like the right of persons to move freely from State to State . . . occupies a more protected position in our constitutional system than does the movement of cattle, fruit, steel and coal across state lines. . . . A decision based on the Fourteenth Amendment . . . would put an end to all obstructionist strategies and finally close one door on a bitter chapter in American history.[120]

Justice Douglas referred to the court's action some quarter of a century earlier (1941) when it voided a California law which would penalize anyone who brought an indigent person into the state.[121] Justice Byrnes, who at that time spoke in behalf of the court, declared that "it is settled beyond question that the transportation of persons is 'commerce' within the meaning of that provision. . . . The issue presented is whether the prohibition . . . against the 'bringing' or transportation of indigent persons into California is within the police power of that state. We think it is not, and hold it as an unconstitutional barrier to interstate commerce."[122]

It is important for our purpose to record excerpts from two concurring opinions of justices who were unhappy with the grounds upon which the majority opinion in that case rested. The one which we have just quoted in part was written by Justice Douglas, in which Justices Black and Murphy joined. "The right to move freely from state to state," said Justice Douglas, "is an incident of national citizenship protected by the privileges and immunities clause of the Fourteenth Amendment against state interference."[123]

The concept of national citizenship is movingly developed in Mr. Justice Jackson's dissenting opinion:

> The migrations of a human being, of whom it is charged that he possesses nothing that can be sold and has no wherewithal to buy, do not fit easily into my notions as to what is commerce. To hold that the measure of his rights is the commerce clause is likely to result eventually either in distorting the commercial law or in denaturing human rights. I turn, therefore, away, from the principles by which commerce is regulated, to that clause in the Constitution by virtue of which Duncan is a citizen of the United States and which forbids any state to abridge his privileges or immunities as such. . . . The power of citizenship as a shield against oppression was widely known from the example of Paul's Roman citizenship which sent the centurion scurrying to his higher up with the message, "Take heed what thou doest, for this man is a Roman." I suppose none of us doubts that the hope of imparting to American citizenship some of this vitality was the purpose of declaring in the Fourteenth Amendment that "All persons born or natura-

lized in the United States and subject to the jurisdiction thereof are citizens of the United States and the state wherein they reside. . . . No State shall make or enforce any law which shall abridge the privileges or immunities of citizens of the United States." . . . For nearly three quarters of a century this court rejected every plea to "the privileges and immunities" clause. . . . The judicial history of this clause and the very real difficulties with many of its practical application to specific cases have been too well and recently reviewed to warrant repetition. . . . But the difficulty of the task does not excuse us from giving these general and abstract words whatever specific content and concreteness they will bear as we mark out their application case by case! That is the method of the common law, and it has been the method of this court with other no less general statements in our fundamental law. This court has not been timorous about giving concrete meaning to such obscure and vagrant phrases as "due process," "general welfare," "equal protection," or even "commerce among the several states." But it has always hesitated to give any real meaning to the privileges and immunities clause lest it improvidently give too much.[124]

The Concept of Sovereignty and the General Welfare

Next to the commerce clause, the concept of state sovereignty, and the consequent police power of the state, which it implies, was in many instances appealed to by the court in order to legitimatize state legislation whose obvious intention it was to promote the general welfare. Neither of the two concepts, state sovereignty and police power, are mentioned in the Constitution. They belong in a sense to the Higher Law, to the principles which are assumed to inhere in the very essence of government.

In 1897 the court had before it the first of the so-called *Granger* cases, which for the first time raised the question of the right of a state legislature to regulate private business. In 1871 Illinois created a commission with power to establish maximum passenger and freight rates and maximum charges for the storage of grain in Chicago, etc. The law authorizing the fixing of charges for grain storage was challenged as a violation of the due process clause of the Fourteenth Amendment. Searching for "the principles upon which this power of regulation rests," Mr. Chief Justice Waite, who delivered the opinion of the court, turned "to the common law, from whence came the right which the Constitution protects, we find that when private property 'is affected with a public interest, it ceases to be *juris privati* only.' This was said by Lord Chief Justice Hale more than two hundred years ago." The justice then continued to show that the case involved private property which is "affected with a public interest," and therefore "the statute in question is not repugnant to the Constitution of the United States."[125]

This decision led to the inevitable problem of defining which businesses were or were not "affected with a public interest." For decades the court spent a good deal of time and energy trying to arrive at a definition acceptable to all its members, but failed. In 1932 Justice Brandeis, in a dissenting opinion, took the position that "the notion of a distinct category of business affected with a public interest . . . rests upon historical error. In my opinion the true principle is that the State's power extends to every regulation of any business reasonably required and appropriate for the public protection. I find in the due process clause no other limitation upon the character or the scope of regulation permissible."[126] Two years later the court accepted this opinion. It ceased to take refuge in the concept of "affected with public interest" and turned instead to the constitutional concept of promoting the public welfare. Justice Roberts, in behalf of the court, declared that "so far as the requirements of due process is concerned a state is free to adopt whatever economic policy may reasonably be deemed to promote the public welfare and to enforce that policy by legislation adapted to its welfare. . . . The Constitution does not secure to anyone liberty to conduct his business in such fashion as to inflict injury upon the public at large or upon any substantial group of the people. Price control, like any other form of regulation is unconstitutional only if arbitrary, discriminatory, etc."[127]

In the same year (1934) the principle of the right of the state to legislate in behalf of the public welfare was reaffirmed on yet another ground. The constitutionality of the Minnesota Mortgage Moratorium Act, which permitted debtors in times of serious economic depression to delay payments in their obligations for a "reasonable" period of time, was challenged as a violation of Article I, section 10(1) of the Constitution prohibiting breaches of contract.[128]

After giving a comprehensive review of previous cases involving the contract clause of the Constitution, the court, in upholding the law, said that "not only is the Constitutional provision qualified by the measure of control which the State retains over remedial processes, but the state also continues to possess authority to safeguard the vital interests of its people. It does not matter that legislation appropriate to this end 'has the result of modifying or abrogating contracts already in effect.' . . . Not only are existing laws read into contracts in order to fix obligations as between the parties, but the *reservation of essential attributes of sovereign power* [emphasis added] is also read into contracts as a postulate of the legal order. . . . the question is no longer merely that of one party to a contract as against another, but the use of reasonable means to safeguard the economic structure upon which *the good of all* [emphasis added] depends."[129]

These and similar court decisions gave well-nigh unlimited power to the states to use all means which the court would deem "reasonable" to safeguard "the good of all." This the court did, not on the basis of any specific provision of the Constitution, but upon its understanding of the implications of the concept of "essential attributes of sovereign power." The question then arose whether the court would apply the same reasoning to the federal government. The test came during the severe economic depression of the 1930s.

Soon after entering office and throughout his first term, President Franklin D. Roosevelt presented to Congress a series of legislative proposals intended not only to lead the country out of the current economic depression but also to prevent its recurrence.

These proposals involved a vast variety of legislation to raise wages, reduce working hours, eliminate child labor, outlaw unfair competitive practices, conserve natural resources,[130] relieve unemployment, establish old age benefits, as well as federal aid to dependent children, maternal and child welfare, public health,[131] and so forth. The National Industrial Recovery Act was voided by the court because "the code-making authority it conferred is an unconstitutional delegation of legislative power."[132] Other aspects of the Act, which had been defended by the government attorneys as coming within the purview of the power of Congress under the commerce clause of the Constitution, were declared void because "there is a necessary and well established distinction between direct and indirect effects of intrastate commerce upon interstate commerce . . . where the effect of intrastate transactions upon interstate commerce is merely indirect, such transactions remain within the domain of State power. If the commerce clause were construed to reach all enterprises and transactions which could be said to have an indirect effect upon interstate commerce, the Federal authority would embrace practically all activities of the people and the authority of the state over its domestic concerns would exist only by sufferance of the Federal Government."[133]

Both these contentions are of interest to us in this inquiry, because both affect the power of the federal government to act under the authority of the "general welfare" clause. This clause came under the specific consideration of the court when the constitutionality of the Agricultural Adjustment Act (1933), which provided among other things for payments to farmers for limiting the growth of certain commodities, was challenged. The government argued "that Congress may appropriate and authorize the spending of moneys for the 'general welfare';[134] that the phrase should be liberally construed to cover anything conducive to national welfare; that decision as to what will promote such welfare rests with Congress alone, and that the courts may not review its determination. . ." The court agreed "that the power of Congress to authorize expenditure of public moneys for public purposes is not limited by the direct grants of legislative powers found in the Constitution," but declared that "the act invades the reserved rights of the states. It is a statutory plan to regulate and control agricultural production, a matter beyond the powers delegated to the federal government."[135]

The same argument was used the following year (1937) in the dissenting opinions of Justices McReynolds and Butler in arguing that the Social Security Act of 1935 was unconstitutional because of its provision for old-age benefits. They argued that it was in violation of the Tenth Amendment in that it trespassed on rights reserved to the states.

But for reasons not too difficult to fathom, the majority of the court, instead of maintaining logical consistency in their legal reasoning, went along with Mr. Justice Cardozo, who declared that "it is too late today for the argument to be heard with tolerance that in a crisis so extreme the use of moneys of the nation to relieve the unemployed and their dependents is a use for any purpose narrower than the promotion of the general welfare."[136] This, then, was a frank and unequivocal use of the general welfare clause per se, without recourse to any other constitutional provision, to validate federal welfare legislation.

We have seen that the right to legislate in the area of general welfare, which Justices McReynolds, Butler, and others believed was reserved to the states, was sanctioned in the case of the states by the concept of the state's sovereign power and its police power, which flowed therefrom. The general assumption was "that the federal government has no police power as such, and that it is the police power of the sovereign state which bestows upon the state the rights 'to pass regulatory laws for the protection of the health, morals, safety, good order, and general welfare in the community.'" Therefore the court, whenever legislation affecting the general welfare was passed by Congress, validated it, usually under the commerce clause. What it could not thus validate it usually declared void.[137] Thus in 1919 the court voided the Child Labor Law of 1916, which had prohibited the shipment in interstate commerce of products of mines or factories in which children under the age of sixteen, or fourteen, were allowed to work, because under the commerce clause Congress could prohibit only the shipment of things which were intended to accomplish harmful results, like lottery tickets, obscene literature, injurious or fraudulent commodities, and so forth. But the goods produced by child labor were harmless and ordinarily were permitted to be transported. "Over interstate transportation or its incidents, the regulatory power of Congress is ample, but the production of articles intended for interstate commerce is a matter of local regulation. . . . If it were otherwise, all manufacture intended for interstate shipment would be brought under federal control to the practical exclusion of the authority of the states—a result certainly not contemplated by the framers of the Constitution when they vested in Congress the authority to regulate commerce among the states."[138]

In a dissenting opinion, Mr. Justice Holmes declared: "I should have thought that the most conspicuous decisions of this court had made it clear that the power to regulate commerce and other constitutional powers could not be cut down or qualified by the fact that it might interfere with the carrying out of the domestic policy of any state. . . .It does not matter whether the supposed evil precedes or follows the transportation. It is enough that in the opinion of Congress the transportation encourages the evil. . . . The Act does not meddle with anything belonging to the States."[139]

The issue found its final solution only some quarter of a century later. In 1938 Congress enacted the Fair Labor Standards (Wages and Hours) Act. The act provided for conditions under which goods intended for interstate commerce should be produced. It established a minimum wage and maximum hours, prohibited child labor, and so forth. Shortly thereafter a lumber company was declared guilty of violating the law. A district court had held the act unconstitutional, and the case came before the Supreme Court. In the opinion delivered by Mr. Justice Stone the court declared:

> Congress, following its own conception of public policy concerning the restrictions which may appropriately be imposed on interstate commerce is free to exclude from the commerce articles whose use in the states for which they are destined it may conceive to be in-

jurious to the public health, morals or welfare, even though the
state has not sought to regulate their use. . . . It is no objection to
the assertion of power to regulate interstate commerce that its exercise is attended by the same incidents which attend the exercise
of the police power of the states. . . . Whatever their motive
and purpose, regulations of commerce which do not infringe some
constitutional prohibition are within the plenary power conferred
on Congress by the Commerce clause.

Mr. Justice Roberts then refers to the "now classic dissent of
Mr. Justice Holmes" in the case of *Hammer* v. *Dogenhart* (1918)
and declared that "the majority decision in that case was a departure
from the principles which have prevailed in the interpretation of the
commerce clause both before and since the decision . . . and that
it should be and is now overruled. . . . The Sherman Act and the
National Labor Relations Act are familiar examples of the exertion
of the commerce power to prohibit or control activities wholly intrastate because of their effect on interstate commerce." As for the
reserved rights referred to in the Tenth Amendment, the opinion
stated that "the Amendment states but a truism that all is retained
which has not been surrendered. . . . From the beginning and for
many years the amendment has been construed as not depriving
the National government of authority to resort to all means for the
exercise of a granted power which are appropriate and plainly
adopted to the permitted end. . ."[140]

Congress was thus declared to have the right to enact whatever
legislation it deemed necessary in order to implement an "end" permitted by the Constitution. To promote the general welfare is admittedly such an end.

America's phenomenal growth and prosperity, said Lincoln,
"is not the result of an accident. It has a philosophical cause. Without the *Constitution* and the *Union,* we could not have attained the
result; but even these, are not the primary cause of our great prosperity. There is something back of these, entwining itself more
closely about the human heart. That something, is the principle of

'Liberty to all'—the principle that clears the *path* for all—gives *hope* to all—and, by consequence, *enterprise* and *industry,* to all.

"The *expression* of that principle in our Declaration of Independence, was most happy, and fortunate. *Without* this, as well as *with* it, we could have declared our independence of Great Britain [sic]: but *without* it, we could not, I think, have secured our free government, and consequent prosperity."[141]

That "principle" and others associated with it, having been embedded in the document most revered by the American people, continued "to lay heavily upon the conscience" of every historically and ethically sensitive American.

It has ever been, and continues to be, the finely pointed goad that pricks and vexes the conscience of America, never permitting it to sink, for unconscionably long periods of time, into a deep quiescent, dreamless slumber. Whenever America was "troubled" and communed with her own heart" and "pondered the days of old" (Ps. 77:5–7), that principle was the "tried and sure foundation stone" (Isa. 28:16), which served as the standard whereby she tested and measured the state of her spiritual health. When, in 1947, President Harry S. Truman appointed a committee to report on the state of civil rights in America, the committee conceived its task to be that of establishing the extent to which "the American ideals still await complete realization." That ideal, the committee states, was set in the Declaration.[142] And when President Dwight Eisenhower set up a Commission on National Goals as Guides for Programs for Action in the Sixties, it was inevitable that the commission should open its report with the statement:

> The paramount goal of the United States was set long ago. It is to guard the rights of the individual, to ensure his development, and to enlarge his opportunity. It is set forth in the Declaration of Independence drafted by Thomas Jefferson and adopted by the Continental Congress on July 4, 1776. The goals we here identify are within the framework of the original plan and are calculated to bring to fruition the dreams of the men who laid the foundation of this country.

The commission then proceeds to quote the Declaration and continues:

> It was an even broader and bolder Declaration than those who made it knew. . . . It inspires us still in the struggle against injustice. . . . In the 1960's every American is summoned to extraordinary personal responsibility, sustained effort, and sacrifice. . . . To preserve and enlarge our own liberties, to meet a deadly menace and to extend the area of freedom throughout the world. These are high and difficult goals. . . . This Report identifies goals and sets forth programs. It is directed to the citizens of this Country, *each one of whom sets his own goals and seeks to realize them in his life, through private groups, and through various levels of government* [emphasis added].[143]

In the approximately four hundred pages that follow, the commission pinpointed the areas in America life to which the principles of the Declaration still had to be more fully applied. Much of what the commission proposed has since been realized.

Thus, almost two hundred years after the Declaration was adopted by a handful of men, who then used it as the basis on which to establish a government, the broad, generous, humanitarian principles embodied in it have, to an extent inconceivable at the time of its adoption, been written into law, thus defining in legally obligatory acts, as well as in legally protected privileges and immunities, what it means to be an American. As this brief review of the long process indicates, the transformation of ideals into legally enforceable realities required *extraordinary perseverance and readiness to sacrifice on the part of many individuals.* Nor is the process completed. It never can be. There are those who warn that the manner in which this process has thus far expressed itself may have within it the seed of future grief. "Every decision that expands constitutional rights, that construes the Constitution so as to make it cover more, protect more, do more than it did before, is a decision that centralizes power."[144] The fear of a federal government in which too much power is concentrated, which haunted the authors of the Constitution, continues to be real and well founded.

There are those, therefore, who are now calling for what they designate as the "new federalism," in which the same purposes may be better achieved through a decentralization of powers. It is not the purpose of this inquiry to advocate any specific method of achieving the goals set by the Declaration. Our purpose is merely to stress the conviction that the decision regarding the method must be made anew by every generation, and that in the making of that decision every citizen is in duty bound to participate to the best of his ability, through exercising his rights to vote, to express his convictions, and to associate with other citizens in various groups to determine how the government should use, or refrain from using, its vast powers to further the ends for which, in accordance with the Declaration and the Preamble, it was established.

To the extent that one participates intelligently, selflessly, and tirelessly in the ongoing process of transforming the self-evident truths of the Declaration into legal realities, to that extent does he define what being an American means to him. To that extent also does he simultaneously incorporate into his own life many of the elements which we previously enumerated as significant components of the good life.[145]

The Limitations of The Declaration and The Constitution

But the self-evident truths of the Declaration require fulfillment not only in enforceable law. They require expression in the social relations between man and man, and between group and group. While the law can do much to further their expression in the social relations as well, very much remains forever beyond the power of the law and completely in the domain of the individual human being.

The founders of this nation worried about the machinery of government, all right; but also about the virtue of the people. The Constitution allows for self-government, without guaranteeing any virtue in the electorate. Modern liberals assume a virtue in

the people, if only people are allowed to speak. Every fault
in government is derived, therefore, from some obstacle that baf-
fled voters' expression of their will. But Nixon was the expression
of that will. If he is a blight, it is because there has been a failure
of virtue in those who expressed their wishes. . . . As long as the
President has the people behind him, he can cater to their vices.
That is because the system does work—it gives the people what
they want. Fooling around with the system will not much improve
matters.[146]

The process whereby the truths of the Declaration can be ever-
more fully embodied in law and in social relations can be vigorously
*sustained only by those of America's citizens who have fashioned
themselves into human beings for whom the fulfillment of that purpose becomes a psychological and spiritual necessity.* To achieve
such a fashioning of one's own personality, one must call upon spiritual and intellectual resources not available to him in the American
tradition per se.

The Father of his country, whose intellectual and spiritual endowments have all too frequently been underestimated, was apparently aware of the spiritual limitations of his exclusively American
heritage. He therefore admonished his countrymen in his Farewell
Address:

Of all the dispositions and habits which lead to political prosperity,
religion and morality are indispensible supports. . . .

In vain would that man claim the tribute of patriotism, who should
labor to subvert . . . these firmest props of the duties of men and
citizens. . . . And let us with caution indulge the supposition that
morality can be maintained without religion. Whatever may be
conceded to the influence of refined education on minds of peculiar
structure, reason and experience both forbid us to expect that
national morality can prevail in exclusion of religious principle.[147]

Moreover, the goals set by the Declaration and the Preamble,
broad and noble as they are, do not include all aspects of the indi-

vidual's life. We are not merely citizens of a body politic. We are also children, parents, neighbors, members of identifiable, self-conscious, historically and often biologically determined ethnic, religious, and cultural groupings. In addition we share with all human beings the well-nigh daily necessity of confronting tragedy, pain, distress; of living with the awareness of the awesome mysteries of life and death—with the psychologically almost unbearable fact that we know not whence we came and whither we are going.

"Eisenhower's report on National Aims, if I had anything to do with it, would have pondered the private and inward existence of Americans first of all."[148]

If Americans are to wrestle with the problem of their "private and inward existence," which all thoughtful persons must inevitably "ponder," they must have recourse to resources other than those that inhere in American citizenship per se.

America wisely avoided the error of imposing upon her citizens a monolithic, dogmatic philosophical or theological system which is presumed to meet all their spiritual, intellectual, and aesthetic needs. She has bestowed upon them the precious freedom to seek wherever they will the answers which best satisfy them. Each citizen is not only permitted but encouraged to turn to his own or to any other religious, ethnic, or cultural heritage as a resource. This freedom is available to the Jew as to every other American citizen. To the extent that each one explores the resources available to him in his own religious and ethnic heritage for the living of the good life, and then seeks to live it within the framework of the goals that America has set for herself in the Declaration of Independence, to that extent he makes his most vital contribution to the preservation and advancement of the new nation that was brought forth upon this continent some two hundred years ago.

3.

ETHICS AND LAW IN JUDAISM

THE INFINITELY COMPLICATED NATURE of man and of human society produces an infinite number of interpersonal situations which no law can possibly foresee and provide for adequately. Hence, to the best of my knowledge, no law governing human relations has ever been so perfectly formulated that it is easily applicable to every situation that may arise within the scope of its reference. It is safe to assume that there is probably no law on the statute books of any society, no matter how noble the purpose which inspired its enactment, which has not at one time or another worked unfair hardships on someone.

Moreover, there is no institution which, by its very nature, is more complicated than the institution of the family. The relationships between husband and wife, parents and children, involve man's most profound biological drives, his most tender emotional endowments, and his most sensitive spiritual aspirations. In addition, the family directly affects the most basic need of society, the need to insure its own stability and continuity as a self-conscious social organism. Hence the laws of marriage and divorce have

157

never been formulated with complete satisfaction. They have been a subject of intense ongoing concern and frequent acrimonious controversy in all civilized societies. The Jewish people has been no exception in this matter. I shall limit my remarks to only one aspect of this many-faceted problem.

The Bible states: "When a man takes a wife and marries her, if then she finds no favor in his eyes because he has found some indecency in her, and he writes her a bill of divorcement and puts it in her hand . . ." (Deut. 24:1). The literal meaning of this verse indicates that the husband is the exclusive initiator of the proceedings that culminate either in marriage or divorce. Rabbi Simeon said: "Why does the Torah say 'when a man takes a wife,' and not 'when a woman takes a husand'? Because it is in the nature of man to seek after the woman and not in the nature of the woman to seek after the man."[1] Although neither Jewish nor general *law* places the woman at a disadvantage in initiating the process culminating in marriage, biology, society, and long-standing tradition have limited her freedom even in this realm much more than that of the man. In the matter of terminating a marriage, however, the biblical law, as at present interpreted and applied, places the Jewish woman, in countries where the Jewish community exercises no legally enforceable authority over its members, completely in the power of her alienated husband. Even though the man may have been granted a civil divorce and even have remarried, he may nevertheless refuse to grant her a *get,* a rabbinically sanctioned religious divorce, or may consent to grant it only on conditions that he sets.

The hardships that this frequently imposes on innocent women were recognized early in Jewish history, and, as we shall see, the Rabbis tried to overcome them. But the problem was not altogether solved even in periods when the Jewish community exercised considerable legal authority over its members and could severely punish those who transgressed its enactments. The scope of the problem infinitely increased in modern times, when most Jewish diaspora communities ceased to exercise any significant legally enforceable authority over their members. Attempts to find a solution, therefore,

were made on the level of both theory and practice, and a vast literature dealing with the subject has been developed over the centuries.[2]
But no solution has as yet been suggested by anyone which has won
widespread acceptance both in theory and in practice. The dimensions of the problem have in the meantime continued to increase
rather than to diminish.

While national and international Jewish women's organiza-
tions have been the most vocal group urging a modification of the
present rabbinical laws regulating Jewish divorce proceedings, they
are not alone among those who feel profoundly unhappy with the
present situation. Equally perturbed are many who are committed
to the continued exercise of the authority of the *halakhah,* biblical-
rabbinic law, in as many areas of Jewish personal and communal
life as possible. Since the dawn of the modern era in Jewish history
and the integration of the Jews as individuals into Western society,
the role of the *halakhah* in Jewish life has steadily diminished. One
of the last significant areas in which it still plays an important role is
that of family life. Its role in this area, however, is ever more seriously threatened because of this particular law. As one of the great
saints and sages of our day has put it:

> The situation has gravely deteriorated. New and difficult problems,
> which the leaders of former generations did not have to deal with,
> have arisen. Matters have reached so sad a pass that many women
> are divorced only in the civil courts without a *get* and are then
> re-married to other Jews, thus multiplying *mamzerim* in Israel.
> Were it a matter of only a few such instances, as was the case in
> former generations, we would still have to deal with the law with
> great seriousness, and seek a way to eliminate the evil. How much
> more then is it incumbent upon us to do so when we are faced
> by a mass phenomenon, when families in which the Jewish law of
> *gittin* has not been observed intermarry with families that have
> remained true to the *halakhah,* without anyone being particularly
> concerned, for we all know the power of love in our lives. There-
> fore, I believe that we should not remain silent and indifferent in
> the presence of so serious a breach. We must assiduously seek

some way to enact regulations that would remove the stumbling blocks before large sections of our people, including many of its most loyal members.[3]

This law, more than any other, tends to undermine the loyalty of those who want to live in accordance with the *halakhah,* because in conforming to it one feels that he often is called upon to act as an accomplice of evilly motivated individuals. This is a law that belongs to the class "which Satan can question"[4] with great cogency.

Law, Hardship, and Justice

The fact that a law of the Torah imposes hardships upon those who observe it, is *ipso facto* no reason for its abolition. If the authority of a law were to depend upon whether or not it involves one who observes it in hardships, neither the ethical nor the ritual laws of the Torah could stand the test. Obedience to the moral imperatives of the Torah, which require holiness in our personal lives, loyalty to one's spouse, and honesty and mercy in all our dealings with our fellow men, repeatedly involve us in hardships and sacrifices great or small. As for the ritual laws of the Torah, until modern sanitary precautions and medical facilities became readily available, circumcision subjected every Jewish male child not only to immediate great physical pain, but also to the possibility of complications which at times ended in serious illness or even in death. The observance of the Sabbath, the dietary laws, and the whole pattern of Jewish life often demand great sacrifices.

Opposition to this law, therefore, does not stem from the fact that it imposes hardships on some women, but rather that it violates our elementary sense of justice and decency. In the hands of a spiteful or greedy husband, it becomes a weapon wherewith to inflict grave injury upon an emotionally alienated, legally divorced—and often altogether innocent—wife.

Rabbi Louis M. Epstein, who devoted much time and energy to this problem, expressed the sentiments of many when he wrote:

The problem of the *agunah,* as far as I am concerned, is not only a matter of the suffering of the unhappy woman, but it is also a matter of the contradiction between the law and justice. My mind cannot accept the thought that our holy Torah based family life upon the foundations of injustice and cruelty. Hence, I have come to the conclusion that there must be some mistake in the manner in which this law has been interpreted over the generations.[5]

Rabbinic Measures on Behalf of the Wife

The Rabbis made great strides toward equalizing the status of the woman with that of the man in many areas of life.[6] This inquiry is concerned, however, only with those measures whereby the Rabbis achieved a substantial equalization of the role of the woman with that of the man both in initiating and in consummating the granting of a *get.* They did so by formulating legal principles, some of which applied specifically to the problem of *gittin* and others which were equally applicable to other legal problems. We shall here present, though not in chronological or hierarchal order, a few of these principles.

1. *Kofin oto 'ad sheyomar rozeh ani.* The court had the right to compel an individual to perform an act and to declare such an act performed under compulsion to be as valid as if it had been performed voluntarily.[7]

Hence, even though the literal meaning of the biblical text is that the *get* is to be given by the husband voluntarily, a *get* given by him under court compulsion was also declared valid. This legal formula made it possible for Jewish communities that could enforce their authority over their members to deal effectively with the overwhelming majority of recalcitrant husbands. It also made it possible for the woman to initiate divorce proceedings wherever there was a Jewish court with power to implement its decisions. Once this principle was established, the reasons for which a court could force a man to grant a divorce became almost entirely a matter of the court's discretion. The seventh chapter of *Ketubot* lists quite a large number of such reasons. The ultimate, the most "liberal" or "modern" of all reasons, that of incompatibility, is already fore-shadowed in the Talmud[8] and clearly formulated by Maimonides. He states: "If she says he is obnoxious to me and I cannot bear having intercourse with him, he is forced to divorce her, for she is not his captive and does not have to live with one hateful to her."[9]

The Rabbis justify the validation of a *get* given under compulsion on the principle that "it is a *mizvah* (and therefore one is in duty bound) to obey the words of the wise." To which Rashi adds, "We have the right (or the duty) to consider him (i.e., the husband) as one who fulfills *mizvot* and that therefore he really had made up his mind to obey the orders of the court."[10] Maimonides justifies the validation of a *get* given under compulsion in great detail.

> Why do we not declare a *get* given under duress to be invalid? . . . because we invoke the principle of duress (to invalidate an action) only in cases where one is compelled to do something which the Torah does not require him to do. . . . But one who when seized by his evil impulse fails to observe a commandment or commits a transgression, is beaten until he does what the Torah requires him to do, or until he desists from doing what he is forbidden to do, he is not to be considered as acting under external duress. On the contrary, he had been previously acting under the duress of his evil impulse. Therefore, one who refuses to give his wife a *get* (when the court orders him to do so), since (we assume that) he wants to remain a member of the people of Israel and wants to perform all the *mizvot* and to desist from performing a transgres-sion, and that it is only his (evil) impulse which has got hold of him (and prevents him from doing what he really wants to do), and since he was beaten until his (evil) impulse was enfeebled so that he said "I am willing," we assume that he granted the *get* volun-tarily.[11]

2. *The takkanah of Rabbenu Gershom, Me'or Hagolah* (ca. 1000). This *takkanah*, which became law for Ashkenazic Jewry, prohibited polygamy and thus made it impossible for a man who did not give his wife a *get* to receive rabbinic sanction for his remarriage. Rab-

benu Gershom also established the practice that a woman cannot be divorced against her will.[12]

3. *Afkainhu rabbanan l'kiddushin minay.*[13] The Rabbis have the power to annul[14] or terminate a marriage without requiring a *get*.

In annulment proceedings the husband had no rights which the wife did not have, for it is in the very nature of such proceedings that the status of the husband is under question. Hence one cannot exercise the rights which such a status bestows. In fact, as we shall have occasion to note later, proceedings in accordance with this rabbinic principle were often weighted to the advantage of the wife, for they occasionally involved the cancellation of rights which, in accordance with biblical law, the previous act of marriage had bestowed upon the husband.

Literally translated, the rabbinic statement regarding the termination of a marriage without a *get* declares that "the Rabbis have withdrawn from (or denied to) the husband the act of *kiddushin*," and hence also all the rights which it bestowed upon him. It obviously implied that the act of *kiddushin* had been effected. On what did the Rabbis base their claim to their power to terminate it? There are two schools of thought on this question.

One school bases itself upon the fact that marriages were most often effected by a financial transaction. The groom gave his bride an object having the value of no less than a *pruta* in consideration of which she became his bride. Now it is a universally accepted rabbinic principle that *hefker bet din hefker*—the court had the right to declare a man's property ownerless.[15] Hence the court could retroactively declare that the *pruta* the groom had given his bride was given as a gift and not as a consideration for marriage.[16] Thus, theoretically, the marriage had never been effected, and the groom never acquired the rights of a husband.

But a marriage could also be effected by sexual intercourse. In such a case, the Rabbis claimed the right to terminate the marriage on the basis of their power "to declare the intercourse to have been merely an act of fornication" and not one that effected a marriage.[17] While the Rabbis cite biblical support for their right to declare property to be ownerless,[18] they nowhere cite biblical or any other sanction for their right to declare an act of intercourse intended by both parties to effect a marriage to be an act of fornication. They seem to have simply arrogated this right unto themselves, and to the best of my knowledge it was not challenged.[19]

The rabbinic power to annul a marriage was thus based upon the power to declare property ownerless and to declare any act of sexual intercourse to have been an act of fornication.

The other school of thought bases the rabbinic power to annul marriages upon the all-encompassing principle that "every Jewish marriage to be valid must accord with the regulations set up by the Rabbis."[20] The power to determine the conditions appropriate to effecting a marriage inhered in the Rabbis by virtue of the fact that "it was a *mizvah* to obey the teaching of the wise."[21] It was then assumed that the right to set the conditions for effecting a marriage also implied the right to terminate a marriage which, in the opinion of the Rabbis, did not conform to their conditions.[22] This broad, general principle is, in the opinion of this school, in itself sufficient to bestow upon the Rabbis all the power they need to annul marriages.[23] The other two principles which were previously discussed, are, in their opinion, only tangentially related to this main principle and are, as it were, only of academic interest. If, having accepted this basic, general prerogative of the Rabbis, one's academic curiosity moves him to ask what happens with the money that was originally used to effect the marriage, or what is the status of the act of sexual intercourse by which it might have been effected, the answer is supplied by these two principles: In the first instance the Rabbis could declare the money to have been retroactively ownerless. In the second instance they could declare the act of sexual intercourse to have been an act of fornication.[24]

Obviously the Rabbis had great compunctions about having even theoretical recourse to so radical a principle.[25] Hence, some suggest an additional nuance, in order to indicate that the mere fact that the Rabbis had the power to do it, made it unnecessary for them ever to use that power. "Since everyone knows that the Rabbis have the power to terminate marriages . . . and since no one wants his relationships with his wife to be declared as having had the status of fornication, hence (in cases to be later discussed) . . . it is as if the husband had decided to give his consent to the annulment."[26] The power to annul, then, becomes analogous to the power of "compelling him to say 'I agree.' "

These were the legal principles which were formulated and applied by the Rabbis in their efforts to equalize the rights of the wife with those of the husband in terminating a marriage. These principles did indeed succeed in large measure in achieving their purpose, especially in times of comparative peace, when rabbinic authority, in long-established Jewish centers, was buttressed by a powerful public opinion and by the executive power exercised by semi-autonomous Jewish communities. But a serious residue of inequality nevertheless remained, and undoubtedly caused great suffering to individual women in every generation.

This inequality became particularly evident in time of war, massacre, and mass migration, when the structure of Jewish communities was disrupted. Before the modern era in Jewish history, there was always the expectation that the authority of the community and the rabbinic courts would soon be re-established. Hence the comparatively widespread grief caused by this law was viewed as a transient phenomenon. However, with the complete collapse of Jewish communal autonomy, and the disappearance of legal authority by the Jewish community over its members, particularly in the democracies of the Western world, rabbinic courts found themselves utterly helpless in the face of a recalcitrant husband.

Failure to Deal with the Agunah

Why, then, did not the Rabbis either of the talmudic period or of modern times formulate legal maxims and procedures whereby the innocent wife, with whom they undoubtedly sympathized, could be spared suffering?

The attempt to explain why others fail to take steps necessary

to correct a situation which to them, as well as to us, obviously
requires correction, must always be undertaken not only with the
utmost caution and hesitation, but also with the utmost sympathy. I
know that there are many who heartily agree with Rabbi Louis
Epstein's estimate of both the judgment and the motives of most of
the Orthodox rabbis of his day. Instead of dispassionately discussing the basic legal issues raised in his well-documented, closely
reasoned *teshuvah* on the subject of the *agunah,* they merely denounced and vilified him for even daring to suggest a possible solution to the problem. Moved by a righteous indignation, Rabbi
Epstein wrote:

> I have come to the conclusion that the injustice which results from
> the law of our holy Torah is hidden and preserved beneath the
> ample garments of those Rabbis who claim that "anything new is
> prohibited by the Torah," because they fear that some unforeseen
> evil or licentiousness may result from it. They are the ones who cry
> "no" to *any* suggestion, even though it conforms in every detail to
> the accepted traditional law. They are the ones who will oppose
> from now to the coming of the Messiah any suggestion that may
> be made in the name of justice.[27]

It may be true that the modern Orthodox rabbinate as an organized body is lacking in courage or in legal creativity. This was
certainly not true of the Rabbis of the talmudic period. Nor can the
members of the modern Orthodox rabbinate as individuals be accused of lack of human sympathy, or lack of appreciation of the
seriousness of the situation, or of utterly failing even to attempt to
cope with it. A vast body of literature exists, expressing the profound sympathy of great rabbinic luminaries of modern as well as
earlier times with the plight of the woman.[28] Moreover, a goodly
number of suggestions have been made by individuals and by groups
of Orthodox rabbis on how to remedy the situation. Not only have
none of these suggestions won general approval, but they all were
violently opposed by overwhelming numbers of Orthodox rabbis,

so that none of them even reached the stage of attempted implementation.[29]

What is there about this biblical law which has made it so impervious to traditional rabbinic legal ingenuity and ethical sensitivity? In the first place, the biblical injunction that "he [the husband] shall write her a bill of divorcement and put it in her hand" (Deut. 24:1) is clear and apparently devoid of patent or latent ambiguity.[30] We know how reluctant the Rabbis always were to reject completely the literal meaning of the biblical text.[31]

But that certainly cannot be the whole answer. As we shall note later in this inquiry, rabbinic enactments very often varied radically from the literal meaning of the text. Indeed, this very verse explicitly states that the husband shall do the writing of the *get* or pay to have it written, yet the Rabbis not only permitted the woman to pay the scribe, but after a while it became the accepted practice for her to pay him. The reason given for this radical variation from the literal meaning of the biblical text is clearly stated. It is to avoid the possibility of having the *get* withheld by the scribe because the husband may unconscionably delay payment or altogether refuse to pay him.[32] Obviously this involves a case where the woman is more anxious than the man to have the *get* become effective, and the Rabbis legislated in her behalf. Permitting the woman to pay the scribe also involved an *extension* of the principle of *hefker bet din hefker,* in the sense that the Rabbis not only deprived a person of his property, but even transferred its ownership to another, for this involved the theoretical transferring to the husband of the ownership of the money paid by the wife to the scribe.[33]

What happened in this instance, however, and proved unfortunate in the long run, is that the principle of *kofin oto,* of *compelling* the husband to give a *get,* had for many generations satisfactorily met the needs of the overwhelming number of cases in which the husband might prove to be recalcitrant. Thus it was a case of the "good" preventing the search for the "better." The other legal formulas for the rabbinic termination of a marriage without a *get,* which we discussed above, were, as we have noted, very rarely used at any time or place. As time passed they were used less and less. The more time that passed without any significant change in the procedures established by the Sages of the Mishnah, the more difficult it became to suggest any further modification,[34] so that the *literal* meaning of this text became especially sacrosanct. The brilliance of the way in which the Rabbis interpreted the text blinded, as it were, the eyes of their followers, so that they could see no other possibility. But this was not the only reason that the Rabbis were so hesitant about dealing with this particular biblical passage. There was the additional factor of primary importance, namely, the rabbinic conception of the relationship which the act of marriage establishes between husband and wife.

Protection of Wife and Preservation of Family

There is no greater travesty of the truth than the oft-repeated statement that underlying the Jewish laws of marriage is the concept of the wife as the property of the husband, he having bought her from her father.[35] If that were so, the Rabbis would have had little difficulty in finding a way to dissolve the marriage without the husband's consent, for we have noted that the power of the court to declare property ownerless was one of the most firmly fixed assumptions of rabbinic legislation. Rabbinic law, however, places marriage in a category all its own. It is not like any other interpersonal relationship. There are aspects to it which give it transcendent ethical significance. Marriage involves man's and woman's total personality —physical, intellectual, and spiritual—more fully than any other relationship into which any two human beings can enter. It is, moreover, a union in which God is to be an ever-present partner; it is sanctioned ultimately by Him and dedicated primarily to His glory. A violation of marriage involving a married woman is punishable by death for both participants (Deut. 22:23–24). It is on a par with idolatry and murder as a transgression which a man is required to avoid even at the price of martyrdom.[36]

It is this conviction that marriage is more than a legal contract between two individuals which causes young people to turn to the Rabbi and ask his blessings upon their marriage. It is this conviction which has bestowed upon marriage the sanctity, the tenderness, and the stability which has made the Jewish family of the past one of the greatest achievements of human civilization. Hence, anyone who on his own authority presumes in any way to change the nature of this relationship, once it is established, is tampering with transcendent elements of which he cannot claim to have real knowledge. He may be doing spiritual violence to the individuals directly involved, and to their offspring, as palpably as if he were performing an act of mayhem against their bodies.

Moreover, the stability and the sanctity of the family are of surpassing importance not only to its immediate members. They have direct bearing upon the essential quality and nature of the life of the whole Jewish people. The family has always been the citadel of our people's strength. Whatever unity the Jewish people has been able to maintain over the centuries, despite their dispersion, has been in large measure rooted in the laws of Jewish marriage. Among the paramount forces which bind Jew to Jew wherever they may be, is the mutual understanding that they may intermarry. When a Jew acts in a manner which in the opinion of many of his fellow Jews disqualifies him from intermarrying with another Jew, he obviously tends to read himself out of the Jewish people and thus to impair its existence as a people. Hence, the preservation of the maximum possible uniformity in Jewish marriage and divorce laws is of the utmost importance to the preservation of the transcendent, intuitive sense of the unity and oneness of the Jewish people.

The outright rejection of the biblical divorce law as interpreted in the rabbinic tradition will inevitably seriously affect the unity of the Jewish people and may ultimately lead to a schism as serious in its consequence as the Karaitic schism. For there can be no gainsaying the fact that the core of the Jewish people has in the past been made up of those who remained loyal to the *halakhah* generally, and to the laws of marriage and divorce in particular. Despite the current rather widespread disregard of these laws, the fact remains that a large percentage of the core of committed Jews continue to be unwaveringly loyal to them. There is good reason to believe that these Jews will tend more and more to refuse to marry Jews who are members of families which have not observed these laws and thus disqualified themselves "to enter into the congregation of the Lord" (Deut. 23:3).

Nor do I have in mind merely the fact that such marriages are today prohibited by the laws of the State of Israel, though that is of very great importance. Of far greater significance for the future of the Jewish people are what I believe to be the increasing number of cases which never come to public notice, in which observant Jews view marriage with Jews who have rejected the law as being to all intents and purposes tantamount to marriage outside the faith.[37] Hence, any action which would tend to impair the sense of the transcendent quality inherent in the family relationship, and reduce it to nothing more than a humanly established relationship to be governed by purely pragmatic considerations, is viewed as a "present and overt danger" not only to the moral and ethical quality of the life of the Jewish people, but to its very physical existence.

The basic factors which motivated the rabbinic builders of Judaism in their attitude toward the biblical laws governing family life—namely, the ascription of divine origin to these laws as to all biblical legislation; the transcendent ethical values which inhere in the marriage relationship; and the role of the family in preserving the Jewish people and determining the quality of its group life—are still, in essence valid.

Moreover, the maintenance, to as great an extent as possible, of the authority of the *halakhah* in Jewish life is of paramount importance. It is the fundamental, indispensable, centripetal force and cohesive agent endowing the scattered segments of the Jewish people with the sense and reality of *Knesset Yisrael,* of their spiritual oneness as a people.

But this does not require one to believe that the Torah intended to put an innocent woman forever in the power of an obviously wicked man. On the contrary, there is ample reason to believe that requiring the husband to write a bill of divorcement and give it to his wife was intended, among other things, to protect her against his irrational, momentary whims.[38] The right of the husband to dismiss his wife with the mere wave of his hand was legally abolished in Tunisia only a short time ago.[39] We know that the Rabbis instituted the *ketubbah,* the written marriage contract obligating the husband to pay a rather substantial sum of money before he could divorce his wife, for her protection.[40]

It is one of the ironies of history that a biblical law which was unquestionably intended to protect the wife should become an instrument for inflicting grief upon her. Hence, to those concerned not merely with the preservation of the authority of the *halakhah,* but also with increasingly making it the embodiment of the moral and ethical teachings of the Torah, the status quo is unacceptable. The suggestions made by Rabbi Louis Epstein and Rabbi Eliezer Berkovits, though halakhically valid, do not constitute a viable solution. They have been rejected by the Orthodox rabbinate for its own reasons. Others have not been ready to implement them because, in one form or another, they require the bride and groom in joint action at the time of their marriage to provide for its possible dissolution.[41]

These suggestions violate the psychologically sound rabbinic principle of *lo makdim inesh puranuta lenafshay*[42]—that no one wants to anticipate misfortune. We should, therefore, be most reluctant to ask anyone to enter upon an enterprise as sacred and as joyful as marriage anticipating that it may come to grief by his own doing. A solution that would subject every Jewish couple to a psychologically repugnant experience at the moment in their lives that should be one of purest joy, in order to avert a future evil that would hopefully befall only a very small number of them, is one in which the good it may accomplish is more than cancelled out by the evil which inheres in it.[43]

Study Guidelines

Since neither the status quo nor its outright rejection is an acceptable alternative, what is called for seems to be an examination of the attitude of the Rabbis to the literal meaning of the biblical text. We know that they did not always feel bound to it and on numerous occasions significantly deviated from it. Was there any principle or principles which consciously or subconsciously guided them and which, they felt, justified their deviations from the literal meaning of the text? If we can discover that principle and formulate it with a fair degree of probability, it should be of help in finding an alternative solution to the problem under discussion that would conform to both the spirit and the letter of the *halakhah* as it developed in its most creative and imaginative eras.

A passage in the Maharsha at the end of his commentary on *Yevamot* will serve as the starting point for this inquiry. The passage directs our attention to an aspect of the inherent dynamism of the *halakhah* which has not been sufficiently explored. It is of supreme relevance not only to the problem immediately before us, but to the fundamental question of the course that must be followed if the potential of the *halakhah* for infinite spiritual and moral, as well as purely legal, development is to be reactivated.

The tractate *Yevamot* ends with the statement of Rabbi Elazar made in the name of Rabbi Ḥanina that "the sages increase peace in the world, as it is written [Isa. 54:13], 'And all thy sons will be learned of the Lord and great will be the peace of thy sons.' " Commenting on this closing passage, Maharsha says,[44] "This aggadic statement is found at the end of three other tractates, *Berakhot, Nazir,* and *Keritot.* Nor can we explain this merely by saying that the Rabbis like to end each tractate with an aggadic passage, since there are other aggadic passages at the end of *Berakhot* which are relevant to the immediately preceding materials, while here [*Yevamot*] the aggadic Midrash is not at all relevant to what precedes it. There must be a reason, therefore, for it in each instance."[45] The reason he gives for placing this Midrash at the end of *Yevamot* is that "this tractate contains many strange things, which appear to uproot biblical injunctions." In regard to them the Rabbis themselves ask, "Does the court have the right to enact regulations which uproot an injunction of the Torah?" Though they answer that these enactments do not constitute an uprooting of biblical injunctions, their answers appear forced and farfetched. Therefore, this tractate ends with the statement that the sages increase peace in the world to indicate that these rabbinical enactments *do not constitute an "uprooting" of biblical law but rather are the implementation of the principle of "peace,"* so that the woman should not remain an *agunah*, as it is written, "Her [the Torah's] ways are ways of pleasantness and all her paths are peace" (Prov. 3:17). Moreover, the tractate concludes[46] with the verse "The Lord gives strength to His people" (Ps. 29:11) to indicate that these enactments do not constitute an uprooting of a biblical law because the Holy One, blessed be He, gave power and strength to His people, who are the *talmidey ḥaḥamim*, the sages, so that they may be lenient in these matters, since the Lord wants to bless His people with peace—and there is no peace where there is an *agunah*. Thus too are we to understand the verse "The Lord will raise up His countenance unto you" as empowering you to uproot an injunction of the Torah because "the Lord will grant you peace" (Numbers, 6:24–26).

What is it that seems to have troubled Maharsha and moved him to write so long a comment on an apparently innocuous rabbinic homily? It is the fact that this homily appears to be completely irrelevant to the subject matter of the tractate. Maharsha senses from this apparent irrelevance that the Rabbis themselves must have had doubts about the adequacy of the ingenious casuistry[47] with which they sought halakhically to justify enactments which obviously "uprooted" biblical law. By this homily they are saying to us that the *ultimate validation* for their enactments is not the legal formula, important as that may be, but the *ethical principle* which the legal formula seeks to implement.

Two fundamental issues are involved in this comment.

The first concerns the question of the power of the Rabbis, *la'akor*, "to uproot," *davar*, "an enactment" of the Bible.

The second concerns the role of ethical concepts in shaping the *halakhah*. Let us turn our attention, then, to these two issues.

Do the Rabbis have the power *la'akor davar min ha-Torah?*[48] The Talmud records the following instance. "It happened that in

Nares a man had betrothed a minor. When she came of age and was sitting on the bridal chair, another man came and snatched her away." Rabbi Bruna and Rabbi Hannanel, the pupils of Rav, who were present on the occasion, did not require her to receive a *get* from the second man.[49] Rav Pappa said they did so because in Nares they first effected the marriage (through intercourse) and then set her on the bridal chair. (Therefore the second marriage was not at all valid and she needed no *get*.) Rav Ashi said, "Since he (the man who snatched her away) acted *shelo kehogen,* improperly, therefore the Rabbis acted *shelo kehogen,* improperly" (and declared the action of the second man to be null and void). Whereupon Ravina said to Rav Ashi, "That is all well and good had he married her by giving her a monetary gift. [The Rabbis could then declare his money as having been ownerless and the transaction would have had no legal validity.] But what if he had effected the marriage through sexual intercourse?" To which Rav Ashi is presumed to have responded, "The Rabbis declared his act of intercourse to be an act of fornication [and not one that effected a marriage]."[50]

The term *shelo kehogen* is used as a synonym of *shelo kedin*— not in accordance with the law.[51] It is surprising, therefore, that Rav Ashi uses it to designate the actions of both the bride-snatcher and of Rabbis Bruna and Hannanel. In accordance with biblical law the action of Rabbis Bruna and Hannanel was legally questionable, since the act of marriage by the bride-snatcher, whether effected by a money transaction or by intercourse, is considered to be valid. What right, therefore, did they have to annul the marriage? The Tosafot *ad locum* is not quite sure. "Rabbi Yizhak ben Shmuel (RI)[52] was not sure whether the marriage in this instance was annulled in accordance with the principle that all marriages must accord with the conditions laid down by the Rabbis, or in accordance with the principle that the Rabbis have the power *la'akor davar,* to uproot an injunction of the Torah, because in this instance [the Talmud] does not *explicitly invoke* the former principle as it does in similar instances everywhere else."

In either case, however, Rabbis Bruna and Hannanel were

apparently acting in accordance with rabbinic law, and yet Rabbi Ashi says that they acted *shelo kehogen*. Why? The only answer that occurs to me is that by equating the action of the snatcher, which violated rabbinic law, with the action of Rabbis Bruna and Hannanel, Rav Ashi implied that they too had violated a law, thus indicating that he must have felt that there was something not altogether right about a rabbinic enactment that "uprooted" a biblical law.

Definition of Terms

We have thus far translated the term *la'akor davar* by "to uproot an injunction." Is that a correct translation? Obviously, the word *davar* does not ordinarily mean an injunction, an enactment, or a law. The key to the meaning of the term as used here is, I believe, to be found in the passage in *Horayot* (3b–4a) where, on the basis of the rabbinic interpretation of the phrase *vene'elam davar* (Lev. 4:13), *davar* is made synonymous with *mikzat* "an aspect of," as contrasted with *kol haguf*, "the whole of," the law. The question of whether the Rabbis could "uproot" *kol haguf*, all of a biblical law, is for obvious reasons never even raised. The concept of an "aspect" of a *mizvah* is not easy to define, and the Rabbis rightly make the point that while a law may be viewed as being only an "aspect" of the whole institution, such as the Sabbath, in and by itself it constitutes *kol haguf*[53]—the whole of the (specific) law.

While this question is in itself of considerable interest, and has some bearing on our problem, we shall not here pursue it. For our purposes it is sufficient to take note of the broad distinction drawn by the Rabbis between *davar* as *mikzat*, "an aspect of," and *kol haguf*, "the whole of."

We translate *la'akor*, for lack of a better word, as "to uproot." "Uproot" is defined as "to tear up, as by the roots; hence to remove utterly, to extirpate." Is that what the word *la'akor* means to the Rabbis? The only way we can find our answer is to examine the passages in which the Rabbis either explicitly use the term *la'akor* or employ a circumlocution which implies it. We shall not quote all the available passages, but only a number we believe to be sufficient to establish its meaning, drawn from various areas of the law.

1.　The Mishnah states: It is forbidden to set aside *trumah,* the portion due the priest, from the unclean for the clean. If one did so by mistake, the *trumah* is valid. If one did so on purpose, it is as if he did nothing. Rav Ḥisda said that the statement in the Mishnah, "It is as if he did nothing," is to be taken literally, so that even the *griva* (the measure of crop which he had set aside as *trumah*) returns to its original state, and no sanctity attaches to it. Rabbi Nathan, son of Rabbi Oshia, says it means merely that it had no effect upon the rest of the crop (that is, he has not fulfilled the obligation to separate *trumah*), but the *griva* (the measure of crop) itself is to be treated as *trumah.*

Rabbi Ḥisda does not agree with Rabbi Nathan, because if you say that the *griva* is *trumah,* then it may well happen that the man will make a mistake and will feel that he does not have to separate other *trumah* for his crop.[54] Rabbah then asked Rabbi Ḥisda, "You say that even the *griva* is not *trumah* because we fear that if we say that it is *trumah,* he may feel that he does not have to separate other *trumah* for his crop. Are we to assume, then, that because we fear a man may err, we have the right to declare as not *trumah* that which the Bible designates as *trumah?* Does the *Bet Din* have the right to 'uproot' a biblical law?" To which Rabbi Ḥisda responded, "And are you, then, not of the opinion that the Rabbis do have the power to 'uproot' a law of the Torah?"

He then goes on to quote the case of a minor who had been married to a *kohen* and died while still a minor. Rabbi Eliezer is of the opinion that the *kohen* is permitted to inherit from her and to defile himself by burying her, if the marriage had been effected by intercourse while she was still a minor. But Rabbi Eliezer is also of the opinion that a minor's acts are of no consequence. Hence, the act of intercourse did not constitute marriage. On what basis, therefore, does he here say that the *kohen* inherits from her and may defile himself for her as if she were his wife, thereby violating a specific biblical law (Lev. 21:1–3)? To this, Rabbah answers that the question of whether the Rabbis have a right to uproot a law of the Torah is not involved in this instance. Other principles are involved. The husband is declared to be her heir, even though biblically the father inherits from the minor, on the basis of the proposition that the Rabbis have the right to confiscate a man's property; and the *kohen* is here permitted, contrary to biblical law, to defile himself by attending to her burial if she dies as a minor because the Rabbis declare her to be a *met mizvah*.[55]

The Tosafot *ad locum*[56] states that "Rabbi Yizhak was of the opinion that the Rabbis declared her to be a *met mizvah*, not on the basis of the principle that since he inherits her she is a *met mizvah*, but rather on the basis of the principle that the Rabbis have the power to uproot a law of the Torah *bedavar hadomeh* [in a case which is similar] as I have explained previously.[57] In this instance, since her relatives do not inherit her, she is like a *met mizvah*, but she is not in every sense of the word a *met mizvah*."[58]

But the discussion does not end there. The case of the blood of a slaughtered animal that had been defiled before it was sprinkled on the altar is quoted. The Rabbis taught that if the sprinkling of the defiled blood was done unintentionally, the sacrifice is acceptable; if intentionally, it is unacceptable. But the biblical law is that regardless of how the sprinkling is done, the sacrifice is acceptable. Whereupon the statement "it is acceptable" is interpreted to mean that the one who brought the sacrifice does not have to bring another in its place, but he may not eat the meat of the sacrifice. But the Bible says specifically, "They [those who bring the offering] shall eat those things with which atonement was made" (Exod. 29:33). Whereupon Rabbah answered that cases of *shev ve'al ta'aseh*, "sit and do nothing," are different.[59] Rashi *ad locum* explains: "This is *not* considered an uprooting of a biblical law. The eating of the meat is a positive commandment and the Rabbis say 'sit and do not eat.' This is not an actual uprooting [literally, "an uprooting with the hands"]. It is uprooted of itself. But in the case of the *trumah*, where Rabbi Hisda says it is as if he had done nothing (and the *griva* separated as *trumah* is to be treated as if it is not *trumah*), he changes what the Bible considers *trumah* into profane food. This is an actual uprooting."

We have thus arrived at what appears to be the Rabbis' self-limitation on their power to uproot a biblical commandment. It applies only in cases which result in "sit and do not act." The Talmud then lists five other cases all belonging to this category.[60]

But this is not yet the end of the matter. We noted above that in the case of the minor married to the *kohen,* Rabbi Yizhak was of the opinion that what is involved there is not merely the principle of rabbinic power to confiscate property or to declare an individual a *met mizvah,* but rather the power to uproot a law of the Bible. In that instance more than merely "sit and do nothing" is involved. The *kohen* actually defiled himself by his own act, contrary to the specific prohibition of the Torah. From this it seems rather clear that Rabbi Yizhak was of the opinion that the rabbinic power to uproot a biblical law goes beyond the limits of *shev ve'al ta'aseh.* That this is so is specifically assumed in another Tosafot in which this case is discussed in greater detail.[61]

> . . . We should carefully examine how the case of the minor wife whom the husband who is a *kohen* may inherit, and for whom he may defile himself, relates to the principle that there is no power to uproot a law of the Torah. Why is he permitted to defile himself for her? It is said he may do so because since her relatives do not inherit her, she will cry and they will not answer. Therefore, we declare her to be a *met mizvah.* Now let us see what is actually involved. If there are no others to busy themselves with her, why does the text tell us that he may do so because she is his wife? In such a case (i.e., when there are no others to take care of her burial), even if she were a stranger to him, she is also a bona fide *met mizvah.* Hence, we must assume that there are others who can busy themselves with her and yet she is considered to be a case of *met mizvah.* Hence, when a dead person is in the presence of a *kohen,* and there is present an Israelite who is not ready to take care of the corpse, such a corpse is considered a *met mizvah.* Rabbi Yizhak

says that in accordance with the law, the minor wife of the *kohen* is not a *met miẓvah,* but because her relatives *mitrashlim bah,* neglect her, the Rabbis declare her to be a *met miẓvah.* Hence, even though generally speaking, the Rabbis have no power to uproot a law of the Torah in a case such as this, which involves *kum ve'asey,* "rise and act," nevertheless where there is *panim veta'am,* an acceptable reason for it, then surely all agree that they have the power to uproot. Note that in the whole discussion there,[62] there is no reference to the fact that a woman is believed when she says her husband died,[63] for this obviously uproots a law of the Torah in a case involving *kum ve'asay* (since it is a woman who is testifying and she is the only witness, both things contrary to biblical law, and yet she is permitted to remarry). Hence, we can be sure that where there is *panim veta'am,* "acceptable reason," there is the power to uproot.[64]

2.   The most famous of the rabbinic *takkanot* is probably the one attributed to Hillel, whereby debts incurred before the Sabbatical year could be collected after the Sabbatical year, contrary to the specific biblical injunction (Deut. 15:2, 9). Regarding the *prozbul,* the Talmud asks "Is it conceivable that where the Bible specifically says that every seventh year automatically brings with it the remission of debt, Hillel could have ordained that it does not remit debts?" To which Rashi adds, "And thus uproot an injunction of the Torah."[65] This *takkanah* is of especial significance for our inquiry, and we shall discuss it in greater detail later.[66]

3.   According to the rabbinic interpretation of the biblical law, a business transaction is not consummated in the case of *metaltin,* "movable objects," until there is *meshikhah*—until the buyer actually, or in some acceptable symbolic fashion, takes possession of what he has purchased. The Talmud does not refer to this rabbinic enactment as a case of the uprooting of biblical law. The Tosafot, however does.[67] It reads as follows: "And if you ask why did the Rabbis *completely uproot*[68] the practice of consummating a transaction by the transfer of money, which is biblically permitted, they could have decreed that both money and *meshikhah* are necessary.

Rabbi Yizḥak explains that they did so for the benefit of commerce, (*takkanat hashuk*), so that two acts should not be needed to complete a transaction."

4. The exercise by the Rabbis of their power to terminate a marriage at times resulted in what the Talmud declares to be an uprooting of a biblical law. This happens in the case of a man who sent a *get* to his wife via a messenger and then changed his mind. If this change occurred before the *get* reached his wife, the original biblically sanctioned practice, as interpreted by the Rabbis, allowed him to convene a court wherever he was and announce his reversal of intention. That was sufficient to invalidate the *get*. Rabban Gamliel the Elder ordained that *mipne tikkun ha'olam,* "to promote the general welfare," this practice be forbidden, and that unless the messenger is overtaken before he reaches the wife, the divorce remains valid, even if the husband's change of mind took place before the messenger reached the wife.[69]

This *takkanah* of Rabban Gamliel the Elder was questioned by Rabbi Yehuda Hanassi but sustained by his father, Rabbi Simeon ben Gamliel, who argued that if you reject the *takkanah* of Rabban Gamliel the Elder, you will be undermining the authority of the court. Whereupon the obvious question is raised: "Is it conceivable that a *get* which is biblically *invalid* can be declared valid merely because we want to sustain the authority of the court and thus permit a woman whom biblical law considers married to marry another man?" And the answer is yes. It is so because every marriage must be performed *adaata d'rabbanan,* in accord with the regulations set by the Rabbis, *ve'afkainhu rabbanan kiddushin mineh,* and the Rabbis therefore have the power to withdraw the marital rights from him (the husband).[70] Rashi's comments *ad locum* are of particular relevance to our immediate purposes. He writes as follows:[71]

All marriages are performed on the assumption that they accord with the regulations of the Rabbis. It is they who ordained that marriages shall be terminated by such a *get* (that is, by a *get* carried by a messenger, even though the husband withdrew it before the messenger reached the wife, but neither the wife nor the messenger knew of the husband's reversal of his original intention). Therefore, the marriage is terminated, for it was on this condition that he married her. In the case where the marriage was effected by money we can say that this rabbinically validated *get* could terminate the marriage because the Rabbis could declare the money to have been given as a gift. If the marriage was effected by sexual intercourse, the Rabbis, by this *get,* declared it to have been originally an act of fornication. They have the power to do so because when he married her, he was presumed to have married her in accordance with their regulations. That is the way I interpret this everywhere, on the basis of my own opinion.

But my teachers taught me that the principle that "all who marry, marry on conditions laid down by the Rabbis" applies only to marriages effected by money, because the practice of effecting marriages by money is in itself a rabbinic enactment.[72] It is not specifically provided for in Scripture. The Rabbis derived it by a *gezerah shavah* because of the use of the same root word *(keeha)* for marriage (Deut. 24:1) and for the acquisition of property (Gen. 23:13). Therefore the Talmud says that the Rabbis may terminate a marriage effected by money. But in the case of sexual intercourse, where it is specifically stated "and he has intercourse with her" (Deut. 24:1), what can we say? How can they uproot a law of the Torah? Therefore the Talmud says that the Rabbis could declare an act of intercourse which was intended to effect a marriage to be an act of fornication, as it is said (*Kiddushin* 12b), Rav flogged anyone who effected his marriage by intercourse because it was considered to be obscene or licentious.

But there are many serious objections to this position. In the first place a law based on *gezerah shavah* is considered to be biblical law. [Rashi then gives a number of examples.] Moreover, the fact that the Rabbis declared it to be an act of fornication does not make it so, for it is specifically designated by the Torah as an act effecting marriage. And as for the statement that Rav punished those who effected their marriage by intercourse, that may be so, but it does not say that he terminated the marriage. The fact is that the Bible provides that a marriage may be effected by money or by intercourse. The Rabbis have the power to terminate marriages which have been thus effected because at the time of marriage, *tala beda'atam,* the groom agreed to effect the marriage in accordance with the conditions that the Rabbis instituted in Israel.

5. Essentially the same legal problem is involved in the case of a man who, before leaving on a journey, gives his wife a *get* on condition that it be declared valid as of the time it was given if he does not return home at a specified time. This *get* is declared valid, contrary to the rabbinic understanding of the biblical law, even if circumstances beyond his control prevent his return, and "even if he is seen on the other side of a flooded river and is heard shouting that he wants to invalidate the *get*."[73]

Rava ventures the opinion that the Rabbis validated a *get* under these circumstances in order to protect the pious woman from being left an *agunah* and to prevent the dissolute woman from becoming the mother of *mamzerim.* Whereupon the question is asked, "Shall we, in consideration of what may happen to a pious or dissolute woman, permit a woman who on the basis of biblical law is already married to a man, to marry another man?"[74] And the same answer as that noted above is again given.

6. There is also the case of the man who, thinking that he is about to die, gives his wife a *get* which if he dies is to become valid from the day it was given. If he recovers, the *get*, by a *gezerah* of the Rabbis, is declared valid even though the Rabbis assume that biblically it is invalid.

Again the Talmud asks, "Is it conceivable that a *get* which is biblically invalid can, on account of a (rabbinic) *gezerah,* be declared valid, thus permitting a married woman to remarry?" And again the same answers are given.[75]

7. Rashi did not hesitate to apply the phrase *La'akor davar min haTorah* to other rabbinic *takkanot* as well. As we have seen, he does so in regard to the *prozbul.*[76] Moreover, he defines the term

takkanot kvu'ot—ra'uy la'asotam keva la'akor aleyhem davar min haTorah as *takkanot* "worthy of becoming a fixed law, and of 'uprooting' a biblical law on account of them."[77]

8. The idea that laws of the Torah could be completely "uprooted," that they could become permanently inapplicable, was not foreign to the Rabbis. Thus the laws regarding the treatment of Ammon and Moab and the seven nations that inhabited Canaan before the Israelite conquest had become obsolete, because these nations could no longer be identified, nor was there any humanly conceivable possibility that they would ever be identified again.[78]

9. There were biblical laws which for a variety of reasons became inapplicable or fell into desuetude. Though the Rabbis never officially declared them to be obsolete and forever inapplicable, and though they continued to discuss them as if they were, or would conceivably again become, applicable, they could not possibly have failed to note that in their day they were not applied, and that the chances were not very likely that they would ever again be applied. Such were the laws of the "water of bitterness" (Num. 5:18) and of "the heifer whose neck was broken" (Deut. 21:1–9).[79]

The laws dealing with animal sacrifice belong to a different category. Though the destruction of the Temple made them inoperative, it did not abrogate them. The restoration of the Temple is not only something within the realm of the possible, but it is an essential ingredient of rabbinic Judaism's hopes for the future. No one can now foresee what will be done about these laws when the Temple is rebuilt, any more than we can foresee the conditions under which the Temple will be rebuilt in the future.[80] The conditions then prevailing will determine the role that these laws will play in Jewish life.

A very widely quoted rabbinic statement has it that "in the future all animal sacrifices will be abolished except the sacrifice of *Todah,* of Thanksgiving." [81] Others did not hesitate to offer the opinion that "in the future all festivals except Purim and Yom Kippur will be abolished."[82]

10. The most radical of all rabbinic statements regarding biblical laws is the apparently overwhelmingly held opinion that at

least three laws of the Bible were never meant to be implemented:
(1) the law of the "disloyal and defiant son" (Deut. 21:18–21);
(2) the law regarding the excommunicated city (Deut. 13:13–19);
(3) the law regarding a house afflicted by a plague (Lev.
14:33–53).[83]

11. Some laws were "uprooted" by a *halakhah le Moshe
miSinai,* "an [*oral*] law that tradition asserts to have been promulgated by Moses at Sinai." "Rabbi Yoḥanan said in the name of
Rabbi Yishmael:[84] In three instances a *halakhah* [Rashi: *leMoshe
miSinai*] uproots[85] [overrules or circumvents] the biblical text. The
Torah says that the blood of the slaughtered animal must be covered
with dirt (Lev. 17:13). The *halakhah* says it may be covered with
anything.[86] The Torah says that the Nazirite is not permitted to
shave with a razor (Num. 6:5). The *halakhah* forbids the use of
any shaving instruments. The Torah says that he shall write her a
'book' of divorcement (Deut. 24:1). The *halakhah* says he may
write it upon anything." A question is raised whether these are the
only three such instances. But that is not of particular relevance to
our immediate purpose.

12. The prophets or the sages could temporarily (*hora'at
sha'ah*) "uproot" a law when in their opinion the special needs of
the nation in a critical hour required it.[87] The Rabbis found biblical
validation for this practice in the verse "It is time for the Lord to
act, for Thy law has been broken" (Ps. 119:126). The Rabbis
understood this verse to say "they [the prophets] have broken Thy
law because there was need to act in behalf of the Lord." Rashi
ad locum is very specific. "There are times when *mevatlim,* we sus-
pend the commandments of the Torah in order to act in behalf of
the Lord, . . . and it is permissible to violate the Torah and to do
even that which appears to be forbidden."[88] It is primarily on the
basis of this verse that the Rabbis justified the violation of the law
by Simon the High Priest, who left the Temple court in his sacred
high-priestly garments to greet Alexander of Macedon.[89]

13. The verse "The Lord your God will raise up for you a
prophet from among your people, like myself; him you shall heed"

(Deut. 18:15) is used by the Rabbis not only to justify Elijah's offering a sacrifice on Mt. Carmel at a time when this was forbidden because there was the Temple in Jerusalem, but also to formulate the general proposition that "even if he, the true prophet, tells you temporarily to violate a biblical commandment, you are duty-bound to obey him."[90]

The Tosafot[91] extends the application of the injunction "him shall you heed" to the rabbinic court as well. "And if you say that the case of Elijah was different since he authorized the violation of the law at the direct inspiration of the Lord, how can we deduce therefrom that we may violate a biblical law because of an enactment of the Rabbis, who are not directly under divine inspiration? [We say that] it is reasonable to assume that. Since one may do so at the direct inspiration of the Lord because of the urgency of the hour, and as a measure for checking lawlessness, one may also do so when not under direct inspiration, since [under any circumstances] even a prophet is not permitted to legislate anything new."[92]

14. In the same spirit Resh Lakish interprets God's use of the words "which you have broken" (Exod. 34:1) to signify that on occasions *bitulah shel Torah zehu yesoda*, "Violation (or suspension) of the law constitutes its (firm) establishment."[93] Rashi's interpretation (*ad locum*) makes it appear as if Resh Lakish's statement is altogether innocuous, and as if what Moses did was comparable to nothing more than temporarily turning from the study of Torah to the performance of such *mizvot* as attending to the burial of the dead or participating in a marriage ceremony. But what Moses did was obviously considered by the Rabbis to have been a much more serious case of "abrogation of the Torah" than Rashi leads us to think, as can be seen from the attempts made by the Rabbis to justify what he did.[94]

15. Despite the well-known rabbinic dictum that the literal meaning of a biblical verse never completely loses its validity,[95] the Rabbis in a number of instances interpreted even legal biblical passages so as to make their literal meaning completely inapplicable legally. The transmutation by the Rabbis of the biblical *lex talionis*

into a money payment,[96] which we shall discuss in some detail later
in this inquiry,[97] is probably the best-known example of this. Similarly, the Rabbis inverted the clearly expressed biblical preference
for *yibbum*—the levirate marriage (Deut. 25:5) over *ḥaliẓah*—
the ceremony of pulling off the sandal (ibid., 6:9), and prohibited
the levirate marriage. They also transmuted the biblical *yumat*
(Exod. 21:29), "shall be put to death," always referring to "judicial
execution," to death "at the hand of God."[98]

16. In a number of instances the Rabbis fixed conditions
which, to all intents and purposes, made the law inoperative. They
did this in the case of the "disloyal and defiant son" (Deut. 21:18–
21),[99] the law regarding capital punishment,[100] and the law regarding the excommunicated city (ibid., 13:13–19).[101]

17. The Rabbis "uprooted" biblical commandments by formulating conditions under which the law may be circumvented. These
conditions are at times designated as *takkanot,* and at times as
ha'aramot. The difference between the two is nowhere clearly defined. The rabbinic attitude toward them is implicit in the designa-
tions. The term *takkanah* usually implies a rabbinic enactment that
effects some easement in a legal requirement. The term *ha'arama*
also effects an easement, but it carries overtones of deviousness bor-
dering on deception. Though *ha'aramot* were considered to be
legally valid, they were generally viewed with disfavor.[102] They were
usually based upon an obviously forced, disingenuous interpretation
of the biblical text.[103] The *takkanot* were usually validated by some
biblically rooted ethical principle.[104] Both had one thing in common: they "uprooted," by circumvention, a biblical law.

We noted above Rashi's definition of *takkanot kvu'ot* as *takkanot* worthy of "uprooting" a biblical commandment. The
ha'arama, too, has been defined "as a device to remove the prohibition from certain acts or deeds." Most of the later *poskim* agreed
that it has the power to "remove" a biblical prohibition.[105]

Let us now return to the question with which we opened this
section of our inquiry, namely, How are we to define the term *la'akor*
as used by the Rabbis in the phrase *la'akor davar min haTorah?* We

have noted how, by means of *takkanot, ha'aramot,* and other principles, the Rabbis either limited or widened the scope of applicability of biblical law, deviating in various degrees from the literal
meaning of the text. At times their enactments prevented the fulfillment of a "positive law," at times they permitted the violation of
a "negative law." But in every instance, the conditions which they
laid down were such that not only did they not constitute an abrogation of the authority of the Bible, but rather they served as a significant affirmation of it.[106] The very fact that the Jew was required
to follow a specific line of action in order to circumvent the biblical
law made him very conscious of its existence and of its authority. If
the *takkanah* or the *ha'aramah* was not followed, the original biblical
law had to be observed.

And what Maharsha is telling us in his comments at the end
of the tractate of *Yevamot* is that these rabbinic limitations and
expansions of the scope of the applicability of biblical laws are not at
all to be understood as being an "uprooting" of them. Indeed, the
question Do the Rabbis have the power to *uproot* a biblical law? is
meaningless if we define "uproot" as it is ordinarily defined in the
dictionary. Rabbinic legislation never uprooted a biblical law. It
always fulfilled the overarching ethical purpose of the Torah, "whose
paths are peace."

Maharsha thus touches upon one of the ultimate questions
facing every society: What is or should be the relationship between
its laws and its ethical values? And we specifically ask: What is
or should be the relationship between the biblically rooted *halakhah*
and biblical ethics?

Ethical Concepts and Legal Enactments

A society that has developed spiritually to the stage at which it consciously differentiates between law and ethics is bound at some
point in its development to become conscious of the disparity that
exists between its laws and its ethics. The nature of ethical concepts
makes the existence of that disparity inevitable, for it is of the very

essence of the ethical concept that it can never be finally either defined verbally or concretized in law and institutions.[107] Nahmanides
was apparently fully aware of the limitations of the law as the embodiment of the ethical. In his comments on the two most comprehensive ethical passages in the Pentateuch, he formulates in
masterful fashion two aspects of the relationship that should exist
between them.

On the commandment, "And thou shalt do that which is upright and good in the eyes of the Lord (Deut. 6:18). Nahmanides
comments:

> This is a matter of very great importance, for it is impossible for
> the Torah to enumerate all the possible relationships between an
> individual and his neighbors and friends, and all matters affecting
> his business dealings, and the welfare of the community and of the
> nations. Hence, after mentioning a number of them, such as, "Thou
> shalt not be a tale bearer" (Lev. 19:16), "Thou shalt not take ven-
> geance or bear a grudge" (ibid., 18), "Thou shalt not curse the
> deaf" (ibid., 14), "Thou shalt rise before the hoary head" (ibid.,
> 32), and similar injunctions, the Bible repeats them all in the form
> of the generalization that one must do that which is good and up-
> right in all his deeds. Under this generalization we include such
> matters as compromising, acting beyond the strict requirements of
> the law, as is expected of us when we plan to sell a plot of land
> whose ownership would be of particular advantage to the owner
> of the plot right next to it, and such other matters as the rabbinic
> injunction that one must be appropriately groomed, and speak
> gently with all people so that he be known in all matters as a man
> of integrity and uprightness.

This, then, is the first great function performed by the ethical
concept. *It indicates the direction in which the law should develop
and suggests possible new social mores and legal forms by which
the ethical may be concretized.* Examples of spiritually enriching
legal and ceremonial innovations which constitute additional concretizations of accepted ethical values are readily available, ranging

from the ḥassidic *gartel* (waistband), used as a garment of prayer in addition to the *tallit,* to the laws that the Rabbis ordained *mipne darkhei shalom,* because "her [the Torah's] ways are ways of peace."[108]

In regard to the already existing law and mores of the society, the ethical concepts fulfill a twofold function. The first of these is formulated by Naḥmanides in his commentary on the commandment "Be ye holy" (Lev. 19:2).

> The Torah exhorts us against sexual immorality and against eating forbidden foods, but permits sexual intercourse between husband and wife and eating meat and drinking wine. Hence, the licentious individual may thus permit himself all kinds of indulgences with his wife . . . and be among the imbibers of wine and the gluttons for meat, and speak profanities, since these are not specifically forbidden in the Torah. He could then conceivably be a disreputable individual without violating any laws of the Torah. Therefore, the Torah, after detailing the things completely forbidden us, commands us in these general terms to be restrained even in matters permitted to us.[109]

The ethical concept cannot define with exactitude just how far we may go in indulging in the legally permitted. It can only alert us to the truth that even the legally permissible becomes ethically repulsive at a certain point. The responsibility for fixing that point rests essentially with each individual, whose moral stature is largely molded by the boundaries he fixes for himself in his pursuit of the legally permissible.

In addition, a people's moral and ethical concepts stand, as it were, in constant and persistent judgment of its already existing mores and laws. "All people, all places and all times are not alike,"[110] and laws and mores which were ethically adequate under one set of circumstances may prove to be ethically deficient under other circumstances. Ethically sensitive individuals are agitated by the discrepancy between the society's laws and its publicly acknowledged values, and seek ways of eliminating it. This never-ending task of adjusting the law to the ethical values is the most significant, ever-present challenge facing every civilized society. The nature of that challenge, and its extent and intensity within any society, depends upon two factors: (1) the degree to which the articulation of the ethical values *and* the sense of law have been refined within its tradition and practice; (2) the extent of the gap between the articulated values and the law.

In a well-ordered society, constant effort is exerted peacefully to narow this gap so that the tension between the ethical values and the law never reaches the point where only radical or revolutionary measures can resolve it. That, in essence, is what the great builders of Judaism in every generation have done. If in the resolution of the tension, whether by peaceful or revolutionary measures, the ethical concepts prevail, we conclude that the society has moved upward on the ladder of civilization. If the law prevails, the best that can be said for the society is that is has maintained the status quo, although historically this has meant, most often, that the society has retrogressed. *The ethical concepts of a culture thus serve as the driving force which makes possible its further development, and simultaneously constitute the cohesive force endowing the culture with continuity, while providing the framework within which each individual and each generation can achieve distinctive personality.*[111]

The extent of the spiritual pressure exercised by the ethical values within any society depends not only upon how widely they are known and how thoroughly they have been internalized by the individuals, but also, in large measure, upon the historical circumstances under which they entered into the thought patterns of the society. Ethical concepts which are intimately associated with the historical experiences of a people will usually commit its members more than those which have no such historical association. The rejection of such historically rooted concepts simultaneously involves a rejection of the society's estimate of the historical experiences of which they form an inseparable part. The rejection of the "self-evident truths" of the American Declaration of Independence involves not only the rejection of the "proposition" to which America was dedicated, but also a re-evaluation of the personalities and events associated with the Declaration.[112] A Frenchman who rejects "liberty, equality and fraternity" is at the same time passing a negative judgment upon the greatest event in his people's history.

Now there is no more intimate relationship between a people's law, its ethical values, and its historical experiences than that which exists between the Jewish people and the Torah—the sum total of its law and its ethics. Whether one views the Torah as the expression of Israel's search for God or as the expression of God's love for Israel, the result, insofar as establishing the relationship between them is concerned, is the same. They are forever inextricably intertwined and interdependent. Neither can be dynamically creative in this world without the other.[113]

Mutual Indispensability of Israel and Torah

One may and should question the theological validity of the frequently repeated misquotation that "God, Torah, and Israel are one,"[114] but one cannot doubt the historical fact that Israel and the Torah are "one" in that they are indispensable to one another. Both, as it were, recognize this mutual indispensability. Israel recognizes it daily in the pronouncement that the Torah "is our life and the length of our days," and the Torah recognizes it by declaring Israel to be the people to whom it was given, and to whose care on this earth it has been entrusted. In attributing indispensability to one another, each of necessity attributes to the other *in relation to itself,* if not an absolute than at least an unmatched and certainly an unsurpassed excellence.[115] For if Israel were to assume that there is a system of ethics and laws which would be less demanding but as effective as the Torah in giving it meaningful life, or one that is more demanding than the Torah, but which would also be more effective in bestowing meaningful life upon it, then rational self-interest would sooner or later persuade Israel to abandon the Torah for the less demanding or the more effective ally. And if the Torah, so to speak, would be able to find a people of greater excellence than Israel that would be as devoted to it as is Israel, then it would, as it were, abandon Israel in behalf of the other people.

Wherein has the excellence of Israel in relationship to the Torah been evidenced? We know that at no time in Jewish history has every single Jew been faithful to all the teachings of the Torah, nor has the Jewish people as an organized body always or ever conducted its affairs in complete conformity with those teachings. Israel's excellence in relation to the Torah has been evidenced, rather, in the fact that Israel alone, from among all the peoples of the earth, has, throughout its long history, never failed to bring forth from among its members a *she'ar yashuv* (Isa. 10:20–22), a "saving remnant," a substantial number who could truthfully say: "All this is come upon us; yet have we not forgotten Thee, neither have we been false to Thy covenant. Our heart is not turned back, neither have our steps declined from Thy path; though Thou has crushed us into a place of jackals, and covered us with the shadow of death. . . . For Thy sake are we killed all the day; we are accounted as sheep for the slaughter" (Ps. 44:16–23).[116]

It is not in every individual Jew that Israel's excellence is evidenced, but in the people as a whole, insofar as it has always been the seedbed of the "saving remnant" of saints, of sages, of *talmiday hakhamim,* and of humble men and women whose lives were as completely devoted to Torah as they could humanly be. These prophets, scribes, rabbis, sages, humble saints, and towering *talmiday hakhamim* were the living, articulate or silent voices whose "lines went out to every corner of the earth" (Ps. 19:4–5) during their lifetimes and even after death. They exerted, in varying but substantial measure, a transforming spiritual effect upon the people as a whole. The individual Jew, whether knowingly or unknowingly, was affected by them. They refined his ethical sensitivities. They revealed to him his own spiritual potentialities. They bestowed upon him not a debilitating sense of guilt or shame, but an inescapable challenge and a firm conviction, conscious or subconscious, that, as a kinsman of these chosen ones, he too has it within him to actualize the divine image in which he was created. It was because of these sons and daughters of Israel that the Lord, through His prophet, was moved to proclaim, "Fear ye not, neither be afraid; have I not announced unto thee of old, and declared it? And ye are My witnesses" (Isa. 44:8).

Biblical Text and Ethical Context

Wherein does the excellence of the Torah consist? Moses says of the Torah, "And what great nation is there, that hath statutes and ordinances so righteous as all this law, which I set before you this day?" (Deut. 4:8). The psalmist sings, "The law of the Lord is perfect, restoring the soul; the testimony of the Lord is sure, making wise the simple; the precepts of the Lord are right, rejoicing the heart" (Ps. 19:8–9). Are we, then, to assume that this excellence is found equally in every word, sentence, and chapter of the Torah? This question is not to be confused with the question of whether or not every single word of the Torah was divinely revealed. One can maintain, as do the Rabbis, that "And Timnah was the concubine of Eliphaz the son of Esau" (Gen. 36:12) was divinely revealed,[117] without thereby necessarily implying that this passage is as significant, as revelatory of the Torah's excellence, as the Ten Commandments.

The Rabbis did not hesitate to ascribe greater significance to one biblical passage over another. They designated such statements as "Thou shalt love thy neighbor as thyself" (Lev. 19:18) and "This is the book of the generations of man" (Gen. 5:1) as being a *klal gadol,* a "comprehensive rule," or as a "principle of surpassing importance."[118] Passages like the Ten Commandments[119] and the nineteenth chapter of Leviticus[120] were considered to be the quintessence of the Torah, or to include within them the whole of the Torah. Nowhere do the Rabbis refer to such passages as those dealing with the war of the kings (Gen. 14) or listing the descendents of Esau (Gen. 36) as being among the *klalim gedolim.* It was not divine revelation per se which ipso facto bestowed surpassing significance upon a biblical passage, even in the eyes of the tradition. That was determined by the intelligible content of the passage.

Wherein, then, is the excellence of the Torah evidenced? In relationship to the Jewish people it is evidenced by the fact that it gave life to the people. The segment of the people that lived by the Torah, that segment alone, maintained the continuous identity of the people and bestowed upon the people a living, vibrant, creative, meaningful reality.

In relationship to human civilization as we know it, the excellence of the Torah is evidenced by the fact that the noblest ideals known to man, the highest moral and ethical principles for the guidance of the conduct of individuals or societies, are found in it. *There is nothing outside the Torah which is superior to the Torah, and before which the Torah as a whole, or any particular passage within it, need be called to stand in judgment.*[121]

Fully aware of all the pitfalls that inhere in any analogy, I yet venture to suggest that just as the excellence of Israel, in relationship to the Torah, is found in the saints, sages, and martyrs of Israel, who gave their all for the Torah and thus left their imprint on the individual Jew, so the excellence of the Torah is found primarily, though not exclusively, in its unsurpassed ethical and moral concepts, whose indelible imprint upon all other legal and non-legal passages of the Torah is clearly evident in most of the accepted traditional interpretations of the biblical text, which constitute the vast sea of rabbinic literature. The great post-biblical builders of Judaism consciously or subconsciously examined and interpreted the injunctions and the narratives of the Torah in the light of these overarching moral and ethical concepts, and where the biblical passage in its literal meaning appeared to them to be in violation of the Torah's overarching ethical injunctions, they *almost* always found a way to interpret it so that it would conform to them.

I say *almost* always, because a passage that may have appeared, in the eyes of one generation, to be in complete conformity with the Torah's ethical requirements may not appear so in the eyes of another generation.[122] Moreover, not every generation is blessed with spiritual leaders that have the insight, the courage, or the authority to modify long-established and widely accepted practices or opinions. There were, however, two factors to which we have previously referred, which above all others buttressed the authority of the biblical formulation of a law as against that of the ethical concept that it may appear to be violating. The first was the fact that the *laws* are as integral to the Torah as the *ethical concepts*. Hence there were always those who would define the ethical concepts in terms of the laws, rather than the laws in terms of the ethical concepts. The second was the fact that it is not possible to establish objective standards for the application of an ethical concept or maxim to any particular situation. In comparison to the clearly formulated law or legal maxim, the moral maxim, because it is associated primarily with the intuition, and because it resists definition, tends in large measure to be subjective. It was this subjectivity which the Rabbis rightly feared, for it had repeatedly proved to be the path leading to sectarianism and ultimately to severance from the main body of the Jewish people. That is why the position of the Rabbis on the question of establishing the *ta'amey hamizvot,* the humanly intelligible purposes which the *mizvot* served, has always been highly ambivalent.[123]

However, despite the frequently articulated opposition to the validation of biblical laws by indicating the moral principle that inheres in them, there was a clearly articulated conviction that the statutes and commandments of the Torah are *zaddikim,* "righteous" (Deut. 4:8), and that to spell out that righteousness constitutes an act of virtue and piety.[124] This conviction was, I believe, one of the conscious as well as subconscious motivations determining many a rabbinic interpretation of the biblical text. Had those who insisted on the absolute authority of the literal text (as did the Karaites) had their way, the tradition would have long ago been condemned to intellectual and spiritual stagnation.

This tension between the halakhic and ethical aspects of the Torah was maintained on the creative level within the tradition by a nonarticulated but generally observed principle that every emotional and rational resource was brought to the defense of the law, up to the point where the ethical flaw in it was established beyond reasonable doubt. At that point the great expounders of Judaism almost always found a way to circumvent the literal meaning of the text.

By and large, the part of the *halakhah* that deals with the laws *beyn adam lamakom*—regarding the individual's relationship to God —has not presented any ethical or moral problems. Ethical and moral problems arise primarily in the case of laws that affect the relationship of man to man, of what one human being may or may not do to or for another human being. We shall discuss three biblical laws and note how the Rabbis, in their interpretation of them, radically departed from the literal meaning of the biblical text and thereby made them conform to the Torah's explicit or implicit moral teachings.

The Lex Talionis

The *lex talionis* is repeated three times in the Bible.[125] In commenting on one of these three passages, the Sifra states:

> You might think that where he put out his eye, the offender's eye should be put out . . . (Not so, for) it is laid down "He that smiteth any man . . . and he that smiteth a beast" (Lev. 24:17–18). Just as in the case of smiting a beast compensation is to be paid, so in the case of the smiting of a man compensation is to be paid. And should this (reason) not suffice, note also that it is stated, "Moreover ye shall take no ransom for the life of a murderer, that is guilty of death" (Num. 35:31), implying that it is only for the *life* of a murderer that you may not take satisfaction (ransom) whereas you may take satisfaction (ransom) (even) for the principal limbs, though these cannot be restored.[126]

The Talmud treats the subject in much greater detail.[127] The Mishnah states: "If a man injures his fellow he becomes liable on five counts. . . . Thus, if he blinded his fellow's eyes . . . his fellow is looked upon as if he was a slave to be sold in the market; they assess how much he was worth and how much he is worth now." The Gemara *ad locum* opens the discussion of this Misnah by asking, "Why? The Torah states an 'eye for an eye.' Why not take it literally?" And the answer given is, "Let not that possibility enter your mind." The Talmud then refers to the above-quoted passage from the Sifra. It then raises the question why a number of biblical verses were required to prove the correctness of the rabbinic interpretation of "an eye for an eye." The answer given is that Leviticus 24:18 contains a law regarding beasts, and "one should not derive a law affecting human beings from a law regarding beasts." The other biblical passage (Num. 35:31) deals with capital punishment, "and one does not derive a law regarding damages from a law regarding capital punishment." Therefore both verses are needed as complementary to one another. Moreover, on the basis of the second verse alone, "one might have assumed that he who inflicted the injury had a choice of either offering his own eye or offering to pay. Hence the first verse is quoted to teach us that just as in the case of the beast, only money is acceptable, so in the case of a human injury only money was to be accepted."

Obviously, this tortuous mustering of biblical verses did not *precede* the practice of compensating financially for a physical injury that had been inflicted. It was an attempt of later generations to find biblical sanction for an already well established practice which contradicted an explicit biblical injunction. The later Rabbis must have sensed this, for they were not content with the explanation found in the Sifra, and tried to find a logically more cogent basis. A number of them did so, not by manipulating biblical texts, but by attempting to prove that the application of the literal meaning of the text would result in an injustice.

> R. Dosthai b. Judah says: . . . you say pecuniary compensation, but perhaps it is not so, but actual retaliation (by putting out an eye) is meant. What then will you say where the eye of one was big and the eye of the other small . . . Rabbi Simon bar Yohai says: . . .

> What then will you say where a blind man puts out the eye of
> another man, or where a cripple cuts off the hand of another man
> . . . Abbaye said . . . The school of Hezekiah taught: Eye for eye,
> life for life, but not life and eye for eye. Now if you assume that
> actual retaliation is meant, it could sometimes happen that eye
> and life would be taken for eye . . .[128]

But this approach does not satisfy the Rabbis. They cannot in
so many words say that a biblical injunction is not to be taken literally because it violates the requirements of justice. As we have noted
previously, the theoretical position of rabbinic Judaism is that while
biblical texts may be explained as concretizations of moral and
ethical principles, their literal meaning may not be explicitly rejected
because it disagrees with an ethical teaching. The Rabbis could not
possibly say that such and such a law can no longer be applied because it is unjust. They would thus be "identifying God's (attributes) laws with mercy, when in reality they are to be accepted as
His (arbitrary) command."[129] The most that they could say was
that the literal meaning of a text was never different from their interpretation of it. It was, or should have been, always so understood.[130]
They then sought to validate their interpretation of the biblical text
by references to other biblical texts. Thus they maintained the basic
framework of justifying their interpretations not on the basis of their
subjective feelings, but on "objectively" established interpretations
of the text.

In this fashion, the discussion regarding the validation of the
rabbinic interpretation of the *lex talionis* ends with the suggestion
made by Rav Ashi, a sixth-century Babylonian Amora. He validates
it by a farfetched *gezerah shavah* based on the use of the word *tahat*
in the case of "an eye *tahat* an eye" (Exod. 21:23) and in the verse
"the man who lay with her shall pay the girl's father fifty shekels
of silver, and she shall be his wife *tahat* [because] he has violated
her . . ." (Deut. 22:29). Just as in the case of the violated girl
tahat is associated by the Bible with financial compensation, so also

is the *tahat* in "eye for an eye" to be understood as referring to financial compensation.[131]

The discussion of this matter in Nimukey Yosef[132] and in the *Hidushey Anshe Shem, ad locum,* is of such relevance to our purpose that we shall translate or paraphrase most of it. Nimukey Yosef states:

> . . . the Gemara quotes Rav Ashi's opinion that this verse refers to money on the basis of *gezerah shavah* of *tahat-tahat*. One cannot but wonder that none of the Tannaim had recourse to that verse. Furthermore, no one may make use of a *gezerah shavah* except when he has received it from his teacher. In the Yerushalmi they said that anything which is not clear, they explain on the basis of references to many places.[133] The commentators, may their memory be for a blessing, have taken that statement to mean that, in a *matter regarding whose validity they had no clear corroboration from a biblical text,* everyone had the right to express his opinion and to suggest a verse.[134]

Upon this, *Hidushey Anshe Shem, ad locum,* comments:

What he (Nimukey Yosef) is telling us is that if we want *ab origino* to draw conclusions from the presence of *tahat* in the case of *ayin tahat ayin*, or of the *tahat* in the case of the ox (Exod. 21:36), then we may not do so. But where we have the tradition that there exists a *gezerah shavah* of *tahat-tahat* then *we* may have recourse to it. But if there is no such tradition, then one cannot draw any conclusion on the basis of this *gezerah shavah*. But this is not at all the case in the matter under discussion, for we are not at all involved in deducing the law (on the basis of *gezerah shavah*), for the law that *one has to pay (the value of an eye) had already been fixed and was universally accepted, and we are concerned only with supporting the rabbinic interpretation of "eye for an eye" by associating it with a biblical verse.* In such a case, every man has the right to suggest his own *gezerah shavah*.

It becomes quite evident from the above that the reinterpretation of the *lex talionis*, which undoubtedly took place generations, if not centuries, before the days of the Rabbis whose discussion is recorded in the Talmud, was not validated *at that time* by reference to any specific biblical passage. Had it been so validated, the tradition would undoubtedly have recorded and transmitted it, for there can be no more radical departure from the literal text than this, and the sages who effected it would unquestionably have wanted to support their interpretation by a specific biblical text if they could have found it. Or they might have designated their understanding of the verse as a *halakhah leMoshe miSinai*. But they did not, thus giving some reason for questioning the antiquity of this interpretation. Indeed as late as the beginning of the second century, Rabbi Eliezer, one of the five great pupils of Rabbi Yoḥanan ben Zakkai, apparently insisted that the literal meaning be implemented.[135] One cannot but wonder whether in the days of Rabbi Eliezer there were still courts that would conceivably implement this law literally, or whether Rabbi Eliezer was thus declaring a procedure universally accepted by his colleagues to be a violation of the biblical law.

Be that as it may, the fact remains that Rav Ashi's suggested *gezerah shavah* is recognized by all rabbinic authorities to be at best but an *asmakhta b'almah*, a mere mnemotechnical aid having no legal validity. The inevitable conclusion seems to be that even though the Rabbis did not officially accept the arguments of their colleagues that "an eye for an eye" is to be interpreted as referring to money compensation, because a literal application of the law is often impossible and more often would result in an injustice, there can be little doubt that on the "non-official" or subconscious level they did reject the literal meaning of the text, so that the law may conform to the over-arching injunction of the Torah "Righteousness, righteousness shalt thou pursue" (Deut. 16:20).

This seems, therefore, to be a perfect halakhic illustration of Dr. Max Kadushin's insightful observation that the fact that an ethical value is not specifically referred to in a given rabbinic passage is not to be interpreted to mean that it is not significantly imbedded in the passage.[136] Ethical values deeply rooted in the conscious and the subconscious of the people determine their actions and judgments even when not explicitly mentioned.

The Prozbul

We had occasion earlier in this inquiry to refer to the *prozbul* and to the fact that the Rabbis found it difficult to accept the thought that Hillel took it upon himself to "uproot" a clearly expressed injunction of the Torah. The third-century Babylonian Amora, Samuel, goes so far as to say that the institution of the *prozbul* is "an *ulbana* of the judges,"[137] *ulbana* being explained by Rashi, *ad locum,* either as a *huzpa* on the part of the judges, who thereby assumed the right to force a man *unjustly* to pay, or as an assumption of authority not from arrogance but from a desire to relieve the judges of overwork. Samuel, therefore, says that if he ever has the authority (or musters the courage), he would abolish the *prozbul*.

Although Rav Nahman took a position diametrically opposed to that of Samuel, saying that he would go even further than Hillel and have a court ordain that every loan made should be considered as if the notes of indebtedness were placed in the possession of the court, and as if a *prozbul* had been written, even though it was not written,[138] the Rabbis generally seemed to be uneasy about Hillel's *takkanah,* and sought in a variety of ways to mitigate the legal radicalism it implied. Thus the Sifre associated Hillel's *takkanah* with a biblical text,[139] on the basis of which there would appear to be two ways whereby the remission of debts could be avoided. First, if the lender has in his possession a security of any kind left with him by the borrower, the Sabbatical year does not remit the debt.[140] The other way was for the lender to hand over his notes of indebtedness to the courts.[141] After thus interpreting the biblical verse the Sifre goes on to say, *mikan amru,* "on the basis of this they said that Hillel ordained the *prozbul* . . ."

In the Sifre the *mikan amru* is in parentheses. The Jerusalem Talmud states specifically, "On the basis of these interpretations of the biblical verse, they claimed that the *prozbul* had biblical root-

age." The Gemara there goes on to ask, "Do you mean to imply that
the *prozbul* is a biblical injunction?" The answer is clear. "After
Hillel ordained it, they associated it with a biblical verse."[142]

But this did not and could not satisfy many of the later Rabbis,
for it would imply that Hillel arrogated to himself the right to abrogate a biblical law. Hence they sought in a variety of ways to prove
that he did not really do that. Abayye suggested that Hillel's *takkanah* refers only "to the present time, and that Hillel was of the
opinion later held by Rabbi Judah the Prince, who maintained that
the law that the Sabbatical year remits debts at the present time is a
rabbinical enactment. Even though Hillel lived during the days of
the second Temple, Abayye is of the opinion that since the law of
the Jubilee year was not then observed, they did not consider the
law of the remission of debts as being biblically obligatory."[143]
Maimonides decides the law according to Abayye's opinion and says
that "the *prozbul* cannot be used at a time when the laws of the Sabbatical year are biblically obligatory."[144] Ravad, *ad locum,* however,
questions Rambam's unqualified statement. "This decision [of
Maimonides] is not at all certain, for this is only Abayye's opinion,
but Rabbah disagrees with him[145] and says that Hillel's *takkanah* is
based on the legal principle of *hefker bet din hefker.*[146] Therefore,
the *takkanah* is valid at all times."[147]

The Gemara attributes to Abayye yet another line of reasoning
in regard to the *prozbul.* "Abayye says that the *prozbul* is another
case of a rabbinic uprooting of a biblical law involving only *shev
ve'al ta'aseh,* 'mere refraining from action.' " This interpretation of
the legal basis of the *prozbul* is ingenious, to say the least, and even
Rashi's explanation of it is difficult to follow. He says, "The borrower merely refrains from fulfilling the *mizvah* to pay his debt, but
does not thereby uproot it [the *mizvah*] with his hands, and it is permissible to uproot an injunction of the Torah in this manner."[148]
There were even those who suggested that Hillel promulgated his
takkanah in anticipation of the destruction of the Temple and as
having validity only at that time. "But this is a very forced interpretation, for even though he might have known that the Temple
would be destroyed, it was not proper to promulgate a *takkanah*

for a time after the destruction of the Temple while the Temple was still functioning."[149]

And again we must ask, why did later generations seek to supply their own interpretations for a tradition when the reasoning supporting it, as found in the earliest versions of the tradition, was so clear and so authentic? The Sifre specifically states, "Hillel instituted the *prozbul mipne tikkun ha'olam*—for the welfare of society. He saw that the people refrained from lending money to one another as the Sabbatical year drew nearer, and thus violated the commandment, 'Beware that there be not a base thought in thy heart, saying: The seventh year, the year of release, is at hand; and thine eye be evil against thy needy brother and thou give him nought; and he cry unto the Lord against thee, and it be sin in thee' [Deut. 15:9]. Therefore he instituted the *prozbul*."[150] In this instance the biblical law which was circumvented was in itself obviously motivated by the high ethical principle of giving one's fellow man a chance to start anew and not to be crushed forever by a debt which necessity had forced him to assume. But the facts of life indicated that *this highly ethically motivated law harmed the very ones it was intended to help.* Hence Hillel decided that it was preferable to circumvent by a *takkanah* the law of the remission of debts rather than encourage the violation of the ethical injunction requiring one to come to the assistance of his fellow man. In this he was true to his fundamental understanding of the Torah. It was he who had said that the essence of the Torah is contained in the commandment, "Do not do unto others what you would not have others do unto you."[151] Hence, when he saw that in the changed times and conditions of his day, the observance of the ethically motivated biblical law would result in the violation of the biblical ethic, he did not hesitate to set the ethical above the legal.

Saving Life—Violating the Sabbath

The First Book of Maccabees reports that in the early stages of the Judean revolt against the Syrians, the pious rebels "did not defend themselves nor did they hurl a stone against them, nor block up the

hiding places" when they were attacked on the Sabbath day, preferring to die in their "innocence" rather than profane the Sabbath.
And when they were attacked, "they, their wives, their children and
their cattle died, to the number of a thousand souls." The narrative
goes on to say that "when Mattathias and his friends heard this,
they mourned greatly over them, each one saying to the other, 'If
all of us do as our brothers have done, and do not fight against the
heathen for our lives and our laws, they will soon destroy us from
off the earth.' " They then made the following decision: "If any
man attack us in battle on the Sabbath day, let us oppose him, that
we may not all die as our brothers did in the hiding places."[152]

We should note two significant aspects of this narrative. The
first is that those who offered their lives rather than violate the Sabbath assumed that the Torah requires them to do so, presumably
because the Torah nowhere indicates the conditions under which its
Sabbath laws may be violated. Moreover, the Torah prescribes
capital punishment for the violation of the Sabbath.[153] Hence, the
refusal to save one's life by violating the Sabbath is an altogether
logical position, for one's life is forfeit anyhow if he does violate it.

Moreover, Mattathias and his friends did not validate their
decision to fight back on the Sabbath by referring to Scripture,[154]
but by appealing to an unimpeachable common-sense argument.
They simply refused to believe that Scripture enjoined them to act
in a manner that could result in the physical extermination of the
nation. The action of Mattathias and his friends therefore established the principle that in war one may violate the Sabbath when
his life is in present and overt danger.[155] But the Mishnah goes far
beyond that, and states that "whenever there is even only *doubt*
whether life is in danger, it overrides the Sabbath."[156]

While Mattathias and his followers apparently sought no biblical sanction for their decision to violate the Sabbath, later generations did seek such sanction. Was it possible to assume that so
important a matter as permitting the violation of the Sabbath in even
a doubtful situation should not somehow be at least indicated in the
Torah? The *Mekhilta* relates[157] that "Rabbi Yishmael, Rabbi Akiba,

Rabbi Elazar ben Azariah, and others were once walking together when the question was asked, Whence do we derive the right to violate the Sabbath in order to save a human life?" Note that the question is not whether it is or is not permissible to violate the Sabbath in such a situation. The right is assumed. The discussion is devoted merely to finding biblical warrant for what was obviously the universal practice. Rabbi Yishmael, Rabbi Elazar, and Rabbi Akiba all offer biblical *laws* upon which, by the principle of *kal vaḥomer,* they base their biblical validation of the practice. Rabbi Yose Hagalili bases it upon the apparently superfluous *akh* (Exod. 31:13), which is taken to imply that there are occasions when you may violate the Sabbath, and those are presumably when life is in danger. Rabbi Simeon ben Menasya bases it upon the word *lakhem* "to you" (ibid., v. 14), taking it to indicate that "the Sabbath *mesurah*—is placed in *your* charge—and not you in the charge of the Sabbath." Rabbi Nathan validates the practice by interpreting the statement "The children of Israel shall observe the Sabbath" (ibid., v. 16) to imply "you violate one Sabbath on his (that is, the endangered person's) account, so that he may then observe many Sabbaths."

One cannot with certainty decide whether this passage in the *Mekhilta* deals only with cases where the danger to life is certain, or whether it also includes the doubtful cases. But the Rabbis were very specific in their opinion that "even in doubtful cases one may violate the Sabbath . . . even when two Sabbaths are involved, as, for example, when the doctors adjudged the sick man to require eight days of the kind of care which involves the violation of the Sabbath, and that medical decision was rendered on the Sabbath. One is not to say 'Let us wait till after dark so that we violate only one Sabbath for him' . . . nor are these violations to be performed by gentiles . . . but by distinguished Israelites . . . and one need not ask a court's permission."[158] Hence they say: "from these passages we can deduce permission to violate the Sabbath in cases of certain danger. But whence do we derive the right to do so in doubtful cases?"[159]

In regard to all these suggested biblical verses, Rabba said, "All of them can be successfully challenged, except that of Samuel, who said, 'Had I been there I would have said my suggestion is better than yours, namely, the biblical verse 'which if a man do them he shall live by them' (Lev. 18:5); 'live, and not die by them.' "[160] Rashi there comments that "one is expected to perform the commandments only when he is *sure* he shall live by them, and not when in the performance of them he *risks* the possibility of losing his life. Therefore we may violate the Sabbath in cases of *safek* [uncertainty]." Maimonides' statement is most instructive. "It is forbidden to delay violating the Sabbath for a sick person whose life is in danger, for it says, 'which if a man do them he shall live by them' and not die by them. We are thus taught that the commandments of the Torah are not intended to inflict punishment upon mankind but to bestow mercy, loving-kindness, and peace. And as for the *apikorsim,* who say that this is a violation of the Sabbath and is forbidden, in regard to them Scripture says, 'I have given them laws which are not good, and commandments by which they cannot live' " (Ezek. 20:25).[161]

Obviously, at the time the Mishnah was edited, it was the accepted practice to violate the Sabbath to save a human life even when death was not the certain alternative. Apparently, when that radical practice was instituted it was not done on the basis of any specific biblical verse, for then a clear tradition on the subject would have existed.

One may ask why men like Hillel or Yoḥanan ben Zakkai did not make the suggestion later made by Rabba of Babylonia. We do not know the answer to such a question. History records numberless cases where geniuses overlooked simple answers to difficult questions, answers which, when later suggested by lesser men, strike one as so obvious that one is astounded that no one thought of them before. In such instances, we may say with Rabbi Judah the Prince, *"Makom hiniḥu lanu avotenu lehitgader bo,"*[162] our ancestors, wittingly or unwittingly, did not make all the discoveries and answer all the questions. They thus made it possible for their descendants to distinguish themselves by making significant contributions.

But how did the earlier generations justify the violation of the

Sabbath when life was not overtly in danger? What seems to have happened is that by the time of Hillel, or perhaps even earlier, the biblically rooted value concept of the sanctity of human life was thoroughly a part of the thought pattern of Jewish life. Thus it was taken for granted that everyone would understand that the permission to violate the Sabbath, even when it was doubtful whether life was at stake, was, in the words of Maharsha, "not uprooting the the Torah but fulfilling it, for it is a tree of life."

Inviolable Laws

Having arrived at the conclusion that one may violate a biblical law in order to preserve life, even when it is questionable whether life is indeed at stake, we must now ask whether there are any laws which one is *obliged* to obey even when life is clearly endangered thereby. The Talmud records that it was decided, in the attic of Bet Nitzah, that in times of religious persecution a Jew must not violate even the least of the laws and customs of his people at the behest of the persecutor, even if refusal may cost him his life.[163] At other times, however, if he thereby saves his life, he may violate all the laws except three—the laws against murder, adultery, and idol worship.[164] Rather than violate any of these, he is expected to choose martyrdom. Rabbi Yishmael is quoted as being of the opinion that if one is accosted in private and his life threatened, he may even worship an idol in order to save himself, because it says that "if a man do them he shall live by them." In the Tosefta, a biblical proof-text is provided to validate the injunction that in times of religious persecution one must "sanctify God's name" and not violate even the least of the *mizvot*. But no proof-texts are offered in the Tosefta to support the statement that one must at all times be ready to accept martyrdom rather than commit murder or adultery or worship an idol. But since biblical sanction was found for the principle that the law is to be violated when life is at stake, the Rabbis felt the need to provide biblical authority for the exceptions to this principle. That one should accept martyrdom rather than worship an idol was based by Rabbi Eliezer on the biblical commandment to love God "with all your soul" (Deut. 6:5). This he interpreted to mean that one is to "love Him even if it involves His taking your soul." That one is to accept martyrdom rather than commit adultery was based by Rabbi on the biblical verse (Deut. 22:26) which compares the raping of a betrothed woman to murder.

But the Talmud then asks: How do we know that one is not allowed to murder an innocent human being in order to save one's own life? The answer is again given not by a Tanna but by the Babylonian Amora Rabba, who maintains that this is a matter of *svara,* of logic. When asked whether one may kill an innocent man in order to save one's own life, he answered, "No! Who is there who can say that your blood is redder [more precious] than his?" Rabba's answer is, of course, far from being a matter of self-evident logic. More precious to whom? Certainly one's life is more precious to oneself than the life of any other man. Rabba's answer is logical only if we assume that a human being has no more right to dispose of his own life than the life of any other human being because all of us belong to God, and in His sight we are equally precious. This concept, in turn, derives from the account of the creation of Adam as found in the first chapter of Genesis and as interpreted by the Rabbis.[165] God created only one man so that every single individual is to be evaluated as *'olam maleh,* the whole of mankind, and each one can, and indeed must, assume and act as if the world were created for his sake. Thus again we note the dependence of the *halakhah* on a biblically rooted ethical concept rather than upon any specific legal passage.

Ethical Validation of Rabbinic Legislation

The verse "And ye shall do that which is good and right in the eyes of the Lord" (Deut. 6:18) occasionally serves as the biblical sanction for rabbinic legislation. "Rav Yehuda said in the name of Rav: One who owns land separating the properties of brothers or partners and this land (according to Rashi) is about to be confiscated by the government, and he does not offer to sell it to the brothers or partners, he is considered to be *hazifa*—impudent or indecent. But one cannot legally compel him to sell it to them." Rav Nahman maintains that he can be legally compelled to sell it to them. If, however, the neighbors are not brothers or partners, then this law, which is known as the *dina d'var mizra,* does not apply. In Nahardea they taught that even though the neighbors were not brothers or partners the law nevertheless can be applied, and he can be compelled to sell to the neighbors because Scripture commands, "And ye shall do that which is right and good in the eyes of the Lord" (Deut. 6:18).[166]

Thus the Rabbis also decreed that even though a borrower whose land had been assigned by the court to the lender in payment of a debt, has no legal right to demand the land back at some future time when he has the funds available to repay his debt, the lender must nevertheless return the land because it is written, "And ye shall do that which is right and good . . ."[167]

The rabbinic passage involving this verse, which is most significant for our purposes, is found in the Tosefta and is concerned with what, on the face of it, seems to be a very minor problem. The Tosefta states that "when the priest was to draw additional funds for the purchase of the daily sacrifices, he was to be searched before he entered and when he left the room where the money was kept.[168] This was to be done in conformity with the injunction 'and ye shall be innocent [clear] in the eyes of God and man' (Num. 32:22). Others add, also in conformity with the commandment 'and ye shall do that which is *yashar,* right, and *tov,* good, in the eyes of the Lord' (Deut. 6:18). Rabbi Akiba interprets the verse to mean 'that which is *tov,* good, in the eyes of the Lord and *yashar,* right, in the eyes of man.' Rabbi Yishmael says, 'that which is right [also][169] in the eyes of God.' Others add that it is to be done also in conformity to the statement 'and find grace and good favor in the eyes of God and man' (Prov. 3:4). The sages decided to accept Rabbi Yishmael's opinion, since it is written, 'if you will do that which is *yashar,* right, in the eyes of God' (Deut. 21:9),[170] and the word *tov* does not occur here at all. Furthermore, it is written, 'The Lord God knows, and Israel he shall know' (Josh. 22:22)."[171]

On the face of it, one cannot but wonder why the Rabbis quoted so many verses to determine whether or not a man is to be searched in order to place him above suspicion. Important as that may be, there is obviously much more involved. Professor Saul Lieberman comments on this passage as follows:[172]

Let us first explain the difference between Rabbi Akiba and Rabbi Yishmael. The Sifre Reah edited by Rabbi Louis Finkelstein reads (p. 145, par. 79): "If you will do *hatov,* that which is good, *vehayashar,* and right, in the sight of the Lord your God (Deut. 12:28); that which is good in the eyes of Heaven and right in the eyes of man." Thus Rabbi Akiba. Rabbi Yishmael says, that which is right in the eyes of Heaven and good in the eyes of man, for thus it is written (Prov. 3:4), "So you will find favor and good repute in the sight of God and man." It appears then that the point of their differences in our case is whether one is to search a trustworthy individual when he enters to take money from the Temple treasury. Rabbi Akiba is of the opinion that while man must be innocent also in the eyes of Israel and must try to be above suspicion, one does not insult an individual by frisking him, because the act does not appear *yashar* right in the eyes of man. Rabbi Akiba finds support in Deut. 6:18, where the word *yashar* (right) precedes *tov* (good) which is placed near "the eyes of God," and later in Deut. 12:28, the word precedes *yashar* which is placed near "the eyes of God." (Since all agree that the Torah uses the two words *tov* and *yashar* because it has both man and God in mind, and since the order of the two words in relation to "the eyes of God" is reversed, we conclude that the act must be "good and right" in the eyes of both man and God.) Our Mishnah, which does not mention frisking, is in accordance with the opinion of Rabbi Akiba. But Rabbi Yishmael is of the opinion that what is right in the eyes of Heaven, is (or should also be) good in the eyes of man. . . . And it is thus explained in the Sifre, par. 96 (on Deut. 13:19) "To do that which is right in the eyes of the Lord your God." [173] This is what Rabbi Yishmael referred to when he said "what is right in eyes of God," for in this instance the word *tov (good)* is not found. Moreover, carrying out the law in regard to the condemned city is not good in the eyes of man, since one destroys the possessions of her righteous inhabitants also. However, all that is right in the eyes of Heaven will in the end be right also in the eyes of men. . . . Hence one frisks the priest and does not mind embarrassing him, because one must guard Temple property, for this is right in the eyes of Heaven.

Professor Lieberman explained the Tosefta's quoting of Deut. 21:9, dealing with the *egla arufa* to support Rabbi Yishmael's position as follows: In *Tanḥuma* on *Mishpatim,* paragraph 7, there is a list of laws whose validity our *yeẓer hara,* our evil inclination, questions, because we have no satisfactory rationale for them. Among them is the *egla arufa.* But since in regard to this law the Bible goes out of its way to state that we should do that which is right in the eyes of God, Rabbi Yishmael deduces from it that it is of no consequence whether a law appears right to us or not. Since it is right in the eyes of God, it should be good in our eyes also. We thus have two instances in which Scripture enjoins upon us to do that which is right in the eyes of God even though it may not appear right in the eyes of man.

It may appear strange that Rabbi Yishmael, who is usually portrayed as being more inclined to the human and rational interpretation of the text than Rabbi Akiba,[174] should in this instance appear more insistent on the letter of the text, and deduce from it that human feelings or opinions should not be taken into consideration when one is called upon to do that which is "right in the eyes of God." But this is strange only if we insist on forcing a logically consistent straitjacket upon the thought of any one of the Rabbis. While all of them undoubtedly were greatly concerned with preserving a logical consistency in their legal thinking and enactments, none of them apparently ever remained so bound to the principle of logical consistency as to exclude the intrusion of the ethical principle which stubbornly resists subordination to the purely legal or logical consideration. And so it lifts one's spirit to note that even in so minor a matter as the treatment of the priest on an occasion when he may come under suspicion, it is Rabbi Akiba, usually pictured as the legalist par excellence, who tempers the law by the non-legal consideration of human dignity, and that even laws which are *right* in the eyes of God" must be executed in a manner that will show them to be *good* also in the eyes of man.

We shall note briefly two more non-legal biblical passages to which the Rabbis on occasion refer in order to validate their legal rulings.

The verse "That thou mayest walk in the way of good men, and keep the paths of the righteous" (Prov. 2:20) was obviously not intended to serve as a legal maxim. Yet Rav based a decision upon it. The Talmud relates[175] that wine caskets belonging to Rabbah Bar Bar Ḥana were broken while being handled by porters. The text is not clear whether it was in any way due to their negligence, but Rashi thus interprets it. Whereupon Rabbah took possession of their clothing. They complained to Rav and he ordered Rabbah to return it to them. Whereupon he said, "Is this the law?" And Rav answered, "Indeed it is, for does it not say, 'Walk in the way of good men'?" Rabbah Bar Bar Ḥana thereupon returned the clothing. The porters then asked for pay, saying, "We have worked all day. We are hungry and have nothing." Rav ordered that they be paid. Again Rabbah Bar Bar Ḥana asked, "Is this the law?" And again Rav answered, "Indeed it is, for does it not say 'And keep the ways of the righteous'?" [176]

Now by all definitions of law and legal procedure, what Rav did was illegal. If there ever was a clear-cut case of "uprooting" a law of the Bible this was it, for the Bible specifically states, "Neither shalt thou favor a poor man in his cause" (Exod. 23:3). Rav does not defend his action by appealing to any legal dictum, such as *hefker bet din hefker.* Instead he quotes an ethical maxim from Proverbs and insists that he is following the law. And his action remains unchallenged in the Talmud.

Rav Joseph interpreted the verse ". . . and shalt show them the way wherein they must walk, and the work they must do." (Exod. 18:20) as follows:[177] " ' And thou shalt show them,' refers to their house of life;[178] 'the way' refers to deeds of loving-kindness; 'they shall walk' refers to visiting the sick; 'wherein' refers to burying the dead; 'and the work' refers to *lifnim mishurat hadin,* to acts beyond the requirements of the law."

The word beyond, which is usually used to translate the Hebrew *lifnim,* misses what I believe to be the basic nuance of the Hebrew. *Beyond* suggests spatial extension, as in the statement "He went beyond the goal he had set for himself." The goal was first reached and then he went beyond it. In that sense, "beyond the requirements of the law" implies that one does all that the law *requires* of him *and then some more. Beyond* may also mean "completely outside the confines" or "altogether not within the scope of," as in the statement "Beyond the call of duty." But the Hebrew word *lifnim* connotes not something "beyond" or "outside" the boundary of the law, but something very much "within." "Within" what? I believe it refers not to that which is within the boundary or realm of applicability of the law, but rather to that which is within the *intent* of the law. It means that you do something which no specific law requires, and which may even be contrary to a specific law, but which the Law, taken as a whole, does value highly. Thus when Rabba permits scholars to do something *delo kehilkhata,* something which was in violation of a specific law, Rashi explains *delo kehilkhata* there to mean *lifnim mishurat hadin.*[179] Now an action which is designated as exemplifying *lifnim mishurat hadin* is always considered to be a highly commendable action, even when, as in this instance, it violates a specific law. It seems reasonable, therefore, to say that *lifnim* here means that one enters, as it were, into the "inwards" of the Law. One acts at times in accordance with the ultimate moral and ethical purpose of the whole legal structure, and not in accordance with any specific law.

In the prayer that follows the recitation of Genesis 22 in the daily morning service, we supplicate the Lord *"vetikanes eetanu,*[180] enter with us, *lifnim mishurat dinekha,* within the *shura* [boundary] of Thy law—and deal with us, O Lord our God, in accordance with the attribute of loving-kindness and of mercy." It is as if at the core, so to speak, there is mercy and there is a *shura,* a boundary, between the realm of *ḥesed* and the realm of *din,* so that to enter *lifnim mishurat hadin* is to enter into the central core of mercy.[181]

I find support for this interpretation of *lifnim mishurat hadin* in the manner in which this phrase was used in the otherwise enigmatic statement attributed to Rabbi Yoḥanan that "Jerusalem was destroyed because *he'emidu dineyhem,* they based their laws, or rather their judicial decisions, on *din Torah,* the law as found in the Torah, and did not judge *lifnim mishurat hadin.*"[182] The commentators have nothing to say about this statement. Another passage states that the destruction of the stores of Bet Hino preceded by three years the destruction of Jerusalem "because *he'emidu dvareyhem,* they based their actions *al divre Torah,* on the biblical text."[183] Rashi here explains that "they found biblical support to permit what the Rabbis had forbidden." The inference drawn from the first passage is that actions based upon the biblical text alone were too harsh. The inference drawn from the second passage is that actions based upon the biblical text alone were lenient and permissive. In either case, one is not to be guided exclusively or even primarily by the patent, literal meaning of the text. One must understand its inner spirit, and this is what the rabbinic interpretation of the biblical text achieves, or certainly seeks to achieve, whether that interpretation appears to be harsher or more lenient than the literal text.

The question was raised whether laws enacted on the basis of these non-legal verses have the status of *midrabbanan*—laws promulgated by the Rabbis, or *mide'orayta*—laws specifically enjoined in the Torah.[184] There are, as was to be expected, conflicting opinions. This question is not generally raised in regard to laws which are based on rabbinic interpretations of legal passages of the Torah, and which by and large are considered to be *mide'orayta.*[185] Nor is it raised in order to establish the measure of their enforceability, or of the consequences resulting from their violation. We know that the Rabbis were inclined to be more exacting in regard to some of their enactments than they were in regard to some biblical laws.[186]

It seems to me that in this instance what is involved is the question of whether a rabbinic enactment based upon an ethical rather than a legal biblical injunction can ever be given the status of *mide'orayta* on any basis other than that of the all-comprehending biblical commandment, "You must not deviate from the verdict that they announce to you, either to the right or to the left" (Deut. 17:11). The "they" is broadly interpreted to include the Rabbis. The same question can be asked about rabbinic enactments that are validated by appeals to such general ethical principles as *tikkun ha'olam* and *mipne darkhai shalom*. The fact of the matter is, however, that the Rabbis treated the laws they validated on the basis of ethical concepts with the same meticulous attention they gave to any biblical law or to any of their enactments which they based on their interpretation of the legal passages of the Bible.[187]

Recapitulation and Proposal

This inquiry started with a presentation of the problem raised by the traditional rabbinic interpretation of Deuteronomy 24:1, which reserves to the husband the exclusive right to grant his wife a *get*. We pointed out the hardships which this interpretation of the biblical verse inflicts upon the wife and the burden it has imposed on the consciences of the most ardent devotees of the *halakhah* in all ages and under all circumstances, but particularly in our day and in a free democratic society. We took note of the various rabbinic enactments whereby the hardships of this law were to a considerable degree circumvented but not entirely removed, and the suggestions that have been made in the last century or so for the elimination of this residue of a universally acknowledged inequity. We pointed out that the suggestions thus far made have been unacceptable to some for halakhic reasons and to others for psychological and other reasons. We then investigated some aspects of the manner in which the great builders of the *halakhah* approached the biblical text, and the conditions under which their interpretations of it obviously varied from its literal meaning. We pointed particularly to the role that ethical considerations played in determining their interpretations.

We pointed out that the tension between the halakhic and the ethical components in Judaism is greatest for those who believe profoundly that both components are equally indispensable to the creative existence of the Jewish people.

The confrontations between these two components do not occur in some abstract, amorphous, nondescript arena, but in specific situations involving a specific *halakhah* and a specific ethical concept. The solution which is sought is one that would satisfy what are believed to be the complete requirements of both the *halakhah* and the ethical concept. But in many instances such happy solutions are not readily available.

These confrontations almost always constitute a dilemma, for the solutions suggested appear *at the time* to be "choices between equally unsatisfactory alternatives" in that they do not satisfy completely what appear to be the logical requirements of either the *halakhah* or the ethical concept. But it is of the essence of the wisdom which inheres in our tradition that it has either consciously or subconsciously resisted the stubborn efforts of reason to force it into the straitjacket of a syllogism. Neither our theology nor our *halakhah,* in their great creative eras, have been unswervingly subjected to the inhuman demands of an inexorable logic.[188] The still small voice of the ethical value was as persistent and, by and large, as persuasive as that of the more strident voice of the logic of the law.

The method adopted by the Rabbis, as presented in the foregoing pages, should guide us in our solution to the specific problem at the center of this inquiry. They never explicitly annulled a law which they believed to be based upon a biblical injunction. They did, however, feel free to determine the literal meaning of the injunction and to establish the conditions under which it is to be applied, circumvented, or suspended.

Hence the millennia-old practice of having the husband order the writing and issuance of the *get* should not be annulled. Every effort should be made to implement it.[189] But when for one good reason or another, all efforts to implement it fail, and the failure involves an obvious injustice to one of the parties, in this case almost always the woman, provision should be made for the circumvention or suspension of the law. Such provision can, we believe, be made altogether within the spirit and practice of the *halakhah,* and thus without in any way impairing its essential structural integrity and stability. There are ample rabbinic legal maxims and practices which, with a very *minimum of extrapolation,* can furnish a valid halakhic basis for such circumvention or suspension of the present traditional practice. As has already been pointed out, the most comprehensive legal maxim is the proposition that "every Jewish marriage, to be valid, must accord with the regulations decreed by the Rabbis."[190] Intimately allied to this maxim is the principle of *tnai bet din* or *lev bet din matne.*[191] These maxims state that there are certain provisions which are assumed by the court to be part of certain agreements, whether they are or are not specifically included in the written document or the verbal agreement. In accordance with these legal maxims, the Rabbis list a number of rights to which the wife is entitled whether they are or are not specifically included in the marriage contract.[192]

Thus, a reasonably valid extrapolation of the principle of *Kofin oto* could also be applied.[193] As we previously noted, the rabbinic rationale for the validation of a *get* given under duress is the assumption that in reality every Jew wants not only "to obey the words of the wise," but above all "to do that which is good and upright in the sight of the Lord" (Deut. 6:18). Though conditions beyond our control make it impossible for us in the United States to force a man to give a *get,* these conditions do not absolve him from his obligation "to do that which is good and upright in the eyes of the Lord." Furthermore, not only do the Rabbis sanction the use of compulsion in order that a man do the right thing, but they even explain the harsh biblical law regarding the "rebellious son" as a law in the interest of the son, for if he were permitted to live he would end up as a murderer.[194] In both instances the law acts in order to prevent one from doing evil, more particularly from doing harm to *another* human being. In both instances the action of the law is considered a *zkhut,* "to the advantage" of the person who is ostensibly being punished by the law.

Hence, in remarrying a civilly divorced woman whose husband refuses to give her a *get,* we can honestly maintain that we are invoking a reasonable extrapolation of the principle of *zakhin l'adam shelo befanov*[195]—one may act in behalf of another individual in his absence, and therefore presumably without his knowledge, and in this case even in opposition to his wish, if the action is intended to be of benefit to him. In the instance of remarrying a woman when the husband is unjustifiably refusing to grant her a *get,* we are acting in the best spiritual and ethical interests of the husband, even as we do when we compel him to give a *get* against his will, because we are preventing him from becoming the cause of another human being's misery.

Those who believe, on the one hand, that Jewish life devoid of an authoritative normative *halakhah* will become hopelessly chaotic and disintegrate, and, on the other hand, that a *halakhah* which continues to defy the ethical imperatives integral to the Jewish tradition will not be able to hold the loyalty of the Jewish people, must strive ceaselessly to halakhically define an area, *limited as it may be,* within which it will dispense with the initiative or even the participation of the husband in granting a *get.*

The fixing of such a "limited area" within which the traditional requirements for a *get* would not be abolished but only relaxed accords with the practice of the great builders of the Biblical-Rabbinic tradition, who tirelessly sought to concretize in the *halakhah* the ethical principles enunciated in the Torah. It would demonstrate anew that the Biblical-Rabbinic tradition has not reached a dead end, but has within it the principles of its own continued growth, and that it is indeed "the unique quality of Judaism that it is fundamentally a system of ethics, which includes ritual law and civil law, as part of the ethical life."[196]

4.

SOME AFFINITIES BETWEEN THE JEWISH AND THE AMERICAN HISTORICAL EXPERIENCE

IN PREPARATION FOR, AS well as during, the Bicentennial year of the American Declaration of Independence, not only Americans, but freedom-loving people everywhere, will naturally want to heed the admonition to "remember the days of old," and to "consider the years of ages past" (Deut. 32:7). For there is hardly a person living today whose life has not been beneficently affected by the course of events initiated in Philadelphia on July 4, 1776, or who will not eventually be so affected by them. None have been greater beneficiaries of those events than the Jews, and none are more gratefully conscious of their indebtedness.

No Jew participated in the convention in Philadelphia in 1776. But the first chapter of Genesis was there and played a determinative role in the deliberations. The proposition that all men are created equal was in 1776 a self-evident truth, not only to those who believed in the divine authorship of the first chapter of Genesis. Well-nigh everyone accepted as a fact the biblical account that all men had the same original progenitor. The social import, if not the theo-

219

logical grounding, of the rabbinic statement that God created only one man so that no one should claim biological superiority over another was almost universally acknowledged. Hence, neither the signers of the Declaration nor the authors of the Constitution viewed slavery as ethically justifiable. There is ample evidence that they felt profoundly uneasy and deeply apologetic about it.

Oscar Handlin points out that men began to think of slavery as being ethically right only after scientists, following the example of Linnaeus, started to classify men into lower and higher races in accordance with "facial angles," "cranial index," and the like. The defenders of slavery obviously readily seized upon these pseudo-scientific speculations in support of their cause. But until Darwin's *Origin of Species,* "the Biblical account of a single creation with all men equally the descendants of Adam prejudged the weight that could be given to racial differences. An occasional venturesome, and eccentric thinker like Lord Kames speculated on the possibility of polygenesis, that is, of a number of acts of creation from which were derived the varieties of mankind. But this notion was so clearly contrary to revelation as to carry no weight."[1]

And the Book of Exodus was present in Philadelphia in 1776, to give unimpeachable testimony that "revolt against tyrants was obedience to God."

Scores of volumes have been devoted to the historical, philosophical and religious antecedents of the Declaration. I shall not presume to add to what has already been said so well. I intend to limit my remarks to a number of what to me are strikingly interesting historical affinities between the American people, whom Abraham Lincoln once called the "almost chosen people," [2] and the people regarding whom God said, "You are My witnesses, My servant whom I have chosen." (Isaiah 43:10)

Neither the American people nor the Jewish people are entirely "natural" nations. Neither of them came into being as self-conscious nations primarily because the individuals who constituted them had a common ancestry, or a common language, or occupied a contiguous territory segregated from their neighbors by natural barriers of mountains or bodies of water, or a common religion, or because they were subjected to the rule of a foreign conqueror or a native tyrant. The inhabitants of the thirteen colonies in 1776 had no common national ancestry nor a common religion. Vast distances and natural impediments separated them from one another. Most of the colonies governed territories far more extensive than most European states. Each colony viewed itself as an independent political unit and took great pride in its institutions and achievements. There was every reason to doubt the feasibility of their ever coalescing into one effective political unit. It required almost a century, and a civil war of unprecedented proportions, before political unity seemed permanently assured. The process of coalescing into one people is as yet far from complete. In much the same way, tribal loyalties and rivalries impeded the process inaugurated by Moses to mold the emancipated slaves into a self-conscious, united people. Centuries passed before that process reached a state where its success was reasonably assured. In both instances, the beginning of the self-conscious process of nation-building is associated with an unsurpassed moment of spiritual exaltation, which found embodiment in treasured and revered written documents. These documents formulate for each people the larger ultimate goals of its national existence and indicate the steps whereby these goals may hopefully be attained. These documents, to me, are the record of divinely inspired communications[3] vouchsafed to the founders of both nations at the beginning of their national careers. Even as the Ten Commandments constitute a divine communication granted to the whole people of Israel at the beginning of its history in the Sinai desert, so do I believe that the opening paragraphs of the Declaration of Independence constitute a divine communication granted to the American people through their representatives who were gathered in Independence Hall on that destiny-laden day in July of 1776.

It is of the essence of a divine communication that those who are its first recipients cannot possibly fully comprehend its spiritual and intellectual implications, for they are infinite in number and scope. At first such a communication appears to many to be compounded of nothing but grandiloquent, empty generalities. As a matter of fact, that is what was said about the Declaration. But those whom a divine communication touches, however so lightly, are never quite the same again. It somehow implants itself within the deepest layers of their spiritual being and challenges them forever after to implement its directives.

Robert Frost formulated this truth perfectly in the unpretentious but profoundly insightful lines spoken by an elderly widow of the Civil War as she reminisces about the proposition that all men are created equal.

> That's a hard mystery of Jefferson's.
> What did he mean? Of course the easy way
> Is to decide it simply isn't true.
> It may not be. I heard a fellow say so.
> But never mind, the Welshman got it planted
> Where it will trouble us a thousand years.
> Each age will have to reconsider it.[4]

During some forty years of wandering in the wilderness, the Israelites are instructed by Moses in a law whose avowed purpose it is to embed the "glowing generalities" communicated to them at Sinai into a pattern of daily behavior for the individual Jew and the people as a whole that would hopefully make them in fact God's witnesses upon this earth. Thus also, between May 14 and September 17 of the year 1787, the American people, through their appointed representatives who were gathered in Philadelphia, were involved in what at many moments appeared to be a pre-doomed effort to erect the legal framework that would give bone and muscle to the vision of government as the guardian of every man's unalienable right to life, liberty, and the pursuit of happiness. Regarding these men, Morison and Commager wrote: "No fair minded person can read their debates without wonder that a country of four million people could produce men of such intellect, common sense, and enlightened vision."[5]

At one of the critical moments during the deliberations of the

Constitutional Convention, when it seemed that the differences were irreconcilable and that the effort to create the new nation would be abandoned, Benjamin Franklin, the universally revered elder statesman, who was somewhat of a skeptic, as we all know, suggested that henceforth the sessions should be opened with prayer. For he said: "If a sparrow can not fall without God's knowledge how can an empire rise without His aid?" That this was not just a momentary reaction, but a deep conviction on his part, is reflected in the fact that after the convention concluded its arduous task, Franklin, "while expressing his disapproval of many provisions in the document, declared his faith in divine guidance in the matter. Standing then within the shadow of death, he wrote of the convention's achievements: 'I can hardly conceive a transaction of such momentous importance to the welfare of millions now existing and to exist in the posterity of a great nation, should be suffered to pass without being in some degree influenced, guided and governed by that omnipotent, omnipresent, and beneficent Ruler, in whom all inferior spirits live and move and have their being.' "[6]

The legally formulated steps toward the implementation of the divine communication into a pattern of mundane reality were in both instances initially so successful that it was almost inevitable that in both nations there should develop the conviction that the larger purposes which they had accepted as the goals of their national existence had been fully articulated in their legal systems. In Israel reverence for the majestically structured, ethically impregnated *Halakhah* seemed to portend the complete eclipse of the *Aggadah* and in America reverence for the successfully functioning Constitution came more and more not only to overshadow, but altogether to supersede, the Declaration in the minds and hearts of many Americans.

But legal patterns for human behavior, by the very fact of their being ultimately subject to the limitations of the finite, mundane creatures for whom they are intended, can never achieve the complete embodiment of ultimate divinely communicated goals. They can at best only gradually progress in the direction of their more complete concretization. Hence the *Aggadah* persisted in confronting the *Halakhah,* even as the Declaration always had its staunch proponents over against the Constitution. When in either of the two nations the confrontation between the two revered sources of its spiritual life was sharply articulated, that nation was passing through a crisis of major significance, the outcome of which would decide whether the nation would spiritually retrogress or progress.

It is these confrontations between *Aggadah* and *Halakhah,* Declaration and Constitution, that bestow a cosmic dimension upon the historical experiences of the American and Jewish peoples, for it is the outcome of these confrontations that determine whether Lincoln was right when he saw the America of his day as "the last great hope of mankind," and whether the Almighty chose wisely when He chose Israel to be an *Or lagoyim,* "a light unto the nations." For me, therefore, the most fascinating and moving aspect of the first two hundred years of American history is the story of American constitutional law, which records the herculean intellectual and spiritual efforts of a determined minority to make the Declaration the soul, as it were, of the Constitution, animating the least of its provisions even as the soul is said to animate every cell of the body. And the most engrossing aspect of Jewish history is the history of the *Halakhah,* which records the herculean intellectual and spiritual efforts of a determined minority to make the quenching of one's thirst, the use of one's tongue, the production and distribution of the tangible goods of this world, and the least of the contacts between a man and his fellow, the embodiment of the awareness that we are ever in God's presence and that He looks to us to be His witnesses before men.

Neither the American nor the Jewish people can ever be at complete peace with itself, for in neither case has the ideal always triumphed, nor can it ever win a final victory. But neither people, even if it would want to, can reject the ideal in order to find peace within itself. Both know in the deepest recesses of their being that such rejection is for them an invitation not only to spiritual death, but ultimately also to physical death as a people.

One of the best known and most beloved theological works in Jewish literature, the *Kuzari*—written by the poet-philosopher Yehuda Halevi in the twelfth century—consists of a dialogue between the King of the Khazars, who is searching for the true religion, and a Rabbi who succeeds in converting him and his people to Judaism. The first question addressed by the King to the Rabbi is, "What do you believe?" To which the Rabbi replies, "I believe in the God of Abraham, Isaac, and Jacob, who led the children of Israel out of Egypt with signs and miracles." The King, who had previously questioned a Christian and a Moslem philosopher, is surprised by this answer, and says: "Should you not, O Jew, have said that you believe in the creator of the world, its governor and guide, and in Him who created and keeps you, etc.?" To which the Rabbi responds, "What you have just said is *religion based on speculation and system,* the research of thought, open to many *doubts.* I answered you the way Moses spoke to Pharaoh when he told him 'The God of the Hebrews sent me to you, the God of Abraham, Isaac, and Jacob.' He did not say the God of heaven and earth, nor 'My creator and thine sent me.' I answered you as was fitting and is fitting for the whole of Israel, who *knew* these things, first from *personal experience,* and afterwards through uninterrupted tradition, which is equal to the former."[7]

What is it that the Jews had known "first from personal experience and afterwards through uninterrupted tradition?" They knew that they had been slaves in Egypt and had been emancipated. They knew that Jewish tradition contains not a single historical or legendary reference to anything which the enslaved Israelites had done in order to emancipate themselves. The tradition insists that the emancipation was achieved not by the action of any angelic or human messenger but only by that of God alone.

How are we to understand the tradition's unequivocal denial of any active role to the Israelites in the drama of their liberation? Are we to assume that our ancestors actually did play a significant role, but that later generations, out of a sense of piety or humility, purposefully suppressed all memory of it? That is hardly likely. It would run counter to all natural human inclinations. What happened was that the tradition, being honest, took cognizance of, and recorded, the fact that the enslaved Israelites had to all intents and purposes done nothing, or almost nothing, for their liberation. They knew of no enslaved population that had ever before been emancipated either through its own action or in any other way. Hence the Israelites in Egypt had no reason to assume that what had never happened to any other people could happen to them. They had no incentive to act in their own behalf. How then were they emancipated? The tradition records that the fabric of the political and social order which held the Israelites in bondage was brought to the brink of disaster by a series of unprecedented catastrophes. All the Egyptians, from "Pharaoh that sat on his throne, to the captive that was in the dungeon," were physically affected and spiritually bewildered. The enslaved Israelites were in a position to take advantage of this confusion because they had a leader who had spoken to them of freedom. He had prepared them for just such a moment. The slaves, then, simply walked out on their masters, who had been so weakened and distracted that they had neither the presence of mind nor the strength to prevent their departure. To whom but to God could the Israelites, standing in safety on the eastern shore of the Sea of Reeds, attribute the events that had brought them physical redemption?

For a substantial portion of the descendants of the enslaved Israelites, the emancipation from Egypt became for all time the absolute, irrefutable proof of the existence of God and His concern with those who are unjustly treated. They kept the memory of the event so vividly alive in their hearts and minds that no matter what happened to them in succeeding centuries, their faith never wavered.

Is there anything that has happened since Israel's emancipation from Egypt which is strikingly analogous to that extraordinary event? I venture to suggest that the abolition of slavery in the United States constitutes such a strikingly analogous event. There was never a serious threat to the institution of American slavery originating with the slaves themselves. Nor could the slaves be blamed for excessive docility. American slavery was more oppressive and efficient than any system of slavery heretofore practiced in Western society.

In his Cooper Union address on February 27, 1860, in replying to the accusation that Republicans were instigating slave insurrections, Lincoln said, "In the present state of things in the United States, I do not think a general or even a very extensive, slave insurrection is possible. The indispensable concert of action can not be attained. The slaves have no means of rapid communication, nor can incendiary free black or white, supply it."

Were the white men of America, then, by and large, or even an effective majority of them, in favor of giving freedom to the slaves!? Nothing in American history is more certain than the fact that by and large the American people were not ready for it. Lincoln judged the temper of the people better than did the abolitionists, who were badgering him to emancipate the slaves. In March of 1862 he had proposed a program for compensated emancipation, but Congress did not consider it of sufficient importance even to give it serious consideration. Five months later, as if to reassure the American people, Lincoln wrote to Horace Greeley, "My paramount object in this struggle *is* to save the Union, and *is not* either to save or to destroy slavery." But he made sure to add, "I have here stated my purpose according to my view of *official duty;* and I intend no modification of my oft-expressed *personal* wish that all men everywhere could be free" (Lincoln to Greeley, August 22, 1862). In his annual message to Congress on December 1, 1862, Lincoln again proposed a program of gradual compensated emancipation which could, if necessary, take to the end of the century— that is, some thirty-seven years—to complete. With carefully mustered facts and figures, he demonstrated beyond reasonable doubt that his program of gradual compensated emancipation would be no burden financially. "The proposed emancipation," he argued, "would shorten the war, perpetuate peace . . . and will cost no blood, no precious life . . . We know how to save the Union. The world knows we do know how to save it. *We* even *we,* here hold the power and bear the responsibility. In giving freedom to the slave, we assure freedom to the free—honorable alike in what we give and what we preserve. We shall nobly save or meanly lose the last, best hope of earth. Other means may succeed; this could not fail. The way is plain, peaceful, generous, just—a way which if followed, the world will forever applaud, and God must forever bless." But neither logic nor sentiment could move the Congress or the people to act, and the war went on. And so Lincoln had to be satisfied for the time being with issuing his Emancipation Proclamation, which was to become effective on January 1, 1863.

Samuel Eliot Morison, the distinguished American historian, wrote that the Proclamation, though "more revolutionary in human relationships than any event in American history since 1776 . . . *actually freed not one slave,* since it applied only to rebel states where it could not be enforced. . . . The South, indignant at what she considered an invitation to the slaves to cut their masters' throats, was nerved to greater effort . . . *the Northern armies received from it no new impetus.* The Democratic party, presenting it to the Northern people as proof that *abolitionists* were responsible for the duration of the war, *gained seats in the autumn elections.* A large section of the press . . . adopted a cynical and sneering attitude toward the Proclamation." [8]

When I contemplate the circumstances under which Lincoln issued the Proclamation, a great sadness overtakes me. Neither as Americans nor as human beings can we take pride or joy in that great act, for it was performed in response, not to the call of justice, or mercy, or human brotherhood, but to a military need. God was doing to America what He had done to Egypt. Circumstances that had brought the American social and political order to the very brink of complete collapse *compelled* the *American* government, in order to save itself, to free, not those whom it held in bondage, but only those whom its enemies held in bondage.

The resolution calling for an amendment to the Constitution to abolish slavery barely passed Congress even in January of 1865, and that only after Lincoln had brought all his political sagacity and prestige to bear in its favor. *To whom, then, but to God does the black man of America owe thanks for his emancipation?* As I think of Lincoln wrestling for weeks and months over every word and comma of the Proclamation he was writing, to make sure that it was legally correct and could not possibly be interpreted as an abolitionist pronouncement, I cannot but weep for him. It seems to me that I know what he would have wanted to say in that Proclamation —because I know what he said on other occasions. He would have wanted, I believe, to associate his Proclamation with the Declaration of Independence, regarding which he said, "I have never had a feeling politically that did not spring from the sentiments embodied in the Declaration of Independence . . . which gave liberty not alone to the people of this country, but hope to all the world, for all future time." And he would, I am sure, have wanted to present his Proclamation as but an *implementation, a further extension, of the sentiments embodied in the Declaration*—as evidence that America continued to be true to the proposition to which it had been dedicated when it was founded. But circumstances denied him that great privilege and denied to America the esteem that would rightfully have been hers. Thus a great act of emancipation was performed without casting any particular glory either upon those who performed the act or those who were the recipients of its blessing. All happened under the compulsion of events which were initiated by human beings to serve their own selfish purposes but which ended by serving the divine purpose. "Many are the plans in the mind of man, but it is the purpose of the Lord that will be established" (Prov. 19:21).

The Jews saw God's intervention in their history not only in their triumphs but also in their defeats. One of the prominent characteristics of the Jewish historic experience, therefore, is that as a people they justified God in all of His relationships to them. The prophets had warned them that their moral and religious transgressions would lead to military and political catastrophes, eventuating in exile and years and years of suffering. When those catastrophes came, they accepted them as due punishment for their transgressions and incorporated this interpretation of the tragedies that befell them into the synagogue liturgy so that it has become central to Jewish theology and philosophy of history.

To the best of my knowledge, the American people is the only people that by a public act of surpassing impressiveness, incorporated into its historical self-consciousness an unfavorable verdict upon itself, justifying God in the face of the greatest national tragedy it has yet experienced. When the Civil War started, everyone thought it could not or would not last more than a few weeks, or at most a few months. As it continued to drag on month after month, Lincoln began to view it more and more as evidence of God's involvement in human history. In a meditation dated September 1862, Lincoln wrote: "In the present Civil War it is quite possible that God's purpose is something different from the purpose of either party; and yet the human instrumentalities, working just as they do, are of the best adaptation to effect his purpose. I am almost ready to say that this is probably true; and that *God wills* this contest, and wills that it shall not yet end. By his mere great power on the minds of the now contestants, He would have either saved or destroyed the Union without a human contest. Yet the contest began, and, having begun, He could give the final victory to either side any day. Yet the contest proceeds."[9] But why should God have wanted the Civil War to continue for so long a time? It was in his Second Inaugural that Lincoln gave his answer. He said: "Fondly do we hope, fervently do we pray that this mighty scourge of war may speedily pass away. Yet, if God wills that it continue until all the wealth piled up by the bondsman's two hundred and fifty years of unrequited toil shall be sunk, and until every drop of blood drawn with the lash shall be paid by another drawn with the sword, as was said three thousand years ago, so still it must be said, 'The judgments of the Lord are true and righteous altogether.' " (Psalms 19:10)

To the best of my knowledge, no leader before or since, exercising the same power Lincoln had at the time he delivered his Second Inaugural, has ever thus spoken to his triumphant followers. How profoundly aware Lincoln was of the full import of what he was saying is reflected in a letter which he wrote shortly after the inauguration to a friend who had congratulated him. "Everyone likes a little compliment. . . . Thank you for yours on the recent inaugural address. . . . But I believe it is not immediately popular. Men are not flattered by being shown that there has been a difference of purpose between the Almighty and them. To deny it however in this case is to deny that there is a God governing the world. It is a truth which I thought needed to be told, and as whatever of humiliation there is in it falls most directly on myself, I thought others might afford for me to tell it."[8]

The majestic, monumental Lincoln Memorial, upon whose walls are inscribed every word of the Second Inaugural, testifies before the world, and for all future generations, that America has accepted Lincoln's judgment on the ultimate cause of the Civil War. Some men may have been fighting to keep their slaves. Some may have been fighting to preserve the Union. Some may have been fighting to keep the Mississippi River open as a passageway to the seas for midwestern wheat and corn. But all were paying the price for stubbornly harboring within their midst the horrendous evil of slavery. Both North and South benefited by the 250 years of the black man's unrequited labor. And the Divine law of justice, even as the law of gravity, cannot be indefinitely violated with impunity, for the Creator of the world is a God in whose presence evil cannot forever abide. God's true and righteous judgment must, in His own good time, have its way.

When I contemplate these and other such affinities between the historical and spiritual experiences of the American and the Jewish peoples, the veritable miracle of the totally unpredictable relationship that has developed between the United States and the State of Israel in our day takes on profounder meaning for me, for it has deeper roots than usually ascribed to it. There apparently are, and I hope there always will be, confluent mutual economic, political, and military interests between the world's mightiest politically democratic state and the world's most beleaguered political democracy. But overreaching, underlying, and impregnating the visible ties that bind them to one another, are the spiritual bonds rooted in, and nourished by, the historical experiences of both peoples. None of us is therefore called upon to perform a service of greater import, not merely to Jews and Americans but to mankind, than that of strengthening and activating those bonds—by helping America to fulfill her vision of herself as "the best hope of the earth," and the Jewish people to be "God's witnesses upon this earth." In so doing we shall be making our finest contribution toward bringing on the day, "when none shall hurt or destroy, for the earth shall be as full of the knowledge of the Lord as the waters cover the sea." (Isaiah 11:9)

NOTES

1. "Any physical explanation of a phenomenon, he (Einstein) urges is epistemologically satisfactory only when there enter into it no non-observable elements: for the law of causality is an assertion concerning the world or experience only when observable facts occur as causes and effect" (Cassirer, *Substance,* p. 376).

2. Regarding the role in science of hypotheses and of concepts whose substantive content cannot be sensibly verified, see ibid., p. 169.

3. "When a 'scientific' hypothesis serves as a sanction for determining the organization of society, and the relation of the individual to himself, his fellow man and the universe, it, and the actions inspired and sanctioned by it take on the character of religion. Dialectical materialism is advanced as a 'scientific' hypothesis which 'functions' for the Communists almost exactly the way a supernatural god serves the purposes of orthodox religion" (J. Cohen, p. 63). See also Blackstone, p. 55.

4. "The idea of a supreme Being . . . and the idea of ourselves . . . would I suppose, if duly considered and pursued, afford such foundations of our duty and rules of action as might place morality among the sciences capable of demonstration: wherein I doubt not but from self-evident propositions by necessary consequences, as

incontestible as those in mathematics, the measures of right and wrong might be made out to anyone that will apply himself with the same indifference and attention to the one as he does to the other of these sciences" (Locke, "Concerning Human Understanding," bk. 4, chap. 3, par. 18; chap. 4, par. 7:7; chap. 12, par. 8, in Burtt, pp. 334, 345, 374).

5. Sidgwick, *Outlines,* pp. 1, 2.

6. Ibid., p. 6.

7. Barnes, p. 5.

8. "In an voluntary action the drive works through the medium of intention, of thinking, decision and motivation on the part of the individual; in an instinctive action the performance is set going by the drive" (Goldstein, p. 139).

9. Broad, p. 274.

10. "For practical men who do not philosophize, the maxim of subordinating self-interest as commonly conceived to 'altruistic' sentiments . . . is I doubt not a commendable maxim; but it is surely the business of ethical philosophy to find and make explicit the rational ground for such action" (Sidgwick, *Methods,* p. xvi).

11. "Whenever therefore the particular end of any action is the happiness of another (though the agent designed thereby to procure to himself esteem and favor, and looked upon that esteem and favor as a means of private happiness) that action is meritorious. And the same may be said, though we design to please God, by endeavoring to promote the happiness of others" (John Gay, in Burtt, p. 779). On the other hand, Kant says of the shopkeeper who is honest that "this is not nearly enough to justify us in believing that the shopkeeper has acted this way from duty or from principles of fair dealing; his interests required him to do so" (Kant, *Groundwork,* p. 65). Hence his action cannot be considered as having been ethically motivated. Kant recognizes, however, that "in actual fact it is absolutely impossible for experience to establish with complete certainty a single case in which the maxim of an action in other respects right, has rested solely on moral grounds and on the thought of one's duty" (*Groundwork,* pp. 74–75).

12. In *Profiles of Courage,* the late President John F. Kennedy pays tribute to men who were not merely physically and spiritually fearless, but who consciously irretrievably impaired their own welfare in order to advance the welfare of others. See also "Three Saints in Politics" by Paul H. Douglas in the *American Scholar,* Spring 1971.

13. "The term moral is commonly used as synonymous with ethical (moralus being a Latin translation of ethicus) and I shall so use it in the following pages" (Sidgwick, *Outlines,* p. 11). Grice, p. 181, uses the term *moral* as we intend to use it.

14. "The search for grounds of judgment of obligation has been impeded by . . . the failure to notice the distinction between judgments of basic obligation and judgments of ultra obligation" (Grice, p. 6).

15. The Rabbis judged subsidiary intentions in their own right and not on the basis of the character of the primary intentions they subserved. Thus Scripture commands: "Thou shalt not despise the Egyptian for you were a stranger in his land" (Deut. 23:8). The Rabbis comment (*Sifre,* p. 278) that though the Egyptians agreed to act as hosts to the Israelites because they wanted eventually to enslave them, nevertheless, they are to be rewarded for the good intention expressed in their willingness to permit the Israelites to settle in Egypt. Thus also Balak is rewarded for the forty-two sacrifices he offered, even though their purpose was to invoke a curse upon the Israelites (*Nazir* 23b). On the other hand, the Rabbis do not hesitate to designate the act whereby Yael lured Sisera to his death as a transgression (*averah*), even though she thereby rid Israel of one of its most dangerous enemies (Judg. 4), and is highly praised for it in the Song of Deborah (Judg. 5:24).

16. Kant, *Doctrine,* p. 122.

17. "Abelard does not shrink from drawing the inference that since rightness of conduct depends solely on intention, all outward acts as such are indifferent; but avoids the dangerous consequences of this paradox . . . by explaining that 'good intention' must be understood to mean intention to do what really is right, not merely

what seems right to the agent" (Sidgwick, *Outlines,* p. 138). But who knows with an absolute certainty and objectivity what "really is right"?

18. *Bava Kama,* 26a, *Sanhedrin* 72a, and Tosafot *Yevamot* 53b. See also Michael Higger, "Intention in Talmudic Law," in Gershfield, pp. 235–93.

19. Spinoza, *Ethics,* pt. 2, prop. 47, p. 93.

20. Though Kant's analysis of the "moral disposition called conscience" leads him to the conclusion that "conscience must be conceived as a subjective principle of responsibility before God for our deeds," it does not mean that Kant is a "religionist" in the commonly accepted use of the word. For he hastens to add, "This is not to say that man is entitled, on the grounds of the idea to which his conscience inevitably leads him, to posit such a supreme Being as *really existing* outside himself—still less that he is obligated to do so." Kant's conception of religion as such is here only a "principle of regarding all duties as if they were divine commands" (*Doctrine,* pp. 104–6). "Existentialism is closer to Kant than to Plato or Aristotle or Leibnitz both in its ethics and in epistemology" (Barnes, p. 95).

21. The goal which Kant set for himself in his *Critique of Practical Reason* was that of establishing "the supreme principle of morality" (*Critique,* p. 7). He believes that "all previous attempts failed to discover the principle of morality . . . because it was not observed that the laws to which he (man) is subject are only those of his own giving, though at the same time they are universal, and that he is only bound to act in conformity with his own will; a will however, which is designed by nature to give universal laws."

"The moral is given as a fact of pure reason of which we are a priori conscious, and which is apodictically certain though it be granted that no experience, no example of its exact fulfillment can be found" (ibid., p. 136).

22. G. E. Moore is concerned with discovering "the reason why an action is right when it is right" (*Ethics,* p. 8). He concludes that the reason which makes a voluntary action right is that "the

agent could not, even if he had chosen, have done any other action instead, which would have caused more pleasure than the one he did" (p. 19). Whether an action is right or wrong, therefore, has nothing to do with "motives" but only with consequences. "Motives are relevant to some moral judgements, though not judgements of right and wrong" (p. 116). Hence "we are committed to the paradox that a man may really deserve the strongest moral condemnation for choosing an action, which actually is right" (p. 121). As we noted in our text, since no one can foretell all the consequences of his act, what he does may be motivated by what we designated as an unethical intention, and yet could have "caused more pleasure" than any other act which the agent might have chosen. I do not see how it helps us to think clearly about ethics if we call such an act "right." A religiously oriented individual sees "the hand of God" in the case where an act motivated by an unethical intention produces more pleasure than any other act the agent might have chosen. Thus Joseph says to his brothers, "You intended to do me harm, but God intended it for good, so that I might this day sustain a great multitude" (Gen. 50:20). But Joseph does not therefore designate the action of his brothers as having been right. Since we cannot possibly know all the consequences of any act, the only rational judgment we can make about a voluntary action when we judge it by its known consequences is not whether it was right or wrong, but whether it was or was not rationally, wisely related to the intent that motivated it.

23. This position is superficially so similar to Kant's position that only the will can be good or evil (*Groundwork,* pp. 61–62) that it may be helpful to point out wherein it differs. Kant's "will" is related directly and exclusively to the categorical imperative (*Groundwork,* p. 88). It requires that one should not determine his acts on the basis of any immediate considerations involving the advancement of his own or anyone else's welfare (*Critique,* p. 16). In this inquiry the ethical intention is directed to the *human* situation, and is identified by its being or not being an intention which

the agent would have wanted the object to harbor toward him if he were in the object's situation.

24. The question of whether the ethical and the moral have biological roots, whether they are in any way "instinctive," became a subject of central significance for moralists after Hobbes apodictically stated that "justice and injustice are none of the faculties neither of the body nor of the mind" (Hobbes, *Leviathan,* end of chap. 13, in Burtt, p. 162). We shall have more to say about this later (pp. 16–17). See also note 40.

25. The problem of human freedom is, of course, basic to any system of ethics. Since we are not engaged upon a presentation of a comprehensive philosophy of ethics, we shall merely state that this inquiry assumes that the human will is, in some significant manner, free. For a good collection of selected readings on the subject, see the books edited by Enteman and by Hook and G. E. Moore, chap. 6.

26. *Makkot* 23b.

27. *Avot,* chap. 2:1.

28. This statement will be clarified in the course of the essay, but is more specifically discussed in the section on Reward and Punishment. (pp. 83–88). "For it was obvious to all of us that the concept of the nature of man that one holds largely determines how one feels about man's dilemma, what one does about it, and how one goes about doing it" (Doniger, p. xi.).

29. "For the atheist, disintegration of the separate consciousness denotes simple annihilation" (Barnes, p. 245).

30. Sidgwick, *Methods,* p. 95.

"In the theory of psychoanalysis we have no hesitation in assuming that the course taken by mental events is automatically regulated by the pleasure principle" (Freud, *Beyond the Pleasure Principle,* quoted by S. Fox, p. 135). G. E. Moore defines the position of egoism as follows: "No agent can ever be under any obligation to do the action whose total consequences will be the best possible, if its total effect upon him personally are not the best possible. . . . it can never be the duty of any agent to sacrifice his own good to the general good. . . . it must always be his positive duty to prefer his own good to the general good" (*Ethics,* p. 141).

31. "The moralist's proper function is to exhibit the coincidence of virtue with private happiness" (Sidgwick, *Outlines,* p. 268). See n. 77.

32. "It is very seldom indeed that men live according to reason; on the contrary, it so happens that they are generally envious and injurious to one another" (*Ethics,* pt. 4, prop. 35, schol., p. 206).

33. Kant himself recognized the difficulty. "Yet even if a rational being were himself to follow such a maxim strictly, he can not count on everybody else being faithful to it on this ground, nor can he be confident that the kingdom of nature and its purposive order will work in harmony with him, as a fitting member, towards a kingdom of ends made possible by himself—or in other words, that it will favour his expectation of happiness" (*Groundwork,* p. 106). Hence, Kant must and does supply a rationale for obeying his categorical imperative other than that of the "expectation of happiness" upon this earth. But about that we shall have more to say later.

34. "Men who are necessarily subject to affects (corol. to pt. 4, prop. 4) and are uncertain and changeable (pt. 4, prop. 33) can beget confidence one in the other and have faith in one another" only when they are "restrained by a stronger and contrary affect and that everyone abstains from doing an injury through fear of a greater injury." Therefore society must and does "claim for itself the right which every individual possesses of avenging himself and deciding what is good and what is evil and possesses the power . . . of promulgating laws and supporting them, not by reason which cannot restrain affects (schol. pt. 4, prop. 17), but by penalties" (Spinoza, *Ethics,* pt. 4, prop. 37, schol. 2, p. 211).

35. Aristotle-McKeon, p. 1081.

36. Malraux, p. 421.

37 The religious existentalism of men like Kierkegaard or Buber "implies a living faith in God and an intuitive insight into His relation to man" (Simon, Ernst).

38. Callahan, p. 142. "Man is a useless passion". . . . "Thus it amounts to the same thing whether one gets drunk alone or is a leader of nations" (Sartre, quoted by Barnes, p. 50). "Sartre claims that existentialism offers the most thorough-going atheism the world has known, because the order of the universe is the pattern which man has put there as his mind has worked with the meaningless chaos around him" (ibid., p. 239).

39. Ardrey, pp. 80–83, 172–73. See also *Human Decency in Animals,* Edward O. Wilson, N.Y. Times Magazine, October 12, 1975.

40. Edel, p. 117. "Instinct is not only a 'basic' concept or principle but it cannot be reduced. . . . in discussing the behavior of a human being nothing further can be said by way of explanation after one has attributed an action to an instinct" (S. Fox, p. 54).

"The fact that the generality of mankind do approve of virtue or rather virtuous actions, without being able to give a reason for their approbation; and also, that some pursue it without knowing that it tends to their own private happiness, nay even when it appears to be inconsistent with and destructive of their happiness" has been established by Francis Hutchinson, in his *Enquiry into the Origin of our Idea of Virtue,* by "so great a variety of instances, that a man must be either very little acquainted with the world, or a mere Hobbist in his temper to deny it. And therefore . . . this excellent author has supposed (without proving, unless by showing the insufficiency of all other schemes) a moral sense to account for the former, and a public or benevolent affection for the latter: And these, viz., the moral sense and the public affection, he supposes to be implanted in us like instincts, independent of reason, and previous to any instruction; and therefore his opinion is that no account can be given, or ought to be expected of them, any more than we pretend to account for the pleasure or pain which arises in sensation . . ." (John Gay, in Burtt, pp. 770–71). See also in Goldstein, p. 203. Also n. 24.

41. Spinoza, *Ethics,* bk. 4, schol. to prop. 18, pp. 193–94.

42. Ibid., pt. 4, demonstration & corollary to prop. 21. "Spinoza's psychology is fundamentally and explicitly egoistic . . . delib-

erate self-sacrifice is literally impossible . . . although (Spinoza says that) the 'Freeman wills the perfection of other men as well as his own, he wills his own as an end, whilst he wills theirs, not as an end, but only as a necessary means to his own' . . . Pleasure and pain are the only ultimate good and evil" (Broad, pp. 35, 41, 52).

43. Ibid., pt. 2, prop. 49, schol., p. 103.

"The point at issue was the value of the non-egotistical instincts. The instincts of compassion, self-denial, and self-sacrifice, which Schopenhauer above all others had consistently gilded, glorified, 'Transcendentalized' . . . I began to understand that the constantly spreading ethics of pity, which had tainted and debilitated even the philosophers was the most sinister symptom of our sinister European civilization. . . . This preference for and overestimation of pity among philosophers, is an entirely new development in Western civilization. The philosophers of the past deny to a man all value to pity. I need only instance Plato, Spinoza, La Rochefoucauld, and Kant, four minds as different from each other as possible yet agreeing in this one regard; the low esteem in which they hold pity" (Nietzsche, *Genealogy*, p. 154).

44. "The heroic sacrifices of scientists . . . patriots . . . saints . . . and other persons who give their lives for society, or for those they love, are usually not considered suicidal, because of the social usefulness of the course chosen. . . . The individual may have wished to destroy himself or he may not—but if the social or reality value of his sacrifice is predominant, therein lies the evidence that the self-destructive forces were not triumphant" (Menninger, p. 79).

45. See note 38.

46. Barnes discusses at length the various implications of the fact that Sartre had in 1943 promised to write an Ethics. But in the sixties he stated that he no longer had any interest in writing an Ethics (p. 29). She admits "that the absence of any philosophical justification by Sartre of love as a positive existential structure of human reality is a serious lack." "Hostile critics maintain that the reason Sartre has not offered a philosophy of love and of human relations in good faith is that he cannot do so consistently with the

view of human consciousness presented in *Being and Nothingness"* (p. 320). Though she does not accept this judgment, she did say earlier in the volume that Sartre "has not lived out his atheism to its logical conclusion. I believe him when he says he has given up God and got rid of the Holy Ghost. He still holds on to the Messiah . . ." (p. 43).

47. Sidgwick, *Methods,* p. 11, for a definition of these terms.

48. Mill, *Utilitarianism,* in Burtt, p. 900.

49. Ibid., p. 903.

50. Having definied *obligation* as "the necessity of doing or omitting any action in order to be happy" (Gay-Burtt, p. 774), Gay goes on to say: "Thus those who either expressly exclude or don't mention the will of God, making the immediate criterion of virtue to be the good of mankind, must either allow that virtue is not in all cases obligatory (contrary to the idea which all or most men have of it) or they must say that the good of mankind is a sufficient obligation. But how can the good of mankind be any obligation to me, when perhaps in particular cases, such as laying down my life, or the like, it is contrary to my happiness" (Gay-Burtt, p. 776).

What to Gay seems obviously irrational, seems to G. E. Moore to be "quite self-evident that it must always be our duty to do what will produce the best effects upon the whole no matter how bad the effects upon ourselves may be and no matter how much good we ourselves may lose by it" (p. 143). Since to him it is "self-evident" he feels no need to tell us why it is so. All he can do under the circumstances apparently is to sympathize with those poor dullards to whom it is not self-evident.

51. "Thus many men sacrifice happiness to fortune or fame, but no one so far as I know, has deliberately maintained that fame is an object which it is reasonable for men to seek for its own sake" (Sidgwick, *Methods,* p. 9).

52. Keats, p. 346.

53. "Some Greek historians viewed History (Fame) as the goddess that bestowed immortality" (Toynbee, p. 49).

54. Herzl Diary, August 1903.

55. (Kant, *Groundwork,* pp. 90–91). The translator, in his note *ad locum,* points to the difficulty: "This is put in a prudential way, but Kant's doctrine is not prudential, as can be seen from p. 11 and p. 68 footnote." But when one examines carefully the passages to which the translator refers, it becomes even more clear that Kant himself sees his difficulty. In the first reference (p. 11, which is p. 66 in this edition), Kant merely says that "to help others where one can is a duty." Now an action done from duty "has its moral worth, not in the purpose to be attained by it, but in the maxim in accordance with which it is decided upon" (ibid., 67–68). Now a maxim is valid if "a universal law of nature can subsist in harmony with this maxim." In the passage we quoted, Kant admits that a universal law could subsist in harmony with the maxim "I won't deprive him of anything . . . only I have no wish to contribute anything to his . . . support in distress." Hence it is, by Kant's own standards, a valid maxim. He neverthless decides that "it is impossible to will such a universal law since he himself may be in need of his fellow man's love."

In yet another passage Kant repeats that "humanity could no doubt subsist if everybody contributed nothing to the happiness of others but at the same time refrained from deliberately impairing their happiness." He there rationalizes "meritorious duties to others" by arguing that the attitude implied in one who says "I will neither help nor harm you" "merely agrees negatively and not positively with humanity as an end in itself," and insofar as "all men seek their own happiness, everyone must endeavor, so far as in him lies, to further the ends of others" (p. 98). Hence, here too Kant associates what he calls "meritorious duties," and what we have called moral intentions, with "men's own happiness," and not merely with duty as such, nor with the categorical imperative.

56. Edel, p. 126.

57. Jesus said "Resist not evil" (KJV) or "one who is evil" (RSV) (Matt. 5:39) and "commanded" his disciples to love their enemies (Matt. 5:44). The problem which even many pious Chris-

tians have with these verses is reflected in Sherman E. Johnson's exegetical commentary on Matt. 5:34–35 in the *Interpreter's Bible,* which states that "it is difficult to escape the conclusion that verses 34–35 and verses 38–42 are laws" and that "how far they [not to resist] can be applied to groups, and especially to political life, is constantly debated" (v. 39). Regarding the teaching to love one's enemies (v. 44), the commentator correctly remarks, "Exodus 23:4–5 and numerous rabbinical sayings look in this direction, but the idea is never made a general maxim for conduct in Judaism." He admits that this "teaching of course has political implications, but how it should be applied is one of the most difficult problems of Christian social ethics."

58. Thucydides, p. 334. It is interesting to note that Hobbes, who was a believing Christian, wrote: "The right of nature whereby God reigneth over men and punisheth those that break the law is derived not from his creating them . . . but from his irresistible power. . . . It is that which gives Him the right to afflict men at His pleasure" (pp. 123–24). Right and power are thus made synonymous. For Spinoza's position, see below pp. 35–36.

59. Edel, p. 116. Compare the following passages from T. H. Huxley: "The ethical process in so far as it tends to make any human society more efficient in the struggle for existence with the state of nature, or with other societies, it works in harmonious contrast with the cosmic process. But it is none the less true that, since law and morals are restraints upon the struggle for existence between men in society, the ethical process is in opposition to the principle of the cosmic process, and tends to the suppression of the qualities best fitted for success in that struggle" (p. 31).

The golden rule "can be obeyed, even partially only under the protection of a society which repudiates it. Without such shelter, the followers of the 'golden rule' may indulge in hopes of heaven, but they must reckon with the certainty that other people will be masters of the earth" (p. 32).

60. Hegel, p. 322.

J. Ruskin had this to say in an address to students at a military academy: ". . . all the pure and noble acts of peace are founded on war; no great art ever yet arose on earth, but among a nation of soldiers. . . . Now, though I hope you love fighting for its own sake, you must I imagine be surprised. . . . All healthy men like fighting, and like the war" (lecture 3). Ardrey more recently added: "Let us not be too hasty in our dismissal of war as an unblemished evil" (p. 330), after which there follows a long list of the beneficial effects of war. Ardrey even sees some possible good in a nuclear holocaust that will have some five hundred million immediate survivors and one hundred million "post-apocalypse" survivors. Of these perhaps half will have descendants suffering mutations. All but a half-million will be doomed. "But a half-million will have descendants with endowments superior to the ancestral line" (p. 328). "Darwin did not invent the Machiavellian image that the world is the playground of the lion and the fox, but thousands discovered that he had transformed political science. Their own tendencies to act like lions and foxes thereby became irresistible 'laws of nature' and 'factors of progress' while moral arguments against them were dubbed 'pre-scientific'. . . . War became the symbol, the image, the inducement, the reason, the language of all human doings on the planet. No one who has not waded through some sizable part of the literature of the period 1870–1914 has any conception of the extent to which it is one long call for blood, nor of the variety of parties, classes, nations, and voices whose blood was separately and contradictorily clamored for by the enlightened citizens of the ancient civilization of Europe" (Barzun, p. 100).

Goldstein (p. 205) is a rather lone voice when he maintains that "man is neither aggressive nor submissive by nature. He is driven to actualize himself and to come to terms with his environment. In doing so he has at times to be submissive and at times aggressive."

61. Man's apotheosis of sheer physical power and his use of it, has been given new "dignity" by the self-proclaimed saviors of mankind who preach that "every Communist must grasp the truth, 'Political power grows out of the barrel of a gun.'. . . The seizure of power by armed force, the settlement of the issue by war, is the

central task and the highest form of revolution. This Marxist-Leninist principle of revolution holds good universally, for China and for all countries" (Mao Tse-Tung, pp. 61–62). "War can only be abolished through war, and in order to get rid of the gun it is necessary to take up the gun" (ibid., p. 63). This is supported by students of human nature who with the best intentions present overwhelming evidence that "aggression is a drive as innate, as natural, as powerful as sex." See viz. Lorenz, *On Aggression.*

62. Hobbes, chap. 14 (Burtt, p. 163).

63. Ibid., end of chap. 13 (Burtt, p. 162).

64. Ibid., p. 164. If it is as simple as all that, one wonders wherein lies the distinction of the Gospel. We shall return to this question later.

65. Ibid., p. 165.

66. S. Fox, p. 41.

67. Ibid., p. 119.

68. Pp. 37–40.

69. "Utilitarianism is the thesis that the reason for any moral judgment of obligation is that the action enjoined produces more good than any other action open to the agent at the time" (Grice, p. 2).

70. In his criticism of utilitarianism, Grice points out, among other things, that "if I can do as much good for 'B' by breaking the promise as I can do for 'A' by keeping it . . . a Utilitarian is committed to saying that it does not matter which I do. It seems to me that this result is transparently absurd" (p. 59, also p. 74).

71. "The forerunner of this principle was the formula 'the common good for all" which was first suggested by Cumberland as the supreme end and standard in subordination to which all other rules and virtues are to be determined" (Sidgwick, *Outlines,* p. 174). There are undoubtedly some "goods" that are for the good of all, such as pure drinking water, but one would have to be divinely wise to define "the common good of all."

72. See n. 50.

"The equation of the greatest good with the greatest number

is the most difficult of all mathematical calculations, for it is to balance two incommensurates, quality and distribution" (Barnes, p. 456). "The framers of the Constitution recognized that the will of the majority must be prevented from infringing, even in the name of the greatest good for the greatest number, upon certain unalienable rights of the individual or the minority group" (ibid., 284).

73. "In the meantime Sartre does not seem to me to avoid the particular trap set for all sincere social reformers—that of sacrificing earlier generations to a Utopia to come, decreeing in advance that if some individuals are not expendable, at least their happiness is" (Barnes, p. 43).

"When a very young man, Winston Churchill once wrote to an American politician, 'The duty of governments is to be first of all practical. I am for makeshifts and expediency. I would like to make the people who live on this world at the same time as I do better fed and happier generally. If incidentally I benefit posterity— so much the better—but I would not sacrifice my own generation to a principle—however high or a truth however great' " (from a talk by Arthur Schlesinger, Jr., "On the 90th Birthday of Franklin D. Roosevelt," Hunter College, June 30, 1971).

74. Some of the best of us fall prey to the conviction that they have the answer to problems for which there are no final answers. Thus Kant believed that "there can be only one true system of philosophy" and only one doctrine of virtue, so that "when the Critical Philosophy proclaims itself a philosophy such that before it there was as yet no philosophy at all, it does nothing more than what every new philosophy has done, will do and in fact must do" (Kant, *Doctrine*, p. 4). "One belief, more than any other, is responsible for the slaughter of individuals on the altars of great historical ideals. . . . This is the belief that somewhere, in the past or in the future, in divine revelation or in the mind of an individual thinker . . . there is a final solution" (Sir Isaiah Berlin, *Four Essays on Liberty*, p. 167, quoted by Finkelstein in *Social Responsibility*, p. 89).

75. Pp. 37–38.

76. Mill explicitly concedes this: "I do not, indeed, consider

the Epicureans to have been by any means faultless in drawing out their scheme of consequences from the utilitarian principle. To do this in any sufficient manner, many Stoic as well as Christian elements require to be included" (p. 900).

77. "No doubt it is commonly believed that it will be ultimately better for a man to do his duty and that this will promote his real interest or Happiness; but it does not follow that the notions of duty and interest are to be identified or even that the inseparable connection between the two may be scientifically known and demonstrated. This connection indeed is often by modern thinkers regarded as a matter of faith as something providentially left obscure in order that duty may be done as duty and not from a mere calculation of self love" (Sidgwick, *Outlines,* p. 6). "That doing well meant both virtuous action and prosperous life was to Socrates as to Plato and Aristotle after him the expression of a fundamental truth" (ibid., p. 11).

78. Pp. 12–13.

79. The term *soul* is here used to designate that component of man which, no matter how it is conceived or how its relation to the body is understood, is itself viewed as being distinguishable from the body. Thus Epicurus, "whose doctrine places supreme happiness . . . in sense pleasure nevertheless taught that the pleasures one should pursue are the pleasures of the soul, even though our soul will end and its ruin takes with it all sentiment and personal life" (Thonnard, pp. 152–62).

80. Kant distinguishes between the sensible world and the intelligible world, "which contains the ground of the sensible world." Man is a member of both worlds, but "it is his membership in the intelligible world by virtue of his Reason, that gives him his unique distinction and endows him with his higher faculties" (*Groundwork,* pp. 120–21). On the distinction between the higher and lower desires, see Kant-Abbott, pp. 108 ff.

81. The emphasis on the supremacy of the intellect in the moral life of man is fully formulated by Aristotle.—Aristotle-McKeon, p. 1108.

82. "Human beings have faculties more elevated than the animal appetites, and when once made conscious of them, do not regard anything as happiness which does not include their gratification. . . . Of two pleasures, if there be one to which all or most all who have experienced both give a decided preference, irrespective of any feeling of moral obligation to prefer it, that is the more desirable pleasure . . . even though knowing it to be attended with a greater amount of discontent and would not resign it for any quantity of the other pleasure which their nature is capable of" (Mill, *Utilitarianism,* in Burtt, pp. 900–901).

83. W. H. Auden, *A Certain World* (Viking Press, 1970), quoted in *New York Times Book Review,* Sept. 13, 1970, p. 2.

84. Sidgwick, *Methods,* p. 94. Indeed, Bentham's logic drives him to the conclusion that "there is no such thing as any sort of motive that is in itself a bad one." "Let a man's motive be ill-will; call it even malice, envy, cruelty: it is still a kind of pleasure that is his motive. . . . Now even this wretched pleasure taken by itself is good. It may be faint, it may be short, it must at any rate be impure; [why impure? S.G.] yet while it lasts, and before any bad consequences arrive, it is as good as any other that is not more intense" (Bentham, *Principles,* in Burtt, p. 816).

In regard to the proposition that all pleasures are equally good, G. E. Moore wrote: "But those who hold that actions are only right because of the quantity of pleasure they produce must hold also that *if* higher pleasures did not in their total effect produce *more* pleasure than lower ones, then there would be no reason whatever for preferring them." This theory "would deny that a world of men is preferable to a world of pigs, even though the pigs might enjoy as much or more pleasure than a world of men" (pp. 33–34).

But this conclusion is repugnant to Moore, and so he develops his theory of intrinsic value and then raises the question of whether "intrinsic value" is always in proportion to quantity of pleasures. He thinks that the probabilities are all the other way (p. 145), though it is impossible to be quite certain because consequences are so many and so unforeseeable (p. 146). But his final argument against a consistent utilitarian position is that "it seems impossible that any one should hold the point of view that quantity of pleasure should be determinative over against intrinsic value. If so, it is possible to assume that a world without love, knowledge, beauty and morality but with more pleasure would be superior to a world with love, etc. It would mean that a drunkard's pleasure could be equal to that of one who appreciates the beauties of King Lear. This constitutes a *reductio ad absurdum* of the view that intrinsic value is always in proportion to quantity of pleasure. But there is no way of proving that the *reductio ad absurdum* is wrong, that is, that the drunkard's pleasure is less than the other. But it is self-evident that such a position is wrong" (p. 147). Hence, again at the most critical point in his argument, Moore appeals not to reason, but to what is "self-evident" to him.

85. S. Fox, p. 129. Freud vacillates on this subject. His dominant attitude is to make no distinctions between pleasures. But he also wrote: "Its success is greatest when a man knows how to heighten sufficiently his capacity for obtaining pleasure from mental and intellectual work. Fate has little power against him then. This kind of satisfaction . . . has a special quality which we shall certainly one day be able to define metaphysically. Until then we can only say metaphorically it seems to us 'higher and finer' but compared with that of gratifying gross primitive instincts its intensity is tempered and diffused; it does not overwhelm us physically. The weak point of this method (to seek pleasure) however, is that it is not generally applicable; it is only available to the few." Freud, *Civilization,* p. 33.

86. Sidgwick, *Methods,* p. 157.

"The apparent paradox that ethical nature, while born of cosmic nature, is necessarily at enmity with its parent. . . . This seeming paradox is a truth as great as it is plain, the recognition of which is fundamental for the ethical philosopher" (Huxley, p. xiii). "If the conclusion that the two are antagonistic is logically absurd, I am sorry for logic, because as we have seen, the fact is so" (ibid., p. 12). So also Edel, pp. 152–53.

87. Thonnard, p. 162.

88. Ibid., p. 161.

89. "The ethical choice as such involves a justification of conduct in reference to a definite concept of what reality is" (Barnes, p. 48).

90. *Groundwork,* pp. 55–56.

91. Kant-Abbott, pp. 220–28; see n. 20.

92. Ibid., pp. 218–20.

93. Russell, pp. 46–58.

94. Ibid., p. 48.

95. Ibid., p. 51.

96. Ibid., p. 56. Huxley says almost the same thing in less eloquent words (p. 45). "That which lies before the human race is a constant struggle to maintain and improve, in oposition to the State of Nature, the State of Art of an organized polity; in which, and by which, man may develop a worthy civilization, capable of maintaining and constantly improving itself, until the evolution of our globe shall have entered so far upon its downward course that the cosmic process resumes its way; and, once more, the State of Nature prevails over the surface of the planet."

97. Niebuhr, Reinhold *Does Civilization Need Religion?,* p. 6.

98. Barnes, pp. 444–45. See also n. 60 for expression of a hope or a faith in the possibility of a mutation that will produce a species higher than man. Apocalyptic visions of man becoming something in essence different from what he is now, are apparently becoming the hope of many a despairing modern secularist. In a promised volume to be entitled *Transformation,* George Leonard suggests that "in the transformation we will pass into one another. . . . Opacity is a condition of our present limited perception. The condition of transformation, I think will be much more one of flux and flow" ("Work in Progress," interview with George Leonard by John Poppy, *Intellectual Digest,* November 1971, p. 10).

99. Strauss, p. 18.

100. Russell, p. 50.

101. Ibid., p. 48

102. Hume "expressly says that we should not, properly speak-

ing, live under restraint of justice with regards to rational beings who are so much weaker than ourselves, that we had no reason to fear their resentments" (Sidgwick, *Outlines*, p. 206).

"There is no friendship nor justice towards lifeless things. But neither is there friendship towards a horse or an ox nor to a slave *qua* slave. For there is nothing common to the two parties; for the slave is a living tool and the tool a lifeless slave" (Aristotle-McKeon, p. 1071).

"The law against killing animals is based upon an empty super-stition and womanish tendency rather than sound wisdom" (Spi-noza, p. 209). See also nn. 105 and 113, and sec. VIII of this chapter.

103. Hobbes-Burtt, p. 159.

104. Ibid., p. 170.

105. Locke, chap. 2 (Burtt, p. 404). Locke also seems to have some doubts about natural equality. "Though I have said above that all men by nature are equal I cannot be supposed to un-derstand all sorts of equality. Age or virtue may give men prece-dency . . . and yet all this consists with the equality which all men are in, in respect of jurisdiction or dominion over one another. . ." (p. 424).

106. Durant, W. and A. p. 261.

107. Myers, p. 18. "The Doctrine of inequality is one of the oldest in the history of thought. It held a central position in Greek philosophy, the sources of many of our intellectual traditions, and has ever since had advocates of unquestionable integrity" (ibid., p. 11).

108. "That men have natural rights was, as I understand it, a presupposition of classical forms of social contract theory" (Grice, p. 147).

109. President William Henry Harrison, in *Inaugural Ad-dresses*, p. 73.

110. Hobbes, in Burtt, pp. 202, 206.

111. Locke-Burtt, p. 405.

112. Ibid., p. 407.

113. Grice, pp. 147–50.

114. Locke-Burtt, p. 424. In the ancient world, children had no unalienable right even to life. Infanticide was widely practiced. (See article "Infanticide" in *Encyclopaedia Britannica*.)

115. For Stoics, "much that from our point of view and to our restricted vision appears evil, if looked at with reference to the whole, or from the standpoint of the divine reason, would be seen to be good." Furthermore, "inasmuch as . . . the well being of the wise man is not affected by physical evils, these are not in the proper sense evil at all. They may, indeed, as discipline of character, be a positive good" (G. F. Moore, *History,* p. 513).

116. Ibid., p. 375.

117. See particularly Kadushin, *The Rabbinic Mind*.

118. G. F. Moore, *Judaism,* vol. 1, p. vii.

119. Mishnah *Yoma,* chap. 8:7.

120. Commentary on Mishnah *Peah* 1:1.

121. Maimonides, ibid., subsumes all of the *miẓvot* in the first category under the concept of *gemilut ḥasadim* (for which see p. 73).

122. See Kadushin, *Worship,* chap. 6.

123. For the identification of the laws of nature with the ethical and moral laws of Moses, see Troeltsch, p. 159.

"There are certain things which the natural reason of every man, immediately and of itself, discerns and judges, as to be done or not to be done; for instance, honor your father and mother, do not kill, do not steal. Things of this sort are of the natural law in absolute fashion. That is to say, not only is their obligation unrestricted, but the perception of their obligation is common and easy to all men. . . . In terms of philosophical explanation, those precepts find place in the Decalogue, 'the knowledge of which each man of himself has from God. These are precepts that can be known, immediately and on slight reflection from the first common principles.' Here is the basic natural law assertion, that the dictates of common human reason are the dictates of God, who is Eternal Reason" (Murray, pp. 115–16). Murray is quoting Thomas Aquinas, *On the Natural Law;* see chap. 13.

124. The most significant effort to rationalize all the laws of the Torah was made by Maimonides in his *Guide,* pt. 3: 26–49.

125. "In Mesopotamia the law was conceived of as the embodiment of cosmic truths. Not the originator, but the divine custodian of justice was Shamash. . . . In theory, then, the final source of the law, the ideal with which the law had to conform was above the gods as well as men; in this sense the Mesopotamian king . . . was not the source of the laws, but only its agent. However, the actual authorship of the laws, the embodying of the cosmic ideal in statutes of the realm is claimed by the king.

"In the Biblical theory, the idea of the transcendence of the law receives a more thorough-going expression. Here, God is not merely the custodian of justice or the dispenser of 'truths' to man, He is the fountainhead of the law, the law is a statement of His will. The very formulation is God's" (M. Greenberg, pp. 9, 11).

126. Thus the Rabbis relate in great detail the story of the extraordinary honor paid by a gentile to his father "even though he was not commanded" to do so (*Kiddushin* 31a). The Rabbis also point to behavior enjoined by the Torah upon Israelites which they could have learned by observing the behavior of animals (*Eruvin* 100b). Maimonides, who was of the opinion that "the existence of God and His being one, are knowable by human speculation alone" (*Guide,* pt. 2:55; p. 364), and that "no one is ever so perplexed for a day as to ask why we were commanded by the Law that God is one, or why we were forbidden to kill and to steal, etc." (Ibid., pt. 3:25, p. 513), is himself not perplexed why, if that is so, God should have taken the trouble to reveal all this to man.

127. Husik, p. 28, Saadia, pp. 31, 140. Spinoza, who believed that human reason was in itself adequate to determine all aspects of human behavior, nevertheless considered "Holy Scripture or Revelation to be of the greatest use and most necessary. . . . For all can

obey completely, and there are but few . . . who acquire the habit of virtue under the guidance of reason alone" (*Ethics,* p. lvii).

For Locke revelation was indeed superfluous since "traditional revelation may make us know propositions knowable also by reason, but not with the same certainty that reason doth" (p. 391).

128. S. Lieberman, *Yevanit ve Yavnut.*

129. This position has been fully and, I believe, cogently expounded by Dr. Max Kadushin in his various works (see bibliography). His summary statement, "We regard ethics not as a system thought out by a philosopher, but as a pattern of concepts developed by society" (*Worship,* p. 8), I would amend as follows: "We regard ethics . . . as a pattern of (value) concepts (revealed to, applied and) developed by society."

130. *Kiddushin* 31a, *Bava Kama* 38a, 87a, *Avodah Zarah* 3a. This paradoxical dictum is attributed to Rabbi Ḥanina bar Ḥama (Bacher-Rabinowitz, vol. 1, p. 12), a first-generation Amora, who came to Palestine from Babylonia as an adult. Rav Joseph bar Ḥiyya, a third-generation Babylonian Amora, expressed surprise when it was brought to his attention.

Maimonides seemed to have a different version of this text. (*Guide,* pt. 3:17, p. 470).

131. Deut. 11:26–28, 30:19; *Avot* 3:19, 20.

132. On the question of whether "a law is good because God commands it, or whether God commands it because it is good," see S. Greenberg, *Foundations,* pp. 95 ff.

133. *Avot* chap. 2:4. See also n. 144.

134. Ibid., chap. 3:8.

135. *Tosafot Avodah Zarah* 3a and *Kiddushin* 31a. *Gadol hameẓuveh.*

"Inclination is blind and slavish whether it be of a good sort or not, and when morality is in question, reason must not play the part merely of guardian to inclination. This very feeling of compassion and tender sympathy, if it precedes the deliberation on the question of duty and becomes a determining principle, is even annoying to right thinking persons . . ." (Kant, *Critique,* p. 214).

One of the perennial problems raised by the biblical narrative is the apparently unfavorable account it gives of Jacob's behavior as contrasted with that of Esau. Esau is the injured party. What flaw, then, in his character made him unworthy of being the bearer of the tradition? Nowhere is hunting for food condemned in the Bible. The Rabbis created legends attributing to Esau acts of moral turpitude nowhere even hinted at in the Bible. On the basis of the Bible narrative alone (Gen. 25:19–34, 26:34, 27:46), the flaw in Esau's character seems to be instability. Esau is a man governed by inclination, or the passion of the moment (Gen. 25:29–34) He is equally inclined to cruelty and mercy (ibid., 33:1–17). Hence Jacob does not accept Esau's offer to go along with him and protect him. He cannot be sure how he will act on another occasion. Such a one cannot be depended upon to carry on a tradition which requires a maximum of self-disciplined devotion.

136. *Mishnah Makkot* chap. 3:16.

137. Cp. Urbach, *Ḥazal,* pp. 320–21, who unconvincingly suggests a different possible interpretation of the Mishnah.

138. Bar Kappara said of this verse that "all the detailed commandments of the Torah stem, so to speak, from it" (literally "hang upon it") (*Berakhot* 63a). See S. Greenberg, *Foundations,* p. 166.

139. *Avot* ch. 2:17.

140. S. Greenberg, *Foundations,* chap. 6. Because a Jew thus has an infinite number of opportunities to serve God by obeying His commandments, Resh Lakish could say that even "the sinners [or, the ignorant] in Israel are as full of *miẓvot* as the pomegranate is full of seeds" (*Eruvin* 19a).

141. Maimonides, *Hilkhot Deot* chap. 3:3. Hence Maimonides includes in his religious code a summary of health laws as the medicine of his day knew them (ibid., chap. 4).

142. "Die Jüdische Ethik is das Prinzip der Jüdischen Religion. Sie ist das Prinzip und nicht die Konsequenz. . . . Sie ist nicht die Folgerung für den Menschen aus dem Prinzip der Gottheit: sondern das Prinzip der Gottheit kann nicht anders entfaltet, nicht

anders definiert werden denn durch die Sittenlehre. . . . Die Jüdische Sittenlehre ist nicht anders als die Jüdische Glaubenslehre" (H. Cohen, p. 6).

Just as secularists divorce ethics from religion, so also are there religionists who do so. "The decision to exclude ethics from religion, to inflate religion with the metaphysical, the metaethical, the metalogical, with dogma, with the people, with the language of myth, foreshadows the structure of *The Star of Redemption*" (A. Cohen, p. 20).

143. *Nazir* 23b.

144. *Mishneh Torah, Hilkhot Melakhim,* chap. 8:11. The *Kesef Mishnah, ad locum,* wonders on what Maimonides bases his opinion. There seems to be no specific statement to that effect in the Talmud. Perhaps Maimonides had in mind the statement in the Mishnah that one who does not believe that the resurrection of the dead is specifically indicated in the Pentateuch has no share in the world to come (*Sanhedrin* 90a). It is not enough for one to say that he believes in the resurrection of the dead on the basis of his own thinking about the matter. As Rashi, *ad locum,* comments: "Since he denies that the resurrection of the dead is indicated in the Torah, what have we to do with his [personal] belief? How does he know that that is so?"

"Price even goes so far as to lay down that an act loses its moral worth in proportion as it is done from natural inclination" (Sidgwick, *Outlines,* p. 226).

For a comprehensive presentation of this subject, see Simon, E. *Pflicht und Neigung,* in Brücken, pp. 184–205.

145. *Berakhot* 17a.

146. *Taanit* 7a.

147. *Pesikta de Rav Kahana,* p. 254. In note to line 8, there are references to other Rabbinic passages dealing with this same problem. See also Jerusalem Talmud, *Ḥagigah* 1, *halakhah* 7.

148. *Nazir* 23a.

149. *Eikha Rabati, Petihta:*2.

150. *Pesaḥim* 50b and *Tosafot, ad locum. Vekan be'osim.*

See also Urbach, *Ḥazal,* 343–44. The question of the status of one who acts *lishmah* and one who acts *shelo lishmah* is not to be confused with the queston of the status of one who, like a gentile or a woman, observes a *miẓvah* even though he or she is not commanded to observe it. On that there is no difference of opinion among the Rabbis. The latter are rewarded, except that their reward is less than that given to one who is commanded and who fulfills the command *lishmah. Kiddushin* 31a, *Tosafot: delo mafkidna ve'avidna.*

"Thus, they [the sages] have made it clear that even he who has not been charged with a commandment is given his reward" (Maimonides, *Guide,* pt. 3:17, p. 470).

151. Resh Lakish is recorded as having said, about scriptural verses which appear far less problematical than those herein discussed, that "[it appears as if] they deserve to be burned [Rashi: that they served no purpose in the Torah and that it was not fitting to associate them with the holy], and yet they constitute the very essence of Torah," if only we can understand them in all their profundity (*Ḥullin* 60b).

152. See, particularly, Maimonides, *Guide,* pt. 3:8–24, Joad, *God and Evil.*

153. *Bava Batra* 34b records the case of two who disputed the ownership of a boat. Neither could legally establish possession, and the court attached the boat. The question that arose then was whether the court should release the boat, "leaving it to the stronger to obtain possession" (whether by argument or by force, Soncino *B.B.,* p. 157). The final decision is that the court should not in the first instance attach the property, but having been attached, it should not be released. See also *Gittin* 60b.

154. *Sotah* 44b.

155. *Sanhedrin* 72a. See also Kimelman, "Non-Violence." Cp. also the principle that "in a case where an irreparable loss is pending, one may take the law into his own hands" (*Bava Kama* 27b).

156. See pp. 77–78.

157. *Ḥullin* 7a.

158. See pp. 77–78.

159. Maimonides, *Yesode HaTorah,* chap. 5:5.

160. Mishnah *Sanhedrin,* chap. 4:5.

161. After analyzing a case in which a seaman was tried for casting some people overboard in order to save the others in the lifeboat, Cahn concludes that "if none sacrifice themselves of free will to spare the others, they must all wait and die together. . . . in such a setting, so remote from the differentiations of normal existence, every person in the boat embodies the entire genus. Whosoever saves one, saves the whole human race; whoever kills one, kills mankind" (Cahn, p. 71).

162. Kadushin, *Rabbinic Mind,* p. 297.

163. See Greenberg, S., *Foundations,* p. 123.

164. "Justice is not an ancient custom, a human convention, a value, but a transcendent demand freighted with divine concern. It is not only a relationship between man and man, it is an *act* involving God, a divine need. Justice is His line, righteousness His plummet (Isa. 28:17). It is not one of His ways, but in all of His ways. Its validity is not only universal, but also eternal, independent of will and experience" (Heschel, *Prophets,* p. 198).

165. Note that the biblical narrative very specifically includes all the inhabitants of Sodom, "from the young to the old, all of the people," in the intention to act wickedly toward Lot's guests (Gen. 19:4). This is apparently in response to Abraham's plea to save the city even if there be but ten righteous inhabitants (ibid., 18:32).

166. (a) If fear of punishment is the primary motivation for one's acting justly, then one who believes in God cannot believe that he can circumvent Him. Human police forces and courts may be circumvented. God's vigilance cannot (*Avot* 3:20, 4:29). (b) If the motivation for acting justly is the desire to fulfill God's law, then no consciously intended violation of justice can be rationalized.

167. *Shabbat* 10a.

168. *Sabbath and Festival Prayer Book,* pp. 87, 89.

169. Lincoln's Second Inaugural Address, in Basler, *Abraham Lincoln,* p. 792.

170. S. Greenberg. *Foundations,* pp. 66–69.

171. On the Rabbinic attempt to mitigate the harshness of the commandment, see the comment of Ramban on Deut. 20:10.

172. A somewhat similar spiritual soul-searching is now taking place among Jews in the State of Israel. See Elon, chaps. 8–10, and Shapira, whose volume is in part devoted to this theme.

173. "As I have written in *The Mystery of Israel* it is strange to see people questioning the right of the Jews to the one land regarding which there is absolute and divine certainty of the unquestionable right of a people to a land. For the people of Israel is the only people to whom a land was given—the land of Canaan—by God, the one and the supreme Creator of the world and of man. And that which God had once given, was given forever" (translation from the Hebrew of an article by Jacques Maritain in *Haarez,* November 27, 1970). See also Rashi's comment on Gen. 1:1.

174. Rav Hamnuna, on the basis of Job 20:22, says, "The Holy One, blessed be He, does not punish one before the measure of his wrongdoing has been filled" (*Arakhin* 15a), not even if it means that His people will be enslaved for four hundred years. Rashi, in his comment on Genesis 15:16, draws the same conclusion regarding a whole people on the basis of Isaiah 27:8.

175. *Sabbath and Festival Prayer Book,* pp. 140, 150.

176. The weakest link in Milton Steinberg's brilliant essay on Kierkegaard and Judaism is his apodictic statement, "Nor does anything in Judaism correspond to Kierkegaard's teleological suspension of the ethical. . . . From the Jewish viewpoint the ethical is never suspended, not under any circumstances and not for anyone, not even for God" (Steinberg, *Anatomy,* p. 147).

For an excellent discussion of this subject, see Jacob L. Halevi, "Kierkegaard's Theological Suspension of the Ethical—Is It Jewish?" *Judaism* 8, no 4 (Fall 1959).

177. *Avodah Zarah* 13a. *Tosafot, Amar Abbaye, amar krah.*

See also *Tosafot, Shavuot* 29b, *Ki hekha delay tehevay.* G. E. Moore provides an excellent analysis of when an action which is generally accepted as having been right because of its consequences, may legitimately be used as a precedent for other actions. "Let us suppose that an action X which is right and whose total effects are A; and let us suppose that the total effects of all possible alternative actions would have been respectively B,C,D, and E. . . . then any action Y which resembled X in both these two respects (1) that its total effects were precisely similar to A and (2) that the total effects of all possible alternatives were precisely similar to B,C,D, and E would necessarily also be right" (*Ethics,* p. 84). Note the emphasis on both conditions and upon the similarity of the effects rather than of the actions. Obviously Moore's two conditions can never be fulfilled in actuality. Hence no action *per se* may logically be used as a precedent for another action, because the consequences can never be "precisely similar."

178. This involves the Rabbinic concept of *hora'at sha'ah,* a temporary suspension of a biblical commandment authorized by one whose prophetic status had been established beyond doubt. See Maimonides, *Hilkhot Yesode HaTorah,* chap. 9. Cf. chap. 3 and p. 184 of this volume.

179. Kierkegaard, pp. 129 ff.

180. See Wolf, *The Almost Chosen People.* See also Sandberg, index, s.v. "Lincoln, Abraham, religion of," and Basler, pp. 568, 610, 655. Note there the statement, "I am almost ready to say that . . . God wills this contest . . ." and that he, Lincoln, was but a "human instrumentality" through whom God was effecting His purpose.

181. For a discussion of the principle that the law of agency does not apply to the performance of a transgression, and the few exceptions to it, see *Encyclopedia Talmudit,* vol. 1, under *Ein shaliah l'd'var averah,* p. 338. See also Levinthal, *Jewish Law of Agency,* and *Bava Kama* 79a.

182. Wolf, p. 149.

183. For the profound impression John Brown made on Emer-

son and many other leading men of his day, see Nevins, vol. 2, chap. 3.

184. *Bava Batra* 12a. Urbach, *Ḥazal,* pp. 514–17.

185. Maimonides, *Yesode HaTorah* chap. 9:1. See also paragraph following the listing of the 613 *miẓvot.*

186. *Bava Meẓia* 59b. Also Greenberg, S. *Foundations,* pp. 18–20.

187. "The well-known four virtues of the Greeks—courage, wisdom, caution or moderation and justice neither include nor imply anything akin to benevolence or brotherly love" (Lazarus, pp. 222–23). "One defect of Aristotle's account of virtue which strikes a modern reader is that benevolence is not recognized except obscurely in the imperfect form of Liberality" (Sidgwick, *Outlines,* p. 66). "Of the lesser goods the first is health, the second beauty, the third strength . . . and the fourth is wealth. . . . Wisdom is the chief and leader of the divine class of goods, and next follows temperance; and from the union of these two with courage springs justice, and the fourth in the scale of virtue is courage" (Plato-Jowett, vol. 2, p. 413).

188. Cp. Mill-Burtt, p. 907.

189. See above p. 31.

190. Sidgwick, *Outlines,* p. 107.

191. Troeltsch, pp. 103–4.

192. W. Kaufmann, *The Faith,* p. 201.

193. "Stoic virtue is the disposition through which man . . . freely and spontaneously, acquiesces to all events of his life as to his veritable good. . . . Every effort devoted to the progress of the universe or of society has a twofold uselessness: universal determinism makes such efforts ineffectual, and, secondly, everything arrives at its best, anyway. . . . Evil does not exist . . . for everything is really good in things themselves" (Thonnard pp. 148–49). Such quietistic tendencies, leading to acquiescence "to all events of life," are characteristic of all pantheistic philosophies. They are, by their very nature, "potential perils to moral values. By identifying God with the natural world they either persuade men to resign themselves to

the inadequacies of nature, under the illusion that divine sanctity
has rendered them immutable, or they blind the eye to the imper-
fections of nature and thus destroy the moral sensitiveness of religion" (R. Niebuhr, *Does Civilization Need Religion?*, p. 190).

194. W. Kaufmann, *The Faith,* pp. 210ff.

"It is worthy of special note that early Christian apologetic
contains no arguments dealing either with hopes of improving the
existing social situation, or with any attempt to heal social ills . . .
ethical considerations always aimed at fostering habits of sobriety
and industry, that is they are concerned with the usefulness of the
Christian as a citizen" (Troeltsch, p. 40). "Lutheranism is the
Protestant way of despairing of the world and of claiming victory
for the religious ideal without engaging the world in combat. . . .
The medieval ascetic flees from the world into the monastery and
there attempts realization of his religious ideal. The Lutheran
quietist flees from the world into the asylum of his inner life where
he comes into the emotional possession of the ideal without risking
its refinements in the world of cruel realities" (R. Niebuhr, *Does
Civilization Need Religion?,* pp. 110–11).

195. Aristotle-McKeon, pp. 1107–8. Maimonides is in complete agreement. He too maintains that the rational virtues are
superior to the moral virtues because through "the conception of
the intelligibles, which teach true opinions concerning the divine
things . . . man is man" (*Guide,* pt. 3:54, p. 635). "Therefore you
ought to desire to achieve this thing, which will remain permanently
with you, and not weary and trouble yourself for the sake of
others . . . The prophets, like the philosophers, clearly state that
neither the perfection of possession nor the perfection of health nor
the perfection of moral habits is a perfection of which one should
be proud or . . . desire. The perfection of which one should be
proud and that one should desire is knowledge of Him . . ." (ibid.,
p. 636).

196. Spinoza, pt. 4, prop. 28, p. 200.

197. Ibid., pt. 5, prop. xxxii, p. 274.

Strauss points out that Spinoza's "intellectual love of God" is really an intellectual love of fate (*amor fati*). "The free and strong man whose mind is open to fate in intellectual love . . . has no faith, because he does not hope and does not fear. He loves fate, he takes joy in contemplation which is the certain good" (Strauss, pp. 218, 220. Spinoza, *Ethics,* pt. 4, prop 47, scholium).

198. *Avot* chap. 2:9.

199. *Kiddushin* 40b. See also *Megillah* 26b–27a, where the question of prayer vs. study is discussed.

200. See comment of Rashi on *mevi liyede ma'aseh, Bava Kama* 17a, also *Tosafot* there on *Veha'amar Mar.*

201. *Bava Kama* 17a. Scores of other passages can be cited in which deeds of lovingkindness are paralleled to or even set above study: *Rosh Hashana* 18b, *Sotah* 14a, *Avodah Zarah* 5b, 17b, *Avot* 1:2. In his educational theory, as in his personal life, Plato wavers between the ideal of action and contemplation(Rutenber, p. 87). In God, contemplation and activity are one; in man, they must be held in equipoise (ibid., p. 91).

202. *Avot* chap. 3:9, 17. *Yoma* 72b.

203. *Sifra d' be Rav* on Lev. 19:2. See also *Torah Temimah, ad locum,* n. 2.

204. "By a virtual change of a system is now understood not only an infinitesimal spacial displacement of its individual parts, but also an infinitely small increase or decrease of temperature, an infinitely small change in the distribution of electricity on the surface of a conducting body; in short, any elementary increase or decrease of one of the variable magnitudes that characterize the total state of the system" (Cassirer, *Substance,* pp. 174–75).

205. To the hard-line Marxist, charity is a sop extended by the rich to the poor in order to avoid the revolution. Hence it is an evil.

206. The Mishnah *Pe'ah* and the tractate of the same name in the Jerusalem Talmud.

207. See Maimonides, *Hilkhot Matnot Aniyim* and *Hilkhot Zedakah,* in *Shulhan Arukh Yoreh Deah,* pars. 247–59.

208. Above p. 45.

209. Maimonides, *Hilkhot Matnot Aniyim,* chap. 1:15. See also Tosafot *Hagiga* 6b, *She-ayn lahem shiur.*

210. *Gittin* 7b. Also Tosefta *Pe'ah* chap. 4:10.

211. *Sifre,* Deut. *ad locum.* Also Tosefta *Pe'ah* chap. 4:10.

212. *Ketubot* 67b.

213. *Avot,* chap. 2:8.

214. *Avot,* chap. 6:4.

215. "The Christian ideal means rather the entire renunciation of the material social ideal of all political and economic values, and the turning towards the religious treasures of peace of heart, love of humanity, fellowship with God" (Troeltsch, pp. 48–49). "Jesus defines the more ultimate possibility toward which the young man is yearning, in the words: *'If thou wilt be perfect,* go and sell that thou hast and give to the poor.' What is demanded is an action in which regard for the self is completely eliminated" (R. Niebuhr, *Nature and Destiny of Man,* vol. 1, p. 287). Cp. Matt. 19:21; Luke 18:22. Note the efforts of the commentators of the *Interpreter's Bible* to tone down the harshness of the attitude there implied towards the possession of material goods.

216. *Ketubot* 50a. Maimonides sees in this Rabbinic formula a limitation upon the biblical injunction to "lend him sufficient for his needs." "If a man's needs exceeds one-fifth of one's possessions he is obligated to give no more than that fifth and then depart and no sin is imputed to him for failing to give him sufficient for his needs" (commentary on Mishnah *Pe'ah,* chap. 1:1). In his code, *Hilkhot Arakhin veHaramin,* ch. 8:13, he says that giving away all of one's possessions is not an act of *hassidut,* exemplary piety, but of *shtut,* folly.

217. *Arakhin* 28a.

218. See pp. 77–78.

219. Some count forty-six such passages, *Bava Mezia* 59b.

220. Glueck, pp. 40 and 16. Also Maimonides, *Guide,* pt. 3:53.

221. *Berakhot* 5a.

222. *Sukkah* 49b, Tosefta *Pe'ah* chap. 4:19.

223. This they do on basis of Gen. 47:29.

224. Grice, pp. 59, 74–76.

225. *Hilkhot Deot,* chap. 6:7.

226. *Arakhin* 16b.

227. Hence also the great virtue attributed to those who are ready to accept criticism. *Tamid* 28a.

228. *Shabbat* 119b. Also *Shabbat* 55a, on Ezek. 9:4.

229. Jer. 15:10–18; Ps. 69:8–13, 139:21–22. To encourage people to fulfill this unpleasant task, the Rabbis quoted Prov. 24:25, and interpreted Prov. 28:23 to infer that he who rebukes a sinner is ushered into the presence of the Lord. *Tamid* 28a.

230. Jerusalem Talmud, *Pe'ah,* 15b–col. 4, lower half. *Tanhuma* on Num. 21:21. See also Kant, *Doctrine of Virtue,* p. 126; Kimmelman, "Rabbinic Ethics of Protest."

"In the Pauline-Protestant tradition the crucial tension is always between the individual and God, to which relation other persons and the community are irrelevant. This conception of primitive Christendom was revived in an extreme form by Luther. . . . Eventually, in the nineteenth century . . . some of its [Lutheranism's] communicants evolved a 'social gospel.' Revealingly enough, to achieve this they had to reach beyond Luther, beyond Paul, beyond even Jesus, to the Hebrew Prophets for sanction and content" (Steinberg, *Anatomy,* pp. 141–42).

"I have as a Christian theologian sought to strengthen the Hebraic prophetic content of the Christian religion" (R. Niebuhr, quoted by Steinberg, ibid., p. 198).

231. *Torah Temima, ad locum; Sanhedrin* 73a.

232. See *Interpreter's Bible, ad locum,* where in the notes on 15:13–17 the same sentiment is attributed to Buddha. Also "The Gospel According to John, I–XII," vol. 29 of the *Anchor Bible,* by Raymond E. Brown, comment on chap. 10:11, "lays down his life," p. 386.

233. *Bava Mezia* 62a. Maharsha, *ad locum,* is of the opinion that Rabbi Akiba would have agreed with Ben Petura if the water

had belonged to both of them, for then neither of them would have had the right to require the other to give up his life, nor would either of them have been morally obligated to do so. See note 161. We shall have more to say about this later. See also Aḥad Ha'am, "Al Shtei Haseipim," in vol. 4 of *Al Parashat Derakhim,* p. 46.

234. Jerusalem Talmud, *Nedarim* chap. 9, *halakhah* 4.

235. *Shabbat* 31a.

236. See above p. 5.

The Rabbis interpreted "neighbor" to refer to Israelites, and "stranger" (*ger*) to "righteous proselytes" (see Maimonides, *Sefer Hamiẓvot,* positive commandments nos. 206, 207, and his Code, bk. 1, *Hilkhot Deot,* chap. 6, pars. 3–8). While the identification of "neighbor" with Israelite may be reasonably justified, nothing in the use of the term *ger* in the Pentateuch indicates that it ever referred to anyone but a non-Jew. Nor can there be any doubt about how Hillel understood the term "neighbor." His response to the prospective convert is obviously just a negative formulation of Lev. 19:18. For Rabbi Akiba's interpretation of this verse in the spirit of Hillel, see Finkelstein, *Social Responsibility,* p. 44, and particularly his *Mabo,* pp. 47–52. For a diametrically opposite attitude towards the Rabbinic interpretation of this verse see E. Simon, *The Neighbor.*

237. In *Shabbat* 128b, the question whether the prohibition of cruelty to animals is biblical or rabbinic is raised, but is not answered, since no biblical verse is quoted to establish a biblical prohibition. The *Midrash Hagadol* on Num. 22:32, quotes Rabbi Yoḥanan as pointing to this verse to prove that cruelty to animals is a biblical prohibition. For our purposes it makes no difference. It is interesting, however, to note that Bentham (Burtt, p. 846, n. 21), in discussing attitudes toward animals, writes: "Under the Gentoo and Mohammedan religions, the interests of the rest of the animal creation seem to have met with some attention." He has nary a word to say about Judaism, and one cannot but wonder why. He did know the Ten Commandments!

238. *Avodah Zarah* 14b. This law obviously placed severe limitations upon the economic activities of Jews, and they were compelled to find some legal fiction with which to circumvent it. See ibid., 15a, Tosafot *Aymor lishhita.*

239. *Bava Mezia* 87a–b., *J. T. Ma'aserot* chap. 2, *halakhah* 4.

240. Dresner, p. 27.

241. Spinoza, *Ethics,* pt. 4, prop. 37, scholium, p. 209.

242. The opening phrases of Deut. 4:9 and of v. 15 are interpreted by the Rabbis as commandments prohibiting one from inflicting any harm upon himself. The word *nefesh* is understood by the Rabbis to refer not merely to the soul, but to the body. Maimonides thus interprets them in *Hilkhot Rozeah* chap. 11:4; that these verses were thus popularly understood, see *Berakhot* 32b.

243. *Sanhedrin* 74a, Soncino translation.

244. *Bezah* 32b.

245. *Nedarim* 64b. Kant, for analogous reasons, places a limitation upon generosity. As an example of "our duty to ourselves regarding the dignity of humanity within us." he says: "Be no man's lackey. . . . Do not accept favors you could do without, and do not be a parasite or a flatterer or (what really differs from these only in degree), a beggar. Be thrifty, then, so that you will not become destitute" (*Doctrine,* p. 101).

246. The question is raised whether there is greater virtue in one who enjoys the activity which the commandment imposes than in one who fulfills the commandment even though he does not get any pleasure in the doing of it. Some commandments cannot possibly be performed with joy, such as the burial of the dead. There are other commandments whose very essence is that they be performed with joy, such as the celebration of the festivals and observance of the Sabbath (Deut. 16:11, 14; Isa. 58:13). The rabbinic consensus is that the "commandments were not given us for our enjoyment" (*Eruvin* 31a). Hence, whether one derives pleasure from the activity prescribed by the commandment is of secondary consequence. This maxim of the Rabbis has legal implications which do not concern us here. The injunction to "serve God with

joy" (Ps. 100:2) and the rabbinic concept of *Simha shel mizvah,* the joy that should accompany the performance of the *mizvah,* should be associated primarily with the joy that derives from the consciousness that one is serving God, and only secondarily from the joy which may inhere in the act itself. Hence, the performance of a *mizvah* merely because one enjoys doing it, should not be classified as a religiously motivated act.

247. *Avot* chap 1:3, translation of Louis Ginzberg in the *Jewish Encyclopedia* article on Antigonos. Professor Ginzberg there interprets the statement in the light of the apologetic mood current among Jews at the end of the nineteenth century. "The naive conception dominant in the Old Testament, that God's will must be done to obtain His favor in the shape of physical prosperity, is rejected by Antigonos—as well as the view specifically called 'Pharisaic' which makes reward in the future life the motive for human action. Thus the first known Pharisee urges that good should be done for its own sake."

248. *Avot de-Rabbi Nathan,* ed. Schechter, nusaḥ A, chap. 5, p. 13, and in the English translation of Judah Goldin, p. 39. For a comprehensive discussion of the history of the text of this passage and of the data it contains regarding the origin of the sects, as well as of the theological doctrines involved, see Finkelstein, *Pharisees,* pp. 764 ff. We are not concerned with the history of the text but with the ethical implications of its doctrine.

249. Urbach, *Ḥazal,* chap. 14, contains an excellent collection of rabbinic statements on this question, and a bibliography of the literature dealing with these statements.

250. This is the oldest passage in which the expression *mora shamayim* is found. Hence its meaning is uncertain (Urbach, *Ḥazal,* p. 251).

251. According to the Sadducees, "Antigonos had not questioned the doctrine of reward and punishment. . . . Apparently, they agreed that what Antigonos was denying was not reward and punishment as such, but reward and punishment in another world" (Finkelstein, *Pharisees,* p. 772).

270 The Ethical in the Jewish and American Heritage

252. J. Goldin in *Wolfson Jubilee Volume,* vol. 3 (Hebrew), p. 90, and note particularly reference to article by E. Bickerman.

253. *Tanḥuma* (Buber ed.) comment on Lev. 5:1, p. 9, par. 15 Schechter, in *Abot,* n. pp. 26–27, quotes a source similar in spirit to that of the Midrash, in which the "fear of God" appears to be set above the love of God, and comments, "The strangeness of this passage is self-evident since it is well known that the sages always set him who serves God out of love above him who serves Him out of fear." Dr. Finkelstein (*Mavo,* p. 33) disagrees with Schechter's evaluation of the authenticity of the text. But he too assumes that "it is impossible to imagine that any one among the later generation of sages should have differed with the accepted point of view that serving God out of love is superior to serving Him out of fear." For Urbach's interesting interpretation of the statement attributed to Antigonos that *mora* includes *ahavah,* or is well-nigh synonymous with it, see Urbach, *Ḥazal,* p. 352.

254. *Sotah* 31a.

255. *Sotah* 27b. I say "we are led to believe" because we cannot be certain that Yoḥanan ben Zakkai really did feel that way. He might very well have been of the opinion that serving God out of fear was in no way less virtuous than serving Him out of love. From what the tradition has recorded regarding the character of Yoḥanan ben Zakkai (*Sukkah* 28a), no one could have served God with greater love. Yet we are told that on his deathbed he wept in fear of meeting his Creator. When his pupils asked him to bless them he said: "May your fear of Heaven be as great as your fear of man." And when his surprised pupils asked "And no more than that?" he responded "Would it would be that great, for when one transgresses he says 'I hope no man saw me'" *Berakhot* 28b. See also Ḥafeẓ Ḥayyim, p. 9, on discussion of *Yira* and *Paḥad.*

256. *Sotah* 31a.

257. Aristotle-McKeon, *Ethics,* p. 938.

258. "Every man has a conscience and finds himself watched, threatened and, in general, kept in an attitude of respect (of esteem coupled with fear) by an inner judge" (Kant, *Doctrine,* p. 103).

259. This is the OJPS translation. The NJPS replaces "fear" by "revere." For the theologian, "reverence for the Lord has an ingredient of fear, although it is far more than an abject cringing before some arbitrary and unfriendly power. . . . wise living does not remove fear entirely. It consists in fearing 'the right things' " (Rolland W. Schloerb, on Prov. 1:7).

260. Thus Maimonides explains Abraham's reaction to God's command to sacrifice Isaac as being due to "his fear of Him, who should be exalted, and because of his love to carry out His command . . ." (*Guide,* pt. 3:24, pp. 500–501).

261. One may not care to receive a reward for his good deeds, but has he a right to assume that he is sinless or that God never punishes sin? And if sin is punished, is there any particular virtue in not fearing to be punished?

262. Barnes, p. 27.

263. "To need happiness, to deserve it, and yet at the same time not to participate in it, can not be consistent with the perfect volition of a rational being. . . . virtue and happiness together constitute the possession of the *summum bonum* in a person, and the distribution of hapiness in exact proportion to morality . . . constitutes the *summum bonum* of a possible world . . ." (Kant-Abbott, p. 206). See also note 272.

264. The use of the "gold and silver dishes" was not due to ostentation, but rather to a "principle of the Sadducean group which insisted on the enjoyment of the pleasures of this world. The Sadducees ascribed more significance to their earthly hedonism which underlay their disbelief in any future life, a conception they considered schismatic and, as we shall see, unethical" (Finkelstein, *Pharisees,* p. 768).

265. See p. 29.

266. *Pesaḥim* 8a.

267. Ibid., 8b. *Tosafot, Sheyizkeh le-olam,* etc.

268. Y. Kaufmann, p. 40.

269. Ibid., pp. 80–86. See also Lev. 19:31 and 20:27.

270. *Yalkut Shimoni, ad locum. Pesikta de-Rav Kahana,* p. 150 (*Piska Shor oh Keves,* par. 2).

271. Since on this earth the ethical and moral life is not always materially rewarded, the opinion was expressed that *skhar mizvah behai alma leka,* it is never rewarded (Kiddushin 39b). This does not, however, reflect the attitude of the main body of the Biblical-Rabbinic tradition.

272. *Kiddushin* 39b; *Taanit* 11a; *Berakhot* 5a–b; and numerous other passages. Kant arrives at his postulate of the immortality of the soul as follows: "The realization of the *summum bonum,* the distribution of happiness in exact proportion to morality in the world, is the necessary object of a will determinable by the moral law. . . . Now the perfect accordance of the will with the moral law is holiness, a perfection of which no rational being of the sensible world is capable at any moment of his existence. Since, nevertheless, it is required as practically necessary, it can only be found in a progress *ad infinitum* towards that perfect accordance. . . . This endless progress is only possible on the supposition of an endless duration of the existence and personality of the same rational being (which is called the immortality of the soul)" (*Critique,* pp. 218–19).

273. See n. 11.

274. Cp. Santayana, p. 48. "What should be the end of life if friendship with the gods is a means only?" One should not, of course, equate the pagan concept of "friendship with the gods" with the psalmist's concept of "nearness to God." There are, however, overtones of meaning common to both of them.

275. *Avot,* chap. 4:2.

276. Urbach, *Hazal,* p. 239.

277. This is the main theme of the volume that should hopefully follow this one.

278. *Sabbath and Festival Prayer Book,* pp. 87, 89.

279. *Avot,* chap. 3:118.

280. See above pp. 9–10. Also Rutenber, *Doctrine.*

281. Ibid., p. 12–13.

282. "The Intellectual Love of the mind towards God is part of the infinite love with which God loves Himself" (Spinoza, pt. 5, prop. 36, p. 276).

283. Heschel, *Prophets,* chaps. 11–18.

284. Maimonides, *Guide,* chap. 1:55, p. 128.

285. Sec. IX of this chapter.

286. *Megillah* 31a.

287. This verse follows upon the verses which relate that Abraham had been circumcised. This visitation, the *Aggadah* says, occurred three days thereafter, when Abraham was in greatest pain.

288. *Sotah* 14a.

289. In his overly harsh criticism of Lazarus's *Ethics of Judaism,* Hermann Cohen wrote: "Zweierlei mussen wir dagegen fragen. Erstlich: warum ist es denn sittlich" das war die frage: der Grund des Sittlichen. Zweitens aber is die Ganze Fragestellung falsch, weil sie auf das Gebot Gottes allein den Grund des Sittlichen bezieht; und nicht auf das Wesen Gottes. Das Gebot ist von sekundaren Bedeutung. 'Du bist Gott wenn du allein warest.' Aber *das Wesen Gottes ist die Sittlichkeit,* ist die Sittliche Gesetz. Diese begriffe sind nicht bloss untrenbars, sondern identisch" (*Schriften,* p. 14). Lazarus seems to make the same point (*Ethics,* vol. 1, pp. 112–13).

290. "If a man were always anxious that he himself above all things could act justly, temperately or in accordance with any other of the virtues and in general were always to try to secure for himself the honorable course, no one will call such a man a lover of self or blame him, but such a man would seem more than the other a lover of self. At all events, he assigns to himself the things that are noblest and best and gratifies the most authoritative element in himself. . . . Therefore the good man should be a lover of self. . . . it is true of the good man so that he does many acts for the sake of his friends and his country and if necessary dies for them; for he will throw away both wealth and honor and in general the goods that are objects of competition, gaining for himself nobility. . . . In this sense

then it has been said, the man should be a lover of self" (Aristotle-McKeon, pp. 1087–88).

291. *Avot,* chap. 4:22, S. Greenberg, *Foundations,* pp. 146–51.

292. *Shabbat* 127a. Also Mishnah *Pe'ah* 1:1.

293. "To repudiate an overall design to history as do Kierke-gaard and Barth, is an impossibility, both Jewishly and as a matter of human sanity and morale," (Steinberg, *Anatomy,* p. 205). "Sanity and spiritual realism—these are the special endowments of Judaism. . . . In Judaism mystery may attend, but no absurdity mars the simple lines of its essential faith nor the elemental humaness of its moral aspirations" (ibid., p. 212).

294. "The only good reason for adopting a mode of life is that one's character decrees it and this is independent of the question of whether the mode of life consists in the service of other or anything else" (Grice, p. 168).

295. For Socrates' rationalization of his action, see Plato's *Dialogues,* "Apology" and "Crito." For Akiba's rationalization, see *Berakhot* 61b.

296. Sidgwick, who was undoubtedly one of the most thought-ful and thorough students of the various philosophies of ethics and morals, "could find no trustworthy method of reconciling the opposition between rational egoism and rational benevolence without the assumption of the moral government of the world, in short, without theism" (*Outlines,* p. 301). But the theism which can effect the reconciliation is not just any theism, not the God of Aristotle or of Spinoza, but the just, the merciful, and the concerned God of the Biblical-Rabbinic tradition.

297. "Nietzsche . . . made clear that the denial of the biblical God demands the denial of biblical morality however secularized, which far from being self-evident or rational, has no other support than the biblical God; mercy, compassion, equalitarianism, broth-erly love or altruism must give way to cruelty and its kin. . . . The efforts of the new thinking to escape from the evidence of the bib-

lical understanding of man, i.e. of biblical morality have failed. . . .
biblical morality demands the biblical God" (Strauss, pp. 12–13).

298. Broad, p. 255.

299. "Oswald Spengler, in his morphology of civilizations,
presents 'religion without God' as the unvarying symptom of a dying
civilization, too sophisticated to believe in the cosmic worth of its
moral values but not quite ready to abandon them" (R. Niebuhr,
Civilization, p. 56).

CHAPTER 2

1. On the attitude toward the Constitution as a "sacred" document, see Miller, p. 181. E. S. Corwin, in *The Higher Law*, attempts to explain the regard in which the Constitution is held by
the American people by reference to the fact that "in the American
written Constitution, higher law at last attained a form which made
possible the attribution to it of an entirely new sort of validity, the
validity of a *statute emanating from the sovereign people*" (p. 89).
But while emanation "from the sovereign people" may bestow a sort
of validity upon a statute, it does not transform a statute into a
"higher law." Earlier (p. 4) he states: "The attribution of supremacy to the Constitution on the ground solely of its rootage in
popular will represents, however, a comparatively late outgrowth of
American constitutional theory. Earlier the supremacy accorded to
Constitutions was ascribed less to their putative source than to their
supposed content, to their embodiment of an essential and unchanging justice."

The Constitution was not, as far as I know, generally conceived
as the "embodiment of an essential and unchanging justice." The
provisions regarding slavery, and regarding a method for amend-
ing it, were clearly a recognition that it was not such an "embodiment." Its greatest virtue was this very recognition on its part of its
own inadequacies, so that it may in time become ever more nearly
"the perfect embodiment of an essential and unchanging justice."

On the Constitution as the Higher Law, see also Gabriel, pp. 403, 406.

2. Becker, p. 24. At one time Alexander Hamilton, who claimed that he had "done more for the present constitution than anyone else, spoke of it as 'the frail and worthless fabric' " (Bowers, p. 95).

3. For the criticism leveled against the Declaration, see Becker, chap. 6. The *Cambridge Modern History* has the following to say about the Declaration: "On July 4, 1776, Congress passed the resolution which made the colonies independent communities, issuing at the same time the well-known Declaration of Independence. If we regard the Declaration as the assertion of an abstract political theory, criticism and condemnation are easy. It sets out with a general proposition so vague as to be practically useless. The doctrine of the equality of men, unless it be qualified and conditioned by reference to special circumstance, is either a barren truism or a delusion" (quoted by Richard H. Niebuhr, pp. 60–61).

4. For the historical and philosophical sources of the Declaration, see Becker, chaps. 2 and 3. See also B. Bailyn, *The Ideological Origins of the American Revolution.*

5. The Gettysburg Address is referred to in a number of Supreme Court decisions on a par with the Declaration and the Constitution. See pp. 132–33. See also Gabriel, p. 407, 413.

6. Emerson called the Fugitive Slave Law of 1850 "this filthy enactment," and wrote in his journal, "I will not obey it, by God!" (Bickel, p. 113). Thoreau (quoted in Becker, p. 242) wrote: "How does it become a man to behave toward the American government today? I answer that he cannot without disgrace be associated with it. I cannot for an instant recognize that political organization as my government which is the slaves' government also."

7. "In justification of their revolt against the established regime, the abolitionists naturally turned to the Declaration of Independence. From the positive law, they appealed to a 'higher law.' . . . They would defend, not the legal rights of American citi-

zens, but the sacred and inalienable rights of all men" (Bickel, p. 113).

8. Statement by Douglas, quoted by Lincoln in speech at Springfield, Illinois, June 26, 1857 (Basler, p. 361).

9. Lincoln's comment on Douglas's statement (ibid., p. 362).

10. Ibid., p. 361, also p. 437.

11. ". . . Lincoln saw the immediate problem underlying the Civil War, Union and Emancipation in their true perspective as subordinate to the necessity of preserving not merely the words of the Declaration of Independence, but its prophetic truth" (Basler, pp. 39–40). . . . "the beauty and cogency of the preamble [to the Declaration], reaching back to remotest antiquity and forward to an indefinite future, have lifted the hearts of millions of men and will continue to do so. . . . These words are more revolutionary than anything written by Robespierre, Marx, or Lenin, more explosive than the atom, a continual challenge to ourselves, as well as an inspiration to the oppressed of all the world" (Morison, p. 223).

12. Frost, p. 76.

13. Justice Louis Brandeis in *Myers* v. *United States,* 272 U.S. 52293 (1926). Quoted in Miller, p. 56.

14. "We are under a Constitution, but the Constitution is what the judges say it is" (Former Chief Justice Hughes when governor of New York, quoted in Corwin, *The Constitution,* p. xv).

15. See Kristol, "American Historians."

16. See Lincoln's statement on this matter, below p. 113.

17. Chief Justice Marshall in *Barron* v. *Baltimore & Peters,* 243 (1833). Cushman and Cushman, *Decisions,* p. 78.

18. See Konvitz, *Bill of Rights Reader.*

19. " 'There are,' remarked James Bryce in *The American Commonwealth,* 'certain dogmas or maxims which are in so far fundamental that they have told widely on political thought, and that one usually strikes upon them when sinking a shaft, so to speak, into an American mind.' Among these, Bryce thought, were notions about man's inalienable rights, popular sovereignty, the distrust of centralized political power, and the conviction that the

functions of government should be kept at a minimum if the community and the individual were to prosper" (Arieli, p. 318). See also Gabriel, pp. 10, 19–20.

20. *McCulloch* v. *Maryland,* 4 Wheaton (U.S.) 316 (1819). Cushman and Cushman, *Cases,* p. 13.

21. For a comprehensive presentation of the state vs. federal sovereignty issue, see address by John C. Calhoun, "Against the Force Bill," delivered in the Senate on February 15 and 16, 1833 (in Brewer, vol. 3).

22. Lincoln's reply to Douglas at Chicago, July 10, 1858 (Basler, p. 309); see also p. 439: "He [Douglas] has done all in his power to reduce the whole question of slavery to one of a mere *right of property;* and as such, how can *he* oppose the foreign slave trade?" (Lincoln at Springfield, June 16, 1858 [Basler, p. 380]). See also p. 395, 291. See also Angle, p. 303.

23. Basler, p. 361. See also Angle, p. 294.

24. *Dred Scott* v. *Sanford* (1857), 19 Howard (U.S.) 393.

25. The intention of the Declaration, Jefferson later wrote, was not to say something new, but "to place before mankind the common sense of the subject, in terms so plain and firm as to command their assent. . . . Neither aiming at originality of principles or sentiments, nor yet copied from any particular and previous writing, it was intended to be an expression of the American mind" (Hofstadter, p. 70).

26. Basler, p. 20.

27. "The America that means most to me is less her rocks and rills, etc. than her Jeffersons and Lincolns" (Roy P. Basler in letter to Newman Basler, p. xix), a sentiment in which I heartily concur.

28. Basler, p. 577.

29. Speech in Chicago, July 10, 1858 (Basler, p. 393).

30. Address at Cooper Institute, New York, February 27, 1860 (Basler, pp. 535–36).

31. For an account of the efforts that were made in the decade preceding the Civil War to prove that slavery was not only morally

wrong but economically ruinous, see Nevins, vol. 2, chap. 5. The question of whether or not slavery was economically viable has recently been raised anew by Professors Robert W. Fogel and Stanley L. Enjerman in *Time on the Cross* (1974). They argue that slavery was profitable (see *New York Times,* May 21, 1974, p. 149).

32. Basler, pp. 309–10.

33. Ibid., p. 359.

34. Ibid., pp. 13, 186–88, 712.

35. Letter to Joshua F. Speed, August 24, 1855 (ibid., p. 336).

36. Springfield speech, June 26, 1857 (ibid., p. 363).

37. Ibid., p. 361.

38. Speech at Chicago, July 10, 1858 (ibid., pp. 401–2).

39. Ibid., pp. 360–61.

40. Speech at Chicago, July 10, 1858 (ibid., p. 403).

41. Lincoln's Bible apparently had "picture" where others have "setting."

42. A fragment: The Constitution and the Union (1860?), ibid., p. 513.

43. Chief Justice Warren in *Brown* v. *Board of Education of Topeka,* 347 U.S. 483 (1954). Cushman and Cushman, *Decisions,* p. 253.

44. Bickel, pp. 211–53, has an excellent detailed presentation of the debates that preceded the final adoption of the Fourteenth Amendment.

45. Ibid., pp. 252–53.

46. "During the first ten years of the Amendment hardly a half dozen cases came before the court under all of its clauses put together. During the next twenty years some two hundred cases most of them under the 'due process clause.' During the ensuing twelve years this number was more than doubled, a ratio which still holds good substantially" (Corwin, *Constitution, p.* 251).

47. Justice Black in *Chamber* v. *Florida,* 309 U.S. 227 (1940). Cushman and Cushman, Cases, pp. 240–41.

48. Justice Fortas, in a dissenting opinion in which Chief

Justice Warren and Justice Douglas concurred. *Forston* v. *Morris,* 385 U.S. 231, 249 (1966). Quoted in Miller, p. 141.

49. Vann C. Woodward, *The Strange Career of Jim Crow* (1961 ed.), p. xvii (Quoted by Miller, p. 110).

50. "The Civil War itself was the only significant interruption in the course of American history, and perhaps some return afterward to antebellum patterns was inevitable. This meant, however, the debilitation of the 14th Amendment" (Miller, p. 115).

51. ". . . there seems no doubt that a deal was made by the Republicans with Southern Democratic leaders, by virtue of which, in return for their acquiescence in Hayes's election, they promised on his behalf to withdraw the garrison and to wink at non-enforcement of Amendment XV, guaranteeing civil rights to the freedmen. The bargain was kept on both sides. On 2 March 1877 the electoral commission. . . declared Hayes the winner by a majority of one electoral vote. And virtually no attempt was made by the federal government to enforce Amendment XV until the Franklin D. Roosevelt administration" (Morison, pp. 733–34).

52. Cushman and Cushman, *Decisions,* p. 74.

53. *Barron* v. *Baltimore,* 7 Peters 243 (1833). Ibid., pp. 75–76.

54. The *Slaughter Houses* cases, 14 Wallace 36 (1873). Ibid., pp. 55–59. Justice Miller ostensibly based his decision on his reading of the Fourteenth Amendment. We need not here enter into the legalistic subtleties to which he has recourse. But it is of importance to note that he does not rest his case on that alone. He appeals not merely to the text of the amendment, but to the *intention* of its authors. He asks a question to which there is no unequivocal answer: "Was it the purpose of the Fourteenth Amendment . . . to transfer the security and protection of all the civil rights which we have mentioned from the States to the Federal Governments?" He answers unequivocally, "We are convinced that no such results were intended by the Congress which proposed the amendments nor by the legislatures of the states which ratified them." The question upon which the jurists of a later generation differed remained the same

as that upon which the interpreters of the Declaration and the Preamble had differed in a previous generation. How is a historic document to be understood? Do we have the right to assume that its framers were fully aware that the document could bear meanings beyond those which they had attributed to it, and that they expected and even hoped that those who followed them would explore these larger meanings? Taney, in the *Dred Scott* decision, had spoken as clearly as anyone could in the negative. "It [the Constitution] speaks not only in the same words, but with the same meaning and intent with which it spoke when it came from the hands of the framers and was voted and adopted by the people of the United States. Any other rule of construction would abrogate the judicial character of this great court and make it the mere reflex of the popular opinion or passion of the day." The position formulated by Lincoln in relation to the meaning of the Declaration was formulated later by Chief Justice Stone in relation to the Constitution. "In determining whether a provision of the Constitution applies to a new subject matter, it is of little significance that it is one with which the framers were most familiar. For in setting up an enduring framework of government they undertook to carry out for the indefinite future and in all the vicissitudes of the changing affairs of men, those fundamental purposes, which the instrument itself discloses. Hence, we read its words, not as we read legislative codes which are subject to continuous revision with the changing course of events, but as the *revelation of the great purposes* [emphasis added] which were intended to be achieved by the Constitution as a continuing instrument of government. If we remember that 'It is a Constitution we are expounding,' we can not rightfully prefer, of the possible meaning of its words, that which will defeat rather than effectuate the constitutional purpose" (*United States* v. *Classic,* 313 U.S. 299 [1941]. Cushman and Cushman, *Decisions,* p. 69).

55. Corwin, *Constitution,* p. 276.

56. *United States* v. *Cruikshank,* (1876). Cushman and Cushman, *Cases,* p. 1110.

57. *Civil Rights* cases, 109 U.S. 3 (1883). Ibid., p. 1100.

58. *United States* v. *Wheeler,* 254 U.S. 281 (1920). Corwin, *Constitution,* p. 251.

59. *Corrigan* v. *Buckley,* 271 U.S. 323 (1926). Cushman and Cushman, *Decisions,* p. 244.

60. *Plessy* v. *Ferguson,* 163 U.S. 537 (1896). Ibid., pp. 249–50. Also, Cushman and Cushman, *Cases,* pp. 1030 ff.

61. Cushman and Cushman, *Decisions,* p. 250, and idem, *Cases,* p. 1032.

62. *Berea College* v. *Kentucky,* 211 U.S. 45 (1908). Cushman and Cushman, *Decisions,* p. 250.

63. *Gong Lum* v. *Rice,* 275 U.S. 78 (1927). Ibid.

64. Cushman and Cushman, *Cases,* p. 1029.

65. *To Secure These Rights,* p. viii.

66. Ibid., p. ix.

67. Ibid., pp. 23–24.

68. Cushman and Cushman speak of "the nationalization of the Bill of Rights" (*Cases,* p. 512).

69. *Cumming* v. *County Board of Education,* 175 U.S. 528 (1899). Cushman and Cushman, *Decisions,* p. 250.

70. *McCabe* v. *Atchinson T. & S. F. Ry. Co.,* 235 U.S. 151 (1914). Ibid.

71. *Henderson* v. *United States,* 399 U.S. 816 (1950). Cushman and Cushman, *Cases,* p. 1036.

72. Ibid.

73. *Gaines* v. *Canada,* 305 U.S. 337 (1938). Chief Justice Hughes stated that Gaines was "entitled to be admitted to the law school of the state university in the absence of other and proper provision for his legal training within the state." Ibid.

74. Chief Justice Vinson, speaking for the court in *Sweatt* v. *Painter,* 339 U.S. 629 (Cushman and Cushman, *Cases,* p. 1037). For Justice Warren's references to "six cases involving the 'separate but equal' doctrine in the field of public education," see *Brown* v. *Board of Education* (Cushman and Cushman, *Decisions,* p. 254).

75. Article I, section 2.

76. "As early as 1875 in *Minor* v. *Happersitt,* 21 Wall 162,

the Court held that the right to vote was not one of the privileges and immunities of citizens of the United States which the states were forbidden by the Fourteenth Amendment to abridge. The amendment did not deprive the states of their rights to establish qualifications for the suffrage" (Cushman and Cushman, *Cases,* p. 1076).

77. *Guin* v. *United States,* 238 U.S. 347 (1915). Cushman and Cushman, *Decisions,* p. 213.

78. *Lane* v. *Wilson,* U.S. 268 (1939). Ibid. See there also the account of the long legal battle (which ended in 1966) to win the Negro the right to participate in state primary elections and to eliminate the poll tax.

79. *Brown* v. *Board of Education,* 345 U.S. 372 (1953). Quoted in Miller, p. 117, n. 51.

80. See above pp. 121–22.

81. Cushman and Cushman, *Decisions,* pp. 255–56.

82. See above pp. 121–22.

83. *Palko* v. *Connecticut,* 302 U.S. 319 (1937). Cushman and Cushman, *Decisions,* pp. 153-55.

84. *Chamber* v. *Florida,* 309 U.S. 227 (1940). Ibid., p. 241.

85. See above p. 123.

86. *Shelley* v. *Kramer,* 334 U.S. 1 (1948), and *Hurd* v. *Hodge,* 334 U.S. 24 (1948). Cushman and Cushman, *Decisions,* p. 244.

87. For an excellent presentation of the legal issues involved in the reapportionment cases, see Miller, chap. 7, and Bickel, chap. 5. Bickel is far less sympathetic to the court's decision than is Miller.

88. Frankfurter, speaking for the court in *Colegrove* v. *Green,* 328 U.S. 549 (Cushman and Cushman, *Cases,* p. 43). Frankfurter maintained his position in 1962 in *Baker* v. *Carr*—to be discussed later. But in 1960, in *Gomillion* v. *Lightfoot,* 364 U.S. 399, Frankfurter, speaking for a unanimous court, held that the blacks of Tuskegee had the right to have the court decide whether the weird redefinition of the boundaries of the city of Tuskegee, which re-

moved from the city "all save four or five of its 400 negro voters while not removing a single white voter or resident," constituted discrimination against them in violation of the due-process and equal-protecton clause of the Fourteenth Amendment and in violation of the Fifteenth Amendment (ibid., p. 45). The lower federal courts, relying on *Colegrove* v. *Green,* had dismissed the complaint attacking the validity of the statute.

89. *Baker* v. *Carr,* 369 U.S. 186 (1962). Cushman and Cushman, *Decisions,* pp. 224, 229–30.

90. Ibid., p. 234. Justice Clark, obviously referring to Frankfurter's opinion, said, "One dissenting opinion, bursting with words that go through so much and conclude with so little, condemns the majority action as a "masive repudiation of the experience of our whole past" (ibid., p. 231).

91. Ibid., p. 237.

92. Miller, p. 119.

93. See Bickel chap. 5, which he titles "Reapportionment and Liberal Myths." Regarding the fear that the Founding Fathers had of universal suffrage and the "mob," see n. 15 and Bowers, chap. 13.

94. Bickel, p. 187.

95. Ibid. The quote from Douglas is from his opinion in *Gray* v. *Sanders,* 372 U.S. 368 (1963).

96. *Reynolds* v. *Sims.* Cushman and Cushman, *Decisions,* pp. 491–92.

97. *Weeks* v. *United States,* 232 U.S. 383 (1914). Cushman and Cushman, *Cases,* p. 684. But the court did not then rule that evidence illegally secured by other agents, whether state or private, was not admissible in a federal court. On the so-called silver-platter doctrine, which maintained that evidence illegally secured by other than federal agents was admissible, see Cushman and Cushman, *Decisions,* p. 104.

98. Cardozo's phrase: see above p. 130.

99. *Wolf* v. *Colorado,* 338 U.S. 25 (1949). Cushman and Cushman, *Cases,* p. 690.

100. Ibid., p. 691.

101. *Mapp* v. *Ohio,* 367 U.S. 643 (1961). Ibid., p. 696.

102. *Ker v. California,* 374 U.S. 23. Cushman and Cushman, *Decisions,* p. 479.

103. Ibid., p. 543.

104. *Griswold* v. *Connecticut,* 381 U.S. 479. Ibid., pp. 545–47. Note the introduction of the concept that a constitutional provision may have a "penumbra" having legal efficacy.

105. Cushman and Cushman, *Decisions,* pp. 547–48. It is interesting to note that about a decade earlier Chief Justice Warren, without referring to the Ninth Amendment, had stated "although the Court has not assumed to define 'liberty' (as found in the 14th Amendment) with any great precision, that term is not confined to mere freedom from bodily restraints. Liberty under law extends to the full range of conduct which the individual is free to pursue, and it cannot be restricted except for a proper governmental objective." *Bolling* v. *Sharpe,* 348 U.S. 496 (1954). Ibid., p. 258.

106. The Fourteenth Amendment states: ". . . nor shall any State deprive any person of . . . liberty, or property . . ."

107. The Social Security Act was challenged, among other reasons, on the ground that "the relation of employment is so essential to the pursuit of happiness that it may not be burdened with a tax."

108. See pp. 132–33, 141.

109. "Mr. Justice Story points out that if it (the view that article 1, section 8 [1]) grants power to provide for the general welfare independently of the taxing power were adopted it is obvious that under the color of the generality of the words, to 'provide for the common defense and general welfare' the government of the United States is in reality a government of general and unlimited powers, notwithstanding the subsequent numeration of specific powers" (Mr. Justice Roberts in *United States* v. *Butler,* 297 U.S. 1. Cushman and Cushman, *Cases,* p. 216).

110. See n. 19.

111. Mr. Justice Peckham—in *Lochner* v. *New York,* 198 U.S. 45 (1905). Cushman and Cushman, *Decisions,* pp. 272–74.

For more instances in which the court used "liberty of contract to void social legislation," see ibid., p. 269.

112. Ibid., p. 278–79.

113. Ibid., p. 273.

114. Article I, section 8, paragraph 3.

115. *Bell* v. *Maryland,* 375 U.S. 226 (1964). For an excellent presentation of the legal aspects of the "sit-in" cases, see Miller, chap. 11, and Bickel, chap. 3.

116. Miller, p. 104, n. 12.

117. Cushman and Cushman, *Decisions,* pp. 529–30.

118. *New York Times,* October 6, 1964.

119. *Heart of Atlanta Motel* v. *United States,* 379 U.S. 241 (1964). Cushman and Cushman, *Decisions,* p. 533.

120. Ibid., pp. 535–36. See also the immediately following discussion of *Edwards* v. *California,* the case referred to by Mr. Justice Douglas.

121. *Edwards* v. *California,* 314 U.S. 160 (1941). The so-called anti-Okie law. Ibid., p. 443.

122. Ibid., p. 446.

123. Ibid., p. 450.

124. Ibid., pp. 450–51.

125. *Munn* v. *Illinois,* 94 U.S. 113 (1877). Cushman and Cushman, *Cases, pp.* 533–37.

126. *New State Ice Company* v. *Leibman,* 285 U.S. 202 (1932). Cushman and Cushman, *Decisions,* p. 261.

127. *Nebbia* v. *New York,* 291 U.S. 502 (1934). Ibid., pp. 261, 267.

128. *Home Building and Loan Association* v. *Blaisdell,* 290 U.S. 398 (1934). Cushman and Cushman, *Cases,* p. 503.

129. Mr. Chief Justice Hughes, speaking in behalf of the court, ibid., pp. 508–10. In the light of our earlier discussions (see n. 54), the following statement by the Chief Justice in this opinion is of particular interest. "It is no answer to say that the public need was not apprehended a century ago, or to insist that what the provision of the Constitution meant to the vision of that day it must

mean to the vision of our time. If by the statement that what the Constitution meant at the time of its adoption it means today, it is intended to say that the great clauses of the Constitution must be confined to the interpretation which the framers, with the conditions and outlook of their time placed upon them, the statement carries its own refutation. . . . The vast body of law which has been developed was unknown to the fathers, but it is believed to have preserved the essential content and spirit of the Constitution. With a growing recognition of public needs and the relation of individual right to public security, the Court has sought to prevent the perversion of the clause through its use as an instrument to throttle the capacity of the States to protect their fundamental interests. This development is a growth from the seeds which the fathers planted" (ibid., pp. 510–11).

130. The National Industrial Recovery Act (1933).

131. The Social Security Act (1935).

132. Mr. Chief Justice Hughes in *Schechter Poultry Corporation* v. *United States,* 295 U.S. 495 (1935). Cushman and Cushman, *Cases,* p. 144.

133. Ibid., p. 415. We quote this at length because it has some bearing on the use of the commerce clause in the Civil Rights cases. See above p. 139.

134. Note that the government's argument is based on article I, section 8(1), and that one of the purposes of the government to be established by the Constitution was "to promote the general welfare." The Preamble, like the Declaration, has no legal standing, but it surely has great moral authority.

135. Mr. Justice Roberts in behalf of the court in *United States* v. *Butler,* 297 U.S. 1 (1936). Cushman and Cushman, *Cases,* pp. 216–17. Justice Roberts there refers also to the fact that the meaning of the phrase "reserved to the States" in the Constitution was a matter of controversy between Madison and Hamilton, the former limiting its application to powers specifically enumerated in the Constitution, the latter arguing that it "confers a power separate and distinct from those later enumerated." "This Court has

noticed the question but has never found it necessary to decide which is the true construction" (ibid).

"In 1918, in *Hammer* v. *Dagenhart,* the court held for the first time that the powers reserved to the states by the Tenth Amendment acted as a limit to the use of congressional power. There the court struck down the use of the commerce clause to control child labor" (ibid., p. 214). See also pp. 442 ff.

136. *Charles C. Steward Machine Co.* v. *Davis,* 301 U.S. 548 (1937). Cushman and Cushman, *Cases,* p. 344. It is interesting and important to note that in this decision Justice Cardozo also refers to a philosophical doctrine and its relation to the law. The law was attacked because the rebates it offered to states that would cooperate, constituted coercion. Justice Cardozo wrote, "every rebate from a tax when conditioned upon conduct is in some measure a temptation. But to hold that motive or temptation is equivalent to coercion, is to plunge the law in endless difficulties. The outcome of such a doctrine is the acceptance of a philosophic determination by which choice becomes impossible. Till now the law has been guided by a robust common sense which assumes the freedom of the will as a working hypothesis in the solution of its problems" (ibid., p. 345).

137. Cushman and Cushman (*Cases,* pp. 442–43) have a good summary of the many welfare acts of Congress which were thus invalidated.

138. Mr. Justice Day, speaking for the court in *Hammer* v. *Dagenhart,* 247 U.S. 251 (1918). Ibid., pp. 444–45.

139. Ibid., pp. 448–49.

140. *United States* v. *Darby,* 312 U.S. 100. Ibid., pp., 452–57.

141. Basler, p. 513.

142 *To Secure These Rights,* p. 3.5.

143. *Goals for Americans,* pp. 1 and 2.

144. Professor Alexander Bickel, quoted by William Safire in *New York Times,* November 15, 1973, p. 45.

145. Chap. 11, Vol. III, in preparation. See Introduction p.xvi.

146. Perry Wills, in the *New York Times Book Review,* pp. 20, 22, in review of *The Imperial Presidency* by Arthur M. Schlesinger, Jr. Mr. Wills also remarks: "The American reaction to any political trouble is to look for a procedural flaw that can be corrected. Our constitution appears by its mechanics of representation and checks to produce good government. If we have bad government, the machinery must have broken down or need repair. We must tinker." Thus Schlesinger concludes with a chapter on various reforms of the Presidency. ". . . on that level, Mr. Schlesinger's book is about as effective as the attempt to cure a fever by taking apart the thermometer."

147. On the relation of morality to religion, see chap. 1 of this volume.

148. Bellow, p. 205.

CHAPTER 3

1. *Kiddushin* 2b. I took liberty with the text on the basis of the marginal note.

2. Freiman's work is an excellent one volume introduction to and summary of this literature.

3. Rabbi Yechiel Yaakov Weinberg, in his introduction to *Tnai beNesuin Uveget* by Rabbi Eliezer Berkovits. This English version is a paraphrase rather than a literal translation. Rabbi Berkovits himself formulates it thus: "As I have remarked on a number of occasions in this inquiry, we rarely have *agunot* in our day. Our problem is the problem of the woman who has been properly married, then, only civilly divorced and re-married without having been given a *get* by her first husband. Her children are *mamzerim.* The truth is that he who sets obstacles in the way of terminating a marriage multiplies *mamzerim* in Israel" (p. 162).

4. *Yoma* 67b.

5. Epstein, *Lishe'aylat Ha'agunah,* pp. 45–46. This translation is a paraphrase of the original.

6. See Aronson, pp. 123 f.

7. *Sifra deBay Rav,* p. 51, on Lev. 1:3; also *Bava Batra* 47b–48a, *Kiddushin* 50a.

8. *Ketubot* 63b.

9. *Hilkhot Ishut,* chap. 14:8.

10. *Kiddushin* 50a.

11. *Hilkhot Gerushin,* chap. 2:20.

12. Baron, vol. 6, p. 135.

13. *Yevamot* 110a, *Gittin* 33a.

14. The word *annul* does not appear to be a precise equivalent for *afkainhu.* Annulment implies that the status of the individual reverts to what it was before the marriage, and it is as if the marriage had never taken place. This raises the question of the status of the children. The problem is discussed in considerable detail in the volume by Berkovits, pp. 33–34, 54–55, 58–59. While this problem does not concern us in this inquiry, it is brought to the attention of the readers merely to indicate that though we shall occasionally use the term *annul* in the context of this rabbinic statement, it is not an exact translation. A more accurate paraphrasing of the statement would be, "The Rabbis terminate his marriage without requiring a *get.*"

15. *Yevamot* 89b.

16. Ibid., 90b; Rashi on *Hatinah kiddesh b'khaspa.*

17. Ibid., *Shavyuha Rabbanan lebe'ilato be'ilat znut.*

18. Ibid., 89b, where they quote Ezra 10:8.

19. Rashi seems to have found difficulty with it. See below p. 181. See also n. 22.

20. *Ketubot* 3a; *Kol d'mekadesh ada'ata d'rabbanan mekadesh.* Rashi seems to be of that opinion; see below pp. 180–81.

21. *Kiddushin* 50a.

22. *Encyclopedia Talmudit,* vol. 2, pp. 137–38.

23. This position is vigorously and elaborately maintained by Berkovits, p. 141, etc., and by Aronson.

24. Berkovits, p. 138.

25. Ibid., p. 156.

26. *Encyclopedia Talmudit,* vol. 2, p. 138, col. 1. Rashbam

in *Bava Batra* 48b on Mar bar Rav Ashi, relates the power to annul and the power to convert a legitimate act of intercourse into an act of fornication as follows: ". . . Moreover, how can [R. Ashi] answer him [Ravina] that the Rabbis declared the act of intercourse to be an act of fornication? Since this act is biblically legitimate, how can they declare it to be an act of fornication? Hence [we must say that] since all who marry, marry upon conditions laid down by the Rabbis, this [act of the bride-snatcher] was not an act of *kiddushin* as prescribed by the Rabbis. Therefore, the act of intercourse automatically becomes an act of fornication." The Rabbis thus do not pass judgment on the act of intercourse directly. They pass judgment only on the status of the marriage. See also, Tosafot *ad locum, Tinah dekiddesh bekhaspah.*

27. *L'she'aylat Ha'agunah,* p. 46.

28. See Kahana, *Letakanat Agunot.*

29. See Berkovits, pp. 156–72, and Freiman, pp. 385–97.

30. "Actually there is no such biblical injunction. Deut. 24:1 mentions 'and he shall write her' only incidentally, as one of the conditions of the protasis. It is no more an injunction than 'she leaves his household and becomes the wife of another man' (ibid., 24:2). See the new JPS *Torah.* I understand 'and he shall write her' to be, rather, an understood step that had to be taken in the clear attestation of an important transaction. I don't regard the necessity of writing deeds so much a protection against light-headed sales of property as a necessity to keep order in the economy. One could say that 'and he shall write her' reflects the solemnity of the divorce, but so does every rule requiring writing a document solemnize a transaction, and in the East most civilized transactions (urban) were recorded in writing" (Moshe Greenberg, in a note to me).

31. *Ein mikra yozeh miyedai peshutai, Shabbat* 63a; see also *Debainan kra kedikhtiv, Sanh.* 45b.

32. *Bava Batra* 168a and Maimonides, *Hilkhot Gerushin,* chap. 2:4. See particularly the *Pilpulta harifta* on Rabbenu Asher, *ad locum,* where the point is made that it is still preferable to have the husband pay the scribe, and that the Rabbis sanctioned the pay-

by the woman only *if* the husband refused, in order to prevent coming an *agunah*.

33. *Torah Temimah* on Deut. 24:1, nn. 16 and 19.

34. See Freiman, p. 385, etc.

35. "As erroneous as the over-emphasis on economics and its hypostasis as the *vera causa* and essence of marriage is also the tearing out of some one economic trait and giving it a special name and thus an artificial entity. This has been done notably with regard to the initial gifts at marriage, especially when given by the husband. More or less, considerable gifts from the husband to his wife's family at marriage occur very widely (see the comprehensive list of references in Westermarck, *History of Human Marriage,* Vol. II, Ch. XXIII). The term 'marriage by purchase' applied to such gifts usually serves to isolate them from their legal and economic context, to introduce the concept of a commercial transaction, which is nowhere to be found in primitive culture as a part of marriage, and to serve as one more starting point for fallacious speculations about the origin of marriage" (Bronislaw Malinowski in *Encyclopaedia Britannica,* 14th ed. s. v. "Marriage," para. 11).

36. *Sanhedrin* 74a.

37. Compare the case of the Bnei Israel of India discussed by Harishon LeZion, Harav Harashi LeYisrael, Rabbi Nissim, in *Bnei Yisrael.*

38. See *Bava Batra* 160b; Mielziner, p. 117; Neufeld, pp. 176, 183.

39. "President Habib ben Ali Bourguiba who became President of Tunisia in 1956, promulgated a code of personal conduct which abolished polygamy, ended the Moslem system by which husbands could divorce their wives by merely repudiating them, and made divorce obtainable only through courts, and gave women the right to sue" (*New York Times,* May 16, 1968). See also *New York Times,* October 9, 1969, regarding the same situation in Tanzania.

40. *Yevamot* 89a, and Tosafot there—*Ma Taama.* See also Epstein, *Jewish Marriage Contract,* p. 195.

41. The Epstein suggestion requires that the husband, immediately after participating in a clandestine-type marriage, and before the public marriage ceremony, execute a legal document appointing his wife as his messenger and scribe to write a *get* for herself should this become necessary (*Lishe'aylat Ha'agunah,* p. 79). The suggestion that the bride and groom sign an "Ante-Nuptial Agreement" stating the conditions for the possible annulment of the marriage into which they are about to enter was adopted by the Committee on Jewish Law and Standards of the Rabbinical Assembly of America. (See the *Rabbinical Assembly Proceedings* of 1968, pp. 229 ff.).

42. *Gittin* 18a; also *Bava Batra* 167a, Tosafot on *Af al pi she' ain ishto.*

43. The same sentiment is forcefully expressed by Freiman, pp. 396–97.

Regarding *Nesuin al tnai,* Rabbi Epstein wrote: "How will the intelligent young Jew take the Rabbi's proposal that he enter into a conditional marriage? I have made that test with some young people and they responded with shock and horror. I therefore humbly counsel you: trying to avoid a minor evil, do not fall into a major one; seeking to overcome a legal difficulty, do not blunder into an ethical immorality" (*Rabbinical Assembly Proceedings* 5 [1933–38]: 230). And yet on p. 232, he suggests instead that the husband appoint his wife as a *shaliah* to write her own *get.*

44. It is a rather long and complicated comment, and I shall translate or paraphrase only the passages relevant to our purpose, hopefully without in any way violating the author's intent. The same will be true for other rabbinic passages that are quoted.

45. Maharsha apparently promises to give a reason for all the four instances. However, he wrote no commentary on *Keritot* and only a few brief comments on *Nazir.* At the end of *Berakhot* he writes: "At the end of *Yevamot* I explained why that tractate ends with the Midrash that the wise increase peace in the world. This tractate [*Berakhot*] also ends with this Midrash. The reason for it

seems to be that the *tefillot* and *berakhot* discussed in this tractate are enactments of the Rabbis, and their purpose is to establish peace in the world—that is, peace between Israel and their Father in heaven. . ."

46. Maharsha must either have had a text of *Yevamot* different from ours, since the verses he here quotes are not found at the end of our text, but are found at the end of *Berakhot;* or he may have assumed that these verses were omitted at the end of our text for the same reason that the Talmud very often does not quote the end of a biblical verse to which it refers. It is assumed that the student knows the whole verse. Similarly, the aggadic passage as it appears in *Berakhot* may have been taken by him to be an integrated unit, only part of which is quoted at the end of *Yevamot.*

47. The term is not here used pejoratively, but rather positively. "Casuistry is perhaps the most carefully elaborated way of taking account of the diversities of behavior while retaining the integrity of the principle according to which behavior is to be judged" (Lehman, p. 290).

48. See Chayas, vol. 1, pp. 31–43, for a discussion of this question. Much of the source material quoted is also found in Aronson's article, pp. 127 ff. See also "Beth din matnin Laakor davar min Hatorah," by Y. D. Gilat in *Bar Illan Sefer Hashanna* 7–8, 5729–30, which appeared just about the same time this essay did.

49. That is, they permitted her to marry the first man without receiving a *get* from the second man.

50. *Yevamot* 110a. The Talmud does not raise the question of whether the "snatcher" was also punished for committing adultery if he did have intercourse with her. The bride could under any circumstances return to her husband (if he were not a *kohen*), since presumably what was done did not have her consent.

51. See *Bava Batra* 48b; Rashbam on *Mar bar Rav Ashi;* see also *Ketubot* 86a.

52. A great grandson of Rashi (d. 1184); one of the greatest

of the Tosafists. See Urbach, *Ba'alei,* chap. 6. We shall have occasion to refer to him frequently in this portion of our inquiry.

53. *Horayot* 4b.

54. *Yevamot* 89a.

55. An unburied body claimed by no one. (Deut. 21:19). Ibid., 89b. See also Rashi, *Berakhot* 20a, on *shev v'al taase.*

56. *Yevamot* 89b—*Kevan d'loh yarte lah.*

57. See ibid., 88a; Tosafot on *Mitokh homer Shehehmarta.*

58. The Talmud *ad loc.,* defines a *met mizvah* as "one who calls and none answers him." Since her relatives do not inherit her, they would not "answer her call," and would not attend to her burial. Hence she is a *met mizvah.*

59. Ibid., 90a.

60. Ibid., 90b. See Chayas, vol. 1, p. 37, where he writes, "Nevertheless I have not been able to find the source on the basis of which the Rabbis taught that *shev ve'al ta'aseh* does not constitute an actual uprooting. . . . I saw only the simple statement that the Rabbis have the power to uproot a law of the Torah in the case of *shev ve'al ta'aseh,* but I do not know the reason for it and how the Rabbis arrived at it on the basis of a biblical verse." See also ibid., p. 90, etc., where he refers to Maimonides' assumption that all of the *mizvot* and *takkanot* of the Rabbis are included under the general statement in Deut. 17:11 and wherein Nahmanides differs from Maimonides. See also S. Greenberg, *Foundations,* p. 160.

61. *Nazir* 43b, Tosafot on *Vehai met mizvah hu.*

62. I presume that the reference is to *Yevamot* 89b–90a. See also n. 64.

63. *Yevamot* 114b.

64. Rabbi Yizhak was apparently a firm protagonist of the principle that the Rabbis have the power to "uproot" even in cases of *kum ve'asey.* In one of his responsa he wrote: "Even where there is no supporting biblical verse, the Rabbis have the power to uproot a law of the Torah even when it involves positive action" (Urbach, *Baalei,* p. 202). The same insistence upon the right of

the Rabbis to uproot laws of the Torah is reflected in Rabbi Yizḥak's interpretation of the reason why the testimony of one witness to a man's death is sufficient to permit the wife to remarry. The Talmud says in the name of Rabbi Zerah (*Yevamot* 88a), "The Rabbis were lenient in permitting her to remarry on the testimony of one witness because of the hardships they imposed upon her if the testimony proved false (and she had remarried). Would it not have been better had they been neither lenient nor stringent? But out of consideration that she might remain an *agunah,* the Rabbis were lenient." Upon this the Tosafot *ad locum* remarks, "It seems to Rabbi Yizḥak that we are not to assume that one witness is believed [in this case] because we are witness to the fact that she investigated the matter carefully before she remarried, and that in such a case one witness is adequate even on the basis of biblical law. We accept his testimony on the basis of a *takkanah* of the Rabbis, and we do not consider it to be an uprooting of a law of the Torah, since it appears plausible [right, reasonable] to believe such testimony, as I will explain later (*Yevamot* 89), that where a matter has *kzat ta'am usmakh* [even a semblance of reason and authority], we do not consider it to be uprooting a law of the Torah." The opinion of Rabbi Yizḥak as expressed in *Yevamot* 89b is invoked also in a Tosafot in *Avodah Zarah* 13a on *Amar Abayye amar krah.* See also *Bava Meẓia* 32b, Tosafot on *Midivrei,* where questions of violating a biblical law to honor kings are discussed; Also *Avodah Zarah* 11a; Tosafot on *Okrin.*

65. *Gittin* 36a.

66. P. 201.

67. *Eruvin* 81b, *Shema yomru.*

68. We should note, however, that even though the Tosafot states that the Rabbis *akru legamre*—abolished completely—purchase by money only, the biblical law as a matter of fact is *not* completely uprooted. There are instances in which it prevails (*Bava Meẓia* 46b, *Ḥullin* 83a, *Eruvin* 81b). There are other instances in which the Rabbis "completely uprooted" biblical law, yet decided in

accordance with it in a limited number of cases. See *Bava Batra* 20a; Tosafot *Ve'akum sheyashav* (involving *tumat akum*).

69. *Gittin* 32a.

70. Ibid., 33a.

71. I shall translate, paraphrase, or summarize Rashi's unusually lengthy comment beginning with *adaata d'rabbanan*.

72. Maimonides is also of this opinion; cp. *Hilkhot Ishut*, chap. 1:2. See also n. 2 of *Torah Temimah* on Deut. 24:1.

73. *Ketubot* 2b.

74. Ibid., 3a.

75. *Gittin* 73a.

76. See p. 179.

77. *Bava Mezia* 112b; Rashi obviously bases his comment on *Shevu'ot* 45a.

78. *Berakhot* 28a; Mishnah *Yadayim* chap. 4, *Yoma* 54a. See *Sefer Hamizvot* of Maimonides, *Mizvat Asey* 187, where it is maintained that even though these nations no longer exist, the law is still in force.

79. *Sotah* 47a.

80. See *Rosh Hashanah* 30a, Rashi on *inami d'ivney balayla;* also *Sukkah* 41a, Rashi on *inami.*

81. *Midrash Tehillim,* on Ps. 56:4. Notes *ad locum* in the Buber ed. indicate the many other sources in which this passage is found.

82. *Midrash Mishley* (ed. Buber), chap. 9, v. 2.

83. *Sanhedrin* 71a.

84. *Sotah* 16a.

85. Two different roots are used to designate the idea of "uprooting." In *Sotah* 16a the word used is *okevet;* Rashi, *ad locum,* understands it as being synonomous with *okeret.* In T.J. *Kiddushin,* chap. 1, *halakhah* 2 (59b in first third of col. 2), the word is *okefet.*

86. The term *anything* is not to be taken literally here. It means "almost anything."

87. See Chayas, vol. 1, p. 23, and note particularly (p. 25) that these "temporary uprootings" often became permanent rulings.

88. *Berakhot* 54a.

89. *Yoma* 69a. Resh Lakish and Rabbi Yoḥanan used this verse to justify writing down the oral law, saying that "it is preferable to 'uproot' one letter of the Torah [in this instance the prohibition of putting the oral law into writing] than to have the Torah forgotten in Israel" (*Temurah* 14b, *Gittin* 60a).

90. *Yevamot* 90b.

91. Ibid., *ad locum veligmar mineh;* and in *Sanhedrin* 89b, Tosafot on *Eliyahu, behar hacarmel.*

92. On differences between the authority of the *navi,* the prophet, and that of the *Bet Din,* the rabbinic court, see Chayas, vol. 1., p. 31.

93. *Menaḥot* 99b.

94. *Yevamot* 62a. See note 3 of *Torah Temina* on Exod. 34:1, also on Deut. 10:2, and Goldin, p. 20. Also, T.J. *Taanit* chap. 4, *halakhah* 8, where it is said in the name of the school of Rabbi Yishmael that God ordered Moses to break the tablets. See, however, Kadushin, "Introduction to Rabbinic Ethics," in *Kaufmann Jubilee Volume,* p. 101, who accepts Rashi's interpretation. Cp. also Lazarus, vol. 1, p. 71, n. 2.

95. See n. 29.

96. *Bava Kama* 83b, cp. also *Yevamot* 24a—Raba's statement regarding the meaning of Deut. 25:6.

97. P. 196.

98. *Yevamot* 39b and *Bekhorot* 13a.

99. *Sanhedrin* 68b–71b.

100. See M. Greenberg, p. 22 and n. 36. See also Tosafot, *Sanhedrin* 15b on *aymah liktala,* and *Sanhedrin* chap. 5. *Makkot* 7a.

101. *Sanhedrin* 111b–113a. Note particularly Rabbi Eliezer's opinion 113a, quoted also ibid., 71a.

102. *Shabbat* 129a. But see also *Temurah* 24b.

103. *Bava Meẓia,* 87b–88a, law regarding tithing, cp. *Pesaḥim* 9a, *d'amar Rabbi Oshia, ma'arim* etc., and see Rashi, *ad locum, v'ee bait.* See also Mishnah, *Ma'aser Sheni,* chap. 4:4 and *Bava Meẓia* 45b–46a.

In a conversation with Professor Zalman Dimitrovsky he suggested that the *ha'aramah* was the legitimatization by the Rabbis of a practice of which they disapproved, but which had become so widespread among the people that they could no longer eradicate it. Thus the Rabbis, noting the frequency with which the law of tithing was violated, suggested a way in which the law could be legally circumvented. This interpretation of the *ha'aramah* I later found also in Chayas, p. 222, He also designates the selling of *hamez* to a non-Jew on the eve of Passover as a *ha'aramah* (p. 223). See also Rabbi Adin Shteinzaltz's interpretation of the *ha'aramah* in his edition of *Berakhot* 31a.

104. The ethical principles most often used to validate a *takkanah* were *tikkun haolam*—advancing the general welfare (Mishnah *Gittin* chap. 4) and *mipne darkhe shalom*—acts that advance the cause of peace between man and his fellow (ibid., chap. 5). King Solomon is presumed to have ordained (*tiken*) the *eruv* (*Shabbat* 14b), whereby the literal meaning of the commandment "Let no man leave his place on the seventh day" (Exod. 16:29) was circumvented, on his own authority, since no verse or other source of sanction is mentioned. In T.J. *Eruvin* 24 at the end of the third column of that page, the *eruv* is associated with *darkhe shalom*.

105. See *Encyclopedia Talmudit*, vol. 9, item *Ha'aramah*. The article there discusses at some length a number of *ha'aramot*, among which *mekhirat hamez* is one. One would be hard pressed to explain why this is considered a *ha'aramah*, while the *eruv* is classed as a *takkanah*.

106. The Rashbam is of the opinion that the Rabbis said that a debtor could have a *prozbul* written only if he had some real estate, because "the Rabbis did whatever they could so that their enactments should not appear to be uprooting a 'biblical law,' and if the debtor owned (or was even presumed to own) real estate, the use of the *prozbul* had, for reasons there explained, greater biblical sanction" (Rashbam on *Bava Batra* 65b–66a—*Haray hi khekarka*).

107. Kadushin, *Rabbinic Mind*, pp. 76–84.

108. *Gittin* 59a.

109. I was in the midst of studying these two biblical passages when the *Niv Hamidrashia* (Winter–Spring 1968), published by the "Friends of the *Midrashia*" in Pardes Ḥannah, Israel, came to my attention. These two passages from the commentary of Naḥmanides are quoted there and discussed in the excellent article by Rabbi Eliezer ben Shlomo, p. 93 (Hebrew sec.). See also Rashi on *vezurva miderabanan in Bava Mezia* 67b.

110. *Yevamot* 120a.

111. Kadushin's *Rabbinic Mind* constitutes the most comprehensive and insightful presentation of the role of the value concepts in the Jewish tradition.

112. Chapter 2 of this volume is devoted to the tension between the Declaration and the Constitution.

113. I realize that this apodictically formulated proposition has been and can be challenged. It cannot be proved or disproved beyond reasonable doubt. I, however, believe it to be true.

114. The statement in the *Zohar* (*Ahare*, p. 73a) reads: *Gimmel dargin inun mitkashran da beda kudsha brich hu, oraita veyisrael.* The three are interwined, as it were but hardly equally interdependent. They are not one in the sense that each loses his own identity in merging with the other. *Nizozeh Zohar* in the margin contains the beautiful image of Israel as the wick, the Torah as the oil, and the *Shekhinah* as the flame. The statement as misquoted equates Israel with God. See also *Tikkune Zohar, tikkun* 21.

115. I prefer to use the term *excellence* rather than *perfection* because the concept of perfection tends to imply the complete and the static. To speak of something as being perfect is to imply that any change in it would detract from its perfection. The term *excellence* connotes "the possession of good qualities in an unusual degree." It does not imply that there is no room for further growth and development.

116. See also *Seder Eliahu Rabba, piska* 19 on *nokhach pnei Adonai*.

117. *Sanhedrin* 99b.

118. T.J. *Nedarim,* chap. 9, *halakhah* 4.

119. *Torah Shlemah,* vol. 16, p. 203.

120. Sifra on Lev. 19:2; see also *ad locum Torah Temimah,* n. 2.

121. On the passage in *Ḥagigah* 3b, *Nitnu mayroeh eḥad,* "They were given by one Shepherd" (Eccles. 12:11), *El eḥad natanan*—"One God gave them," *Parness eḥad amaran,* "One leader taught them"—Rashi comments, "None of the rabbinic disputants quotes the Torah of any other god, but only the Torah of our God. . . . None of them quotes the sayings of any other prophet as evidence against Moses, our teacher."

122. I have in mind particularly such biblical laws as those dealing with the *nakhri* (Deut. 23:21) and the *akum* (Deut. 7:25–26), which, in the opinion of many in our generation, the rabbinic tradition reinterpreted only partially in accordance with the standards articulated and implied in the biblical ethic.

123. For a fuller discussion of this matter, see S. Greenberg, *Foundations,* chap. 3. See also Nachmanides on Deut. 22:6 and the *Torah Temimah,* n. 68 toward the end, which refers to the crucial rabbinic passage in *Berakhot* 33b dealing with this subject.

124. Maimonides in his *Guide,* pt. 3, did exactly that. See also *Hilkhot Shabbat,* chap. 2, par. 3, quoted on p. 206 in this inquiry.

125. Exod. 21:24, Lev. 24:20, Deut. 19:21, where *b'ayin* is used rather than *taḥat ayin.*

126. *Parashat Emor,* chap. 20, par. 7.

127. *Bava Kama* 83b.

128. Ibid., 84a.

129. *Berakhot* 33b.

130. Doron, "A New Look at an Old Lex," attempts to prove this thesis scientifically in regard to the *lex talionis.*

131. *Bava Kama* 84a.

132. *Hilkhot Rav Alfas* 30a. In the paragraph beginning with *Gemara Yerushalmi,* I start about seven lines from the end of the page.

133. T.J. *Eruvin* chap. 10, *halakhah* 1, and with some slight variation also in T.J. *Berakhot* chap. 3., *halakhah* 3.

134. From this point to the end of the passage the text is not clear. In the *Ḥidushey anshe shem, ad locum,* which I shall also translate, this portion of the text is rejected.

135. *Bava Kama* 84a. Later authorities could not conceive that Rabbi Eliezer really meant what he is reported to have said. Hence, they interpret the statement attributed to him to mean the opposite of what it says. For a full discussion of this matter, see Professor Louis Finkelstein's article, "Od Mitorato shel Reb Neḥunyah ben Hakanah," in *Hagut Ivrit b'Amerika.*

136. Kadushin, *Rabbinic Mind,* pp. 51–52.

137. *Gittin* 36b.

138. Ibid.

139. Sifre on Deut. 15:3, par. 113.

140. See *Bava Meẓia* 48b or Shevu'ot 44b.

141. In *Makkot* 3b, Rashi interprets the statement "hands over his notes of indebtedness to the courts" as a reference to the *prozbul.* Tosafot, *ad locum,* disagrees and takes it to refer to a procedure other than the *prozbul,* and that the procedure of handing over the notes to the court in order to avoid the cancellation of the debt has biblical sanction, while the *prozbul* is only a rabbinic enactment.

142. T.J. *Shevi'it,* chap. 10, *halakhah* 3.

143. Rashi's comment on *Bashviit bizman hazeh, Gittin* 36a.

144. *Hilkhot Shmitah* chap. 9:16.

145. *Gittin* 36b.

146. See above p. 163.

147. See Korban Nethanel, on *Gittin* 36b. He is of the opinion that "Rava too assumes that Hillel's *takkanah* refers only to times when the Sabbatical year is not biblically obligatory. For Rava himself admits that on the basis of the principle of *hefker bet din hefker* we cannot uproot for all times one of the 613 mizvot."

148. *Gittin* 36b. Rashi on *shev ve'al taaseh.*

149. Rabbenu Nissim, at the very end of the *piska, Hitkin*

Hillel Hazaken prozbul, which starts on p. 18b of Rif on *Gittin.* See also Tosafot *Hitkin Hillel. Arakhin* 31b, at end.

150. Thus the text in the Sifre, par. 113. In the Mishnah this statement is divided between *Shevi'it* 10:3 and *Gittin* 4:3. For the same reason the Rabbis do not require *ḥakira udrisha*—the hypermeticulous questioning of witnesses in cases involving money matters—which is required in cases involving capital punishment, although they consider it to be a biblical requirement. *Sanhedrin* 32a.

151. *Shabbat* 31a.

152. Tedesche, p. 85.

153. Num. 15:32–36; Exod. 31:14; etc.

154. See Krochmal, *Moreh-Sha'ar* 10, p. 69.

155. Weiss, *Dor Dor Vedorshav,* vol. 1, p. 143, and others, see a direct relationship between the action of Mattathias and the later development of the law regarding the saving of life on the Sabbath. Others do not. See Moshe D. Har., "Leba'ayat Hilkhot Milḥama Beshabbat Beyemay Bayit Sheni Uvitkufot Hamishna Vehatalmud," *Tarbiẓ* 30, no. 3 (Nisan 5721): 247, n. 28. I want to thank Professor David Halivni (Weiss) for bringing this article to my attention.

156. *Yoma* 83a. See also Tosefta *Moed,* ed. Saul Lieberman; *Shabbat* chap. 15:16–17 and commentary on those passages in *Tosefta ki-fshuṭah.*

157. *Mekhilta d'Rabbi Shimon bar Yoḥai,* on *Ki Tisa* 31:13. Also in *Mekhilta d'Rabbi Yishmael.* Ibid.

158. *Yoma* 84b.

159. Ibid., 85b; see also Rashi, *ad locum,* on *ashkeḥan.* See also T.J. *Yoma* chap. 8, *halakhah* 5.

160. In the passage in Tosefta *Moed* (see n. 156), this biblical proof-text is attributed to Rabbi Akiba. The Talmud (*Sanhedrin* 74a) attributes it to Rabbi Yishmael. Professor Lieberman in *Tosefta ki-fshuṭah* on *Moed,* p. 262, notes on lines 83–84, lists the various places where this verse is used as Samuel used it. Obviously the tradition was not certain about the origin of the use of this proof-

text for this specific purpose. If it were used by Rabbi Akiba and Rabbi Yishmael, it would be very strange that the fact should not have been known in the schools of Babylonia. My conjecture is that it was first used by Samuel, and then later attributed to earlier authorities, for it is too significant a use of a biblical verse to have been forgotten once it was thus used by Rabbi Akiba or any other Tanna. See also Abramowitz, section on *Pikuaḥ nefesh behalakhah*.

161. *Hilkhot Shabbat,* chap. 2, par. 3.

162. *Ḥullin* 7a.

163. *Sanhedrin* 74a; see also Tosefta *Shabbat,* the end of chap. 15, and Professor Lieberman's notes on lines 85–87, pp. 262–63, in *Tosefta ki-fshuṭah,* on *Shabbat.*

164. The passage in *Sanhedrin* does not clearly indicate whether the distinction between public and private violation of the law in order to save life was part of the decision arrived at inᵗ the 'attic' or a later modification of it.

165. *Sanhedrin* 37a. See S. Greenberg, *Foundations,* chap. 4.

166. *Bava Meẓia* 108a.

167. Ibid., 16b.

168. Tosefta *Moed Shekalim* chap. 2:2. The Mishna, Shekalim 3:2 which is in accordance with the opinion of Rabbi Akiba does not require that the priest be searched but only that his garments have no pockets.

169. Ibid. The word *also* is missing in some manuscripts and is not essential to the meaning here.

170. The reference to the Bible here in Lieberman, *Tosefta Moed,* should be 21:9. From Professor Lieberman's comment *ad locum,* it would appear that this verse refers to the case of the *ir hanidaḥat* (Deut. 13:13–19). But the verse (Deut. 21:9) here quoted in the *Tosefta* refers to the *eglah arufa.* I discussed this with Professor Lieberman, and he pointed out that a passage had been omitted here from his commentary. This will be further clarified in what follows.

171. "Hence we see that they (the priests) must appear pure also in the eyes of the people" (*Minḥat Bikkurim, ad locum*).

172. *Tosefta ki-fshuṭah, Moed,* p. 677. I translate revelant selections from the comments on lines 7–9 and 11–12, and add in parenthesis further elucidation of the matter, on the basis of what Professor Lieberman told me in my conversation with him referred to above.

173. This verse refers to the law of the condemned city. Deut. 13:13–19.

174. See Heschel, *Torah Min Hashamayim,* vol. 1, pp. xxxvii–lvi.

175. *Bava Meẓia* 83a.

176. Rashi interprets it to mean "act *lifnim mishurat hadin,"* go beyond the requirements of the law. We shall have more to say about this concept in what follows.

177. *Bava Meẓia* 30b.

178. Rashi here takes this to mean that he should teach them some trade. In *Bava Kama* 100a, Rashi takes it to mean to teach them Torah.

179. *Bava Batra* 22a.

180. *Berakhot* 7a has it *ve'ekanes lahem,* "and I shall enter for their sake" *lifnim,* etc.

181. See Tosafot *Bava Meẓia* 24b, on *lifnim mishurat hadin.*

182. *Bava Meẓia* 30b.

183. Ibid., 88a.

184. See Ben-Shlomo, p. 95.

185. For an excellent discussion of this question, see the comments in Maimonides, *Sefer Hamiẓvot* on *Hashoresh Harishon.*

186. *Eruvin* 77a; Tosafot *Bava Meẓia* 55b on *vekhiasu dvarayhem.*

187. Thus the *dina d'var miẓra,* discussed above on p. 209, occupies twenty-seven columns in vol. 4 of the *Encyclopedia Talmudit.*

188. I again refer the reader to Kadushin's *Rabbinic Mind.*

189. For a detailed statement of the steps that I believe should be taken to implement the present law of *gittin,* see *Conservative Judaism* 24, no. 3 (Spring 1970) p. 135.

190. See above p. 164.

191. *Menaḥot* 79b, *Shevu'ot* 11a.

192. Mishnah, *Ketubbot,* chap. 4:7–12.

193. See above, p. 161.

194. *Sanhedrin* 71b. See also ibid., 73a; Tosafot on *lehazilo b'nafsho,* which Tosafot says may be interpreted to mean that you are permitted to kill a man who is pursuing another man, not because you are thereby saving his victim, but because you are preventing the pursuer from committing a mortal sin.

195. *Eruvin* 81b.

196. Professor Louis Finkelstein, in a letter addressed to members of the Rabbinical Assembly, dated London, July 22, 1969.

CHAPTER 4

1. Handlin, pp. 59–60.
2. See Wolf, W. A.
3. Greenberg, S., *Foundations*, pp. 45–72.
4. Frost, p. 75.
5. Morison and Commager, p. 282.
6. Beard and Beard, p. 330.
7. Hallevi, p. 44–47.
8. Morison, p. 654.
9. Basler, p. 655.
10. Ibid., p. 794.

BIBLIOGRAPHY

Abot d'Rabbi Natan. See Schechter, S., and Goldin, J.

Abramowitz, Hayim Yizhak. *Vehai Bahem.* Israel: Hozaat Orot, 5717 = 1957.

Aḥad Ha-Am. *Al Parashat Derakhim.* 4 vols. Berlin: Yiddisher Verlag, 1921.

Angle, Paul M. *Created Equal: The Complete Lincoln-Douglas Debates.* Chicago: University of Chicago Press, 1958.

Ardrey, Robert. *African Genesis.* New York: Dell Publishing Co., 1961.

Arieli, Yehoshua. *Individualism and Nationalism in American Ideology.* Baltimore: Penguin Books, 1964.

Aristotle. *The Basic Works.* Edited with an introduction by Richard McKeon. New York: Random House, 1941.

Aronson, David. "Kedat Moshe Veyisrael." *Rabbinical Assembly Proceedings* (1951).

Avot. "The Sayings of the Fathers." In Hertz, *The Daily Prayer Book.*

Bacher, W., and A. S. Rabinowitz. *Agadot Amorai Erez Yisrael.* Tel Aviv: Dvir, 5686 = 1925.

Bailyn, Bernard. *The Ideological Origins of the American Revolution.* Cambridge: Harvard University Press, 1967.

Barnes, Hazel E. *An Existentialist Ethics.* New York: Vantage Books, 1971.

Baron, Salo. *A Social and Religious History of the Jews.* 2d ed. Philadelphia: Jewish Publication Society, 1958.

Barzun, Jacques. *Darwin, Marx, Wagner*. Boston: Little, Brown & Co., 1941.

Basler, Roy P., ed. *Abraham Lincoln: His Speeches and Writings*. New York: World Publishing Co., 1946.

Beard, Charles A., and Mary R. Beard. *The Rise of American Civilization*. New York: Macmillan Co., 1934.

Becker, Carl. *The Declaration of Independence*. New York: Alfred A. Knopf, 1966.

Bellow, Saul. *Herzog*. New York: Viking Press, 1964.

Ben-Shlomo, Eliezer. *Berur Hamusag Veasita Hatov Vehayashar*. Pardes Hana: Niv Hamidrashia, 1968.

Bentham, Jeremy. *An Introduction to the Principles of Morals and Legislation*. In Burtt, *The English Philosophers*.

Berkovits, Eliezer. *Tnai be Nesuin Uveget*. Jerusalem: Mosad Harav Kook, 5727 = 1967.

Bickel, Alexander M. *Politics and the Warren Court*. New York: Harper & Row, 1965.

Blackstone, William T. *The Problem of Religious Knowledge*. Englewood Cliffs, N.J.: Prentice-Hall, 1963.

Bowers, Claude G. *Jefferson in Power*. Boston: Houghton Mifflin Co., 1936.

Brewer, David S., ed. *World's Best Orations*. 10 vols. St. Louis: Fred P. Kaiser, 1900.

Broad, C. D. *Five Types of Ethical Theory*. Patterson: Littlefield, Adams Co., 1959.

Brown, Raymond E. *The Gospel according to John I–XII*. Anchor Bible. Garden City, N. Y.: Doubleday, 1966.

Burtt, Edwin A., ed. *The English Philosophers from Bacon to Mill*. New York: Modern Library, 1939.

Cahn, Edmond. *The Moral Decision*. Bloomington: Indiana University Press, 1959.

Callahan, Daniel, ed. *The Secular City Debate*. New York: Macmillan Co., 1966.

Cassirer, Ernst. *Substance and Function and Einstein's Theory of Relativity*. New York: Dover Publications, 1953.

Chayas, Zebi Hirsch (Mahariz). *Kol Sifrei*. Jerusalem: Hoza'at Sfarim Divre Hakhamim, 1958.

Cohen, Arthur A. *"Franz Rosenzweig's Star of Redemption."* *Midstream* 18, no. 2 (February 1972) pp. 13–33.

Cohen, Hermann. *Jüdische Schriften.* Vol. 3. Berlin: C. A. Schwetschke & Sohn, 1924.

Cohen, Jack. *The Case for Religious Naturalism.* New York: Reconstructionist Press, 1958.

Corwin, Edward S. *The "Higher Law" Background of American Constitutional Law.* Ithaca, N.Y.: Cornell University Press, 1955.

―――. *The Constitution and What It Means Today.* Princeton, N.J.: Princeton University Press, 1958.

Cushman, Robert E., and Robert F. Cushman. *Leading Constitutional Decisions.* 13th ed. New York: Appleton-Century-Crofts, 1966.

―――. *Cases in Constitutional Law.* 3rd ed. New York: Appleton-Century-Crofts, 1968.

Doniger, Simon, ed. *The Nature of Man.* New York: Harper & Bros., 1963.

Doron, Pinchas. "A New Look at an Old Lex., *Journal ANE Society Columbia University* 1, no. 2 (Spring 1969).

Dresner, Samuel, and Seymour Siegel. *The Jewish Dietary Laws.* New York: Burning Bush Press, 1959.

Durant, Will and Ariel, *Reader's Digest,* December, 1968.

Edel, Abraham. *Ethical Judgment.* Glencoe, Ill.: Free Press, 1964.

Eicha Rabbati. Ed. Salomon Buber. Wilna: Witte & Gebrüder Romm, 1869.

Elon, Amos. *The Israelis.* New York: Holt, Rinehart & Winston, 1971.

Encyclopedia Talmudit. Edited by S. J. Zevin and others. Jerusalem: *Yad Harav Herzog,* 1955–.

Enteman, W. F. ed. *The Problem of Freewill.* New York: Charles Scribner and Sons, 1967.

Epstein, Louis M. *Lishe'aylat Ha'agunah.* New York, 5700 = 1940.

―――. *The Jewish Marriage Contract.* New York: Jewish Theological Seminary, 1927.

Finkelstein, Louis. *Mabo L'massekhot Abot v'Abot d'Rabbi Natan.* New York: Jewish Theological Seminary, 1950.

―――. *The Pharisees.* 3rd ed. Philadelphia: Jewish Publication Society, 1962.

————. *Social Responsibility in an Age of Revolution.* New York: Jewish Theological Seminary, 1971.

Fox, Marvin, ed. *Modern Jewish Ethics: Theory and Practice.* Columbus: Ohio State University Press, 1975.

Fox, Seymour. *Freud and Education.* Springfield, Ill.: Charles C. Thomas, 1975.

Freiman, Avraham Ḥayyim. *Seder Kiddushin Unsuin.* Jerusalem: Mosad Harav Kook, 5707 = 1945.

Freud, S. *Civilization and Its Discontents.* Translated by Joan Riviere. London: Hogarth Press, 1949.

Frost, Robert. *Complete Poems.* New York: Holt, Rinehart & Winston, 1964.

Gabriel, Ralph H. *The Course of American Democratic Thought.* New York: Ronald Press, 1940.

Gay, John. *Concerning the Fundamental Principle of Virtue and Morality.* In Burtt, *The English Philosophers.*

Gershfield, Edward M., ed. *Studies in Jewish Jurisprudence.* New York: Hermon Press, 1971.

Glueck, Nelson. *Ḥesed in the Bible.* Translated by Alfred Gottschalk. Cincinnati: Hebrew Union College Press, 1967.

Goals for Americans: The Report of the President's Commission on National Goals. Englewood Cliffs, N.J.: Prentice-Hall.

Goldin, Judah. *The Fathers according to Rabbi Nathan.* New Haven: Yale University Press, 1955.

Goldstein, Kurt. *Human Nature.* Cambridge: Harvard University Press, 1951.

Greenberg, Moshe. "Some Postulates of Biblical Criminal Law." In *Kaufmann Jubilee Volume.*

Greenberg, Simon. *Foundations of a Faith.* New York: Burning Bush Press, 1967.

Grice, G. R. *The Grounds of Moral Judgement.* New York: Cambridge University Press, 1967.

Ḥafez Ḥayyim (Rabbi Israel Meir Hakohen). *Al Agadot Haṣhas.* Edited by Shmuel Charlap. Jerusalem, 5726.

Hagut Ivrit B'Amerika. Tel Aviv: Yavne Publishing House, 1972.

Hallevi, Judah, *Kitab al Khazari.* Translated by Hartwig Hirschfeld, Bernard B. Richards Co., N.Y., 1927.

Handlin, Oscar. *Race and Nationality in American Life*. Garden City, N.Y.: Doubleday, 1957.

Hegel, Georg Friedrich. *The Philosophy of Hegel*. Edited by Carl J. Friedrich, New York: Modern Library, 1953.

Hertz, J. H. *The Authorized Daily Prayer Book*. London: National Council for Jewish Religious Education, 1943.

Herzl, Theodor. *Diaries*. New York: Dial Press, 1956.

Heschel, Abraham J. *The Prophets*. New York: Harper and Row, 1962.

———. *Torah Min Hashamayim*. London and New York: Soncino, 1962–65.

Hobbes, Thomas. *Leviathan*. In Burtt, *The English Philosophers*.

Hofstadter, Richard. *Great Issues in American History*. Vol. 1, 1765–1865. New York: Vantage Books, 1959.

Hook, Sidney ed. *Determinism and Freedom*, N.Y. University Press, 1958.

———. *Dimensions of the Mind*, N.Y.: Collier Books, 1961.

———. *Language and Philosophy*, N.Y. University Press, 1966.

Hume, David. *An Enquiry Concerning Human Understanding*. In Burtt, *The English Philosophers*.

Hurewitz, Isaac S. *Yad Halevi: Commentary on Maimonides, Sefer Hamitzvot* (Hebrew). Jerusalem, 1926.

Husik, Isaac. *A History of Mediaeval Jewish Philosophy*. New York: Macmillan Co., 1916.

Huxley, Thomas H. *Evolution and Ethics and Other Essays* New York: D. Appleton Co., 1903.

Inaugural Addresses of the Presidents of the United States. Washington: U.S. Government Printing Office, 1961.

Interpreter's Bible. 12 vols. New York: Abingdon-Cokesbury Press, 1952.

Joad, C. E. M. *God and Evil*. New York: Harper & Bros., 1943.

Johnson, Sherman E. "Commentary on Matthew." *Interpreter's Bible*, vol. 7.

Kadushin, Max. *The Rabbinic Mind*. 2d ed. New York: Blaisdell Publishing Co., 1965.

———. *Worship and Ethics*. Evanston, Ill.: Northwestern University Press, 1964.

Kahana, Yizḥak. *Letakanot Agunot,* Maḥzikay Hadat, Jerusalem, 5703.

Kant, Immanuel. *Critique of Practical Reason and Other Works on the Theory of Ethics.* Translated by T. K. Abbott. London: Longmans, Green & Co., 1909.

―――. *The Doctrine of Virtue: Part II of the Metaphysics of Morals.* Translated with an introduction and notes by Mary J. Gregot. New York: Harper & Row, 1964.

―――. *Groundwork of the Metaphysics of Morals.* Translated and analyzed by H. J. Patton. New York: Harper Torchbooks, 1964.

Kasher, M. H. *Torah Shlemah: A Talmudic and Midrashic Encyclopaedia to the Pentateuch.* New York: American Biblical Encyclopedia Society, 1949–.

Kaufmann Jubilee Volume. Jerusalem: Hebrew University–Magnes Press, 1960.

Kaufmann, Walter. *The Faith of a Heretic.* New York: Doubleday, 1961.

―――. *Critique of Religion and Philosophy.* New York: Anchor Books, 1961.

Keats, John. *The Poems of John Keats.* London: Chapman & Hall n.d.

Kennedy, John F. *Profiles in Courage.* New York: Harper, 1956.

Kerner, George C. *The Revolution in Ethical Theory.* New York: Oxford University Press, 1966.

Kierkegaard, Soren. *A Kierkegaard Anthology.* Edited by Robert Bretall. Princeton: Princeton University Press, 1942.

Kimelman, Reuven. "The Rabbinic Ethics of Protest." *Judaism* 19, no. 1 (Winter 1970) pp. 38–58.

―――. "Non–Violence in the Talmud." *Judaism* 17, no. 3 (Summer 1968) pp. 316–318.

Konvitz, Milton. *The Bill of Rights Reader.* Cornell University Press, Ithaca, N.Y., 4th ed. 1968.

Kristol, Irving. "American Historians and the Democratic Idea." *American Scholar* (Winter 1969).

Krochmal, N. *Kitve N. Krochmal.* Edited by S. Rawidowicz. Berlin-Charlottenburg: Verlag Aganoth, 1924.

Lazarus, M. *The Ethics of Judaism.* Philadelphia: Jewish Publication Society, 1900.

Lehman, Paul. *Ethics in a Christian Context.* New York: Harper & Row, 1963.

Levinthal, Israel. *The Jewish Law of Agency.* Philadelphia: Conat Press, 1923.

Lieberman, Saul. *Tosefta ki-fshuṭah: A Comprehensive Commentary on the Tosefta.* New York: Jewish Theological Seminary, 1955–.

———. *The Tosefta, according to Codex Vienna, etc., together with references to parallel passages in Talmudic literature and a brief commentary.* New York: Jewish Theological Seminary, 1955.

———. *Yevanit ve Yavnut b'Eretz Yisrael.* Jerusalem: Mosad Bialik, 1962.

Locke, John. *An Essay Concerning Human Understanding.* In Burtt, *The English Philosophers.*

Lorenz, Konrad. *On Aggression.* Translated by Marjorie Kerr Wilson. New York: Harcourt, Brace, & World, 1963.

Maimonides, Moses. *Commentary on the Mishnah.* Translated from the Arabic by Joseph Ben-David Kapah. Jerusalem: Mosad Harav Kook, 5723 = 1963.

———. *The Guide to the Perplexed.* Translated by Shlomo Pines. Chicago: University of Chicago Press, 1963.

———. *Sefer Hamitzvot.* Edited by Rabbi Isaac S. Hurewitz. Jerusalem, 1926.

———. *Mishne Torah.* New York: Shulsinger Bros., 1947.

Malraux, André. *Anti-Memoirs.* N.Y.: Holt, Rhinehart & Winston, 1968.

Mao Tse-Tung. *Quotations from Chairman Mao Tse-Tung.* Peking: Foreign Languages Press, 1967.

Mekhilta de-Rabbi Simon b. Yohai. Edited by D. Z. Hoffmann. Frankfurt, 1905.

Mekhilta de Rabbi Yishmael. Edited by Meir Ish Shalom. Vienna, 5630; New York: Om Publishing Co., 1948.

Menninger, Karl. *Man against Himself.* New York: Harcourt, Brace & Co., 1938.

Midrash Hagadol on Numbers. Edited by Shlomo Fisch. Jerusalem, 5723 = 1963.

Midrash Mishley. Edited by S. Buber. Wilna: Romm, 1893.

Midrash Tanḥuma. Edited by S. Buber. Wilna: Romm, 5673 = 1913.

Midrash Tehillim. Edited by S. Buber. Wilna: Romm, 1891.

Mielziner, M. *The Jewish Law of Marriage and Divorce.* New York: Bloch Publishing Co., 1901.

Mill, John Stuart. *Utilitarianism.* In Burtt, *The English Philosophers.*

Miller, Charles A. *The Supreme Court and the Uses of History.* Cambridge: Harvard University Press, 1969.

Moore, G. E. *Ethics.* Oxford: Oxford University Press, 1949.

Moore, G. F. *History of Religions.* New York: Charles Scribner's Sons, 1925.

———. *Judaism in the First Centuries of the Christian Era: The Age of the Tannaim.* Cambridge: Harvard University Press, 1927.

Morison, Samuel Eliot. *The Oxford History of the American People.* New York: Oxford University Press, 1965.

———, and Henry Steele Commager. *The Growth of the American Republic.* New York, 1950.

Murray, John Courtney. *We Hold These Truths.* New York: Sheed & Ward, 1960.

Myers, Henry Alonzo. *Are Men Equal?* Ithaca, N.Y.: Cornell University Press, 1955.

Neufeld, B. *Ancient Hebrew Marriage Laws.* London: Longmans, Green & Co., 1944.

Nevins, Allen. *The Emergence of Lincoln.* 2 vols. New York: Charles Scribner's Sons, 1950.

Niebuhr, H. Richard. *The Meaning of Revelation.* New York: Macmillan Co., 1960.

Niebuhr, Reinhold. *The Nature and Destiny of Man.* New York: Charles Scribner's Sons, 1949.

———. *Does Civilization Need Religion?* New York: Macmillan Co., 1960.

Nietzsche, Friedrich. *The Genealogy of Morals.* Translated by Francis Golfong. New York: Doubleday Anchor Books, 1956.

Nissim, Rabbi Isaac. *Bnai Yisrael.* Jerusalem: Hoẓaat Harabanut Harashit le Yisrael, 5722 = 1962.

Pesikta de Rav Kahana. Edited by Bernard Mandelbaum. New York: Jewish Theological Seminary, 1962.

Plato. *The Dialogues of Plato.* Translated by B. Jowett. New York: Random House, 1937.

Ross, Sir David. *Kant's Ethical Theory.* Oxford: Clarendon Press, 1954.

Ruskin, John. *The Crown of Wild Olive—Sesame and Lilies.* New York: A. L. Burtt, n.d.

Russell, Bertrand. *Mysticism and Logic.* London: Longmans, Green & Co., 1921.

Rutenber, C. G. *The Doctrine of the Imitation of God in Plato*. New York: King's Crown Press, 1946.

Saadia Gaon. *The Book of Beliefs and Opinions*. Translated from the Arabic by Samuel Rosenblatt. New Haven: Yale University Press, 1948.

Sabbath and Festival Prayer Book. New York: Rabbinical Assembly of America and United Synagogue of America, 1946.

Sandburg, Carl. *Abraham Lincoln: The War Years*. New York: Harcourt, Brace & Co., 1939.

Santayana, George. *Reason in Religion*. New York: Charles Scribner's Sons, 1921.

Schechter, Solomon. *Abot d'Rabbi Nathan*. Vienna, 1887.

Schloerb, Rolland W. "Commentary on Proverbs." *Interpreter's Bible*.

Shapira, Avraham. *The Seventh Day*. New York: Charles Scribner's Sons, 1970.

Shteinzaltz, Adin, ed. *B'rakhot*. Jerusalem: Israel Institute for Talmudic Publications, 1968.

Shulhan Arukh by Joseph Karo. Wilna: Romm Bros., 1869.

Sidgwick, Henry. *Outlines of the History of Ethics*. 6th ed., enlarged with an additional chapter by Alban G. Widgory. Boston: Beacon Press, 1968.

―――. *The Methods of Ethics*. New York: Dover Publications, 1966.

Sifra de-Bay Rav. Edited by I. H. Weiss. Vienna, 1862.

Sifra on Leviticus. Vienna: J. Schlossberg, 1862.

Sifre on Deuteronomy. Edited by Louis Finkelstein. New York: Jewish Theological Seminary, 1969.

Simon, Ernst. *Brücken*. Heidelberg: Verlag Lambert Schneider, 1965.

―――. *"The Neighbor (Rea)."* In Fox, M. *Modern Jewish Ethics*.

Spinoza, Baruch. *Ethics of Benedict Spinoza*. Translated by W. Hale White and Amelia H. Stroling. 3d ed. Oxford: Oxford University Press, 1927.

Steinberg, Milton. *Anatomy of a Faith*. New York: Harcourt, Brace, 1960.

―――. *A Partisan Guide to the Jewish Problem*. New York: Bobbs-Merrill Co., 1945.

Strauss, Leo. *Spinoza's Critique of Religion*. New York: Schocken Books, 1965.

Talmud
  Babylonian
    Avot
    Arakhin
    Avodah Zarah
    Bava Batra
    Bava Kama
    Bava Meẓia
    Berachot
    Eruvin
    Gittin
    Ḥagigah
    Ḥullin
    Ketubot
    Kiddushin
    Makkot
    Megillah
    Nazir
    Sanhedrin
    Sotah
    Taanit
    Tamid
    Yevamot
    Yoma
  Jerusalem (T. J.)
    Eruvin
    Kiddushin
    Maaserot
    Nedarim
    Peah
    Sheviit
    Taanit
    Yoma

Tanḥuma. See *Midrash Tanḥuma*.

Tedesche, Sidney. *The First Book of the Maccabees*. New York: Harper & Bros., 1950.

Thonnard, F. J. *A Short History of Philosophy.* Translated from the revised and corrected edition by Edward A. Marziarz. New York: Society of St. John the Evangelist Dezcles & Cie., 1955.

Thucydides. *The Complete Writings.* New York: Modern Library, 1934.

Torah Shlemah. See Kasher, M. H.

Torah Temima on the Pentateuch. Edited by Baruch Halevi Epstein. New York: Hebrew Publishing Co., 1928.

To Secure These Rights: Report of President Truman's Commission on Civil Rights. Washington: U.S. Government Printing Offiice, 1947.

Toynbee, Arnold J. *Greek Historical Thought.* New York: New American Library, 1952.

Troeltsch, Ernst. *The Social Teachings of the Christian Churches.* New York: Macmillan Co., 1931.

Urbach, Ephraim E. *Ba'alei Hatosafot.* Jerusalem: Bialik Institute, 1955.

_____. *Hazal-Pirke Emunot Vedayot,* Magnes Press, Jerusalem, 1969.

Weiss, Isaac Hirsh. *Dor Dor Vedorshav.* New York and Berlin: Platt & Minkus, 5684 = 1924.

Wolf, William A. *The Almost Chosen People: A Study of the Religion of Abraham Lincoln.* New York: Doubleday, 1959.

Wolfson Jubilee Volume. 3 vols. New York: American Academy for Jewish Studies, 1965.

Yalkut Shimoni. Horeb edition. New York and Berlin, 5086.

Zohar. *Sefer Hazohar al Hamishe Humshei Torah with notations on Nizoze Zohar.* Edited by Reuben Margaliyot. 5 vols. Jerusalem: Mosad Harav Kook, 1940–54.

INDEX OF BIBLICAL REFERENCES

INDEX OF NAMES

INDEX OF SUBJECTS

325